Structures & construction in historic building conservation

This book is part of a series on historic building conservation:

Understanding Historic Building Conservation
Edited by Michael Forsyth
9781405111720

Structures & Construction in Historic Building Conservation
Edited by Michael Forsyth
9781405111713

Materials & Skills for Historic Building Conservation
Edited by Michael Forsyth
9781405111706

Other books of interest:

Managing Built Heritage: the role of cultural significance
Derek Worthing & Stephen Bond
9781405119788

Conservation and Sustainability in Historic Cities
Dennis Rodwell
9781405126564

Building Pathology
Second Edition
David Watt
9781405161039

Architectural Conservation
Aylin Orbaşlı
9780632040254

Structures & construction in historic building conservation

Edited by

Michael Forsyth
**Department of Architecture and Civil Engineering
University of Bath**

Blackwell
Publishing

Blackwell Publishing editorial offices:
Blackwell Publishing Ltd, 9600 Garsington Road, Oxford OX4 2DQ, UK
Tel: +44 (0)1865 776868
Blackwell Publishing Inc., 350 Main Street, Malden, MA 02148-5020, USA
Tel: +1 781 388 8250
Blackwell Publishing Asia Pty Ltd, 550 Swanston Street, Carlton, Victoria 3053, Australia
Tel: +61 (0)3 8359 1011

Designations used by companies to distinguish their products are often claimed as trademarks. All brand names and product names used in this book are trade names, service marks, trademarks or registered trademarks of their respective owners. The Publisher is not associated with any product or vendor mentioned in this book.

This publication is designed to provide accurate and authoritative information in regard to the subject matter covered. It is sold on the understanding that the Publisher is not engaged in rendering professional services. If professional advice or other expert assistance is required, the services of a competent professional should be sought.

First published 2007 by Blackwell Publishing Ltd

ISBN: 9781405111713

Library of Congress Cataloging-in-Publication Data

Structures & construction in historic building conservation / edited by Michael Forsyth.
p. cm.
Companion volume to Understanding historic building conservation and Materials & skills for historic building conservation.
Includes bibliographical references and index.
ISBN-13: 978-1-4051-1171-3 (hardback : alk. paper)
ISBN-10: 1-4051-1171-2 (hardback : alk. paper) 1. Historic buildings–Conservation and restoration. 2. Structural engineering. I. Forsyth, Michael, 1951– II. Title: Structures and construction in historic building conservation.

TH3301.S77 2007
720.28'8–dc22
2007014545

A catalogue record for this title is available from the British Library

Set in 10 on 12.5pt Avenir by SNP Best-set Typesetter Ltd., Hong Kong
Printed and bound in Singapore by Fabulous Printers Pte Ltd

The publisher's policy is to use permanent paper from mills that operate a sustainable forestry policy, and which has been manufactured from pulp processed using acid-free and elementary chlorine-free practices. Furthermore, the publisher ensures that the text paper and cover board used have met acceptable environmental accreditation standards.

For further information on Blackwell Publishing, visit our website:
www.blackwellpublishing.com/construction

Contents

Preface

This is the second in a series of volumes on Historic Building Conservation that combine conservation philosophy in the built environment with knowledge of traditional materials and structural and constructional conservation techniques and technology. The chapters are written by leading architects, structural engineers and related practitioners, who together reflect the interdisciplinary nature of conservation work.

While substantial publications exist on each of the subject areas – some by the authors of Historic Building Conservation – few individuals and practices have ready access to all of these or the time to read them in detail. The aim of the Historic Building Conservation series is to introduce each aspect of conservation and to provide concise, basic and up-to-date knowledge, sufficient for the professional to appreciate the subject better and to know where to seek further help.

Of direct practical application in the field, the books are structured to take the reader through the process of historic building conservation, presenting a total sequence of the integrative teamwork involved. *Materials & skills for historic building conservation* describes the characteristics and process of decay of traditional materials which inform the selection of appropriate repair techniques. *Understanding historic building conservation* provides understanding of the planning, legislative and philosophical background, followed by the process of researching the history of a building and the formulation of a conservation policy and plan.

The present volume, *Structures & construction in historic building conservation*, discusses conservation engineering philosophy, exposes the conflict between building codes and conservation legislation, and offers solutions, including fire safety issues. Leading-edge, on-site metric survey techniques are described and a range of structural advice is given, including methods of repair in relation to philosophical principles, not all readily available in published form elsewhere. Causes of induced movement in historic buildings are explained, together with basic soil mechanics and the assessment and diagnosis of structural failure, and there are chapters on the conservation of different types of construction: masonry, iron and steel, and concrete and reinforced concrete.

The series is particularly aimed at construction professionals – architects, surveyors, engineers – as well as postgraduate building conservation students and undergraduate architects and surveyors, as specialist or optional course reading. The series is also of value to other professional groups such as commissioning client bodies, managers and advisers, and interested individuals involved in house refurbishment or setting up a building preservation trust. While there is a focus on UK practice, most of the content is of relevance overseas – just as UK conservation courses attract many overseas students, for example from India, Greece, Australia and the USA.

Michael Forsyth

Contributors

Bill Blake

English Heritage surveyor and cartographer. Has worked for English Heritage since qualification in 1989, first with the Ancient Monuments Drawing Office, later as Measured Survey Manager at the Metric Survey Team responsible for quality assurance in metric heritage documentation. Publications on applied survey include the *English Heritage Metric Survey Specification*, 2000, and *Measured & Drawn* (English Heritage, 2003). Develops tools and skills in measured survey for conservation professionals through the English Heritage Summer School, the Raymond Lemaire Centre for Conservation (Katholieke Universiteit Leuven, Belgium) and the International Committee for Architectural Photogrammetry (CIPA), one of the international committees of ICOMOS (International Council on Monuments and Sites). Has developed an international heritage documentation standard for best practice in heritage documentation.

Michael Bussell

Structural engineer specialising in the appraisal and reuse of existing buildings of the nineteenth and twentieth centuries. Has written and lectured widely on the historical development of structural iron, steel, and reinforced concrete. His *Appraisal of existing iron and steel structures* (Steel Construction Institute, 1997) is the first full-length study of its subject. Currently deeply involved in the various railway and regeneration projects in the King's Cross and St Pancras area of London.

David Cook

Geotechnical engineer. Joined the School of Architecture and Civil Engineering at the University of Bath in 1966, following ten years' varied experience with consulting engineers, earthworks and site investigation contractors. Developed a curriculum content for Soil Mechanics and Engineering Geology within the newly developing courses in civil engineering and architecture. The varied nature of the regional geology provided a supportive backdrop for this teaching. The city's architecture also formed a springboard for collaborative research funding with the Institut für Tragkonstruktionen, Universität Karlsruhe. Research embodied field investigations of cracking and deformation of historic brick and masonry structures, its analysis and development of repair techniques.

Dina F. D'Ayala

Senior lecturer, Department of Architecture and Civil Engineering, University of Bath. Holds first degree and Doctorate of the Faculty of Engineering, Università di Roma La Sapienza. Research associate, Martin Centre, University of Cambridge; joined University of Bath 1996. Research interests: the structural performance of historic buildings, especially in earthquake-prone areas, and structural behaviour of three-dimensional structures, especially masonry domes and vaults. Developed non-linear finite and discrete element procedures to analyse these structures. Member, Editorial Board, *International Journal of Architectural Heritage: Conservation, Analysis, and Restoration*. Expert consultant, *Ethiopian Cultural Heritage Project* sponsored by the World Bank.

Steve Emery

Fire safety adviser for English Heritage. Serving fire fighter with Avon fire brigade for twenty-seven years; working as a fire safety officer in Bath for ten years. Seconded to English Heritage in 1992 as their national fire safety adviser. Has extensive experience of fire risk assessments and applying sympathetic fire safety measures to historic buildings.

Michael Forsyth

Architect and director of the postgraduate degree course in the Conservation of Historic Buildings, University of Bath. Studied, University of Liverpool, held the Rome Scholarship in Architecture and, after residence in Italy, moved to Canada, working on the design of the new concert hall for the Toronto Symphony Orchestra with the architect Arthur Erickson. Lectured at University of Bristol, 1979–89 and has lived and practised in Bath since 1987. Books include *Bath – Pevsner Architectural Guides* (Yale University Press, 2003) and *Buildings for Music: The Architect, the Musician, and the Listener from the Seventeenth Century to the Present Day* (MIT Press and Cambridge University Press, 1985), which won the 19th Annual ASCAP–Deems Taylor Award. The book was translated into French, German, Italian and Japanese. Holds a Doctor of Philosophy degree of the University of Bristol.

Ian Hume

Structural conservation engineer. Worked for English Heritage for twenty-two years, ten as Chief Engineer, and was project engineer for work at Ironbridge, Castle Howard Mausoleum, the National Gallery, the British Museum and the Palace of Westminster. Advised on projects ranging from prehistoric to the 1960s, including earth, stone, brickwork, timber, iron and modern materials. Took early retirement in 1997 and is now in private practice. Lectures to postgraduate students and organises courses on Conservation Engineering. Chairs the Conservation Accreditation Register for Engineers (CARE).

Peter Norris

Chartered surveyor, an approved inspector and fire safety adviser. Started career in building control in 1975 working in West Dorset, with its abundance of vernacular buildings; then moved to Bath City Council in 1986, specialising in major projects and historic buildings. Co-founded Rexon Day Building Control in 1997. Lectures on the Building Regulations and fire safety at the University of Bath for the postgraduate degree course in the Conservation of Historic Buildings and to the RIBA Part 3 students. Also an art historian; holds a degree in art history and is the biographer of the artist Arthur Henry Knighton-Hammond.

1 What is conservation engineering?

Dina F. D'Ayala and Michael Forsyth

Introduction

In the words of Sir Bernard Feilden, the conservation of historic buildings is a complex series of actions taken coordinately by several professionals in order to prevent the decay of a building while preserving and enhancing the cultural values embedded in it (Feilden, 2003).

The successful preservation of a historic building or environment, unless it has become a museum, depends on its continued use and the daily care and maintenance that come with this. The possibility of continued use depends on the adaptation of the building to present-day standards and ways of living, and in turn these invariably require changes in some of the constructional or structural features of the building. Conservation engineering can thus be defined as the branch of conservation that deals with managing the structural well-being of a building, minimising alteration and extending its life for future generations.

Structure is the prime determinant of a building's shape and hence it ultimately determines the building's aesthetic value, notwithstanding the frequent denial of structure that can be traced throughout the history of architecture (Warren, 2004). Structure is the skeleton on which the building's envelope is draped, with its architectural details, decorations and finishes. Hence it is essential to understand the structure and its condition in order properly to preserve the architecture.

The understanding of a structure comes from accurate analysis, whether numerical or qualitative or involving the study of historical records, in order to comprehend the evolution of its behaviour with time, to formulate a diagnosis relating to its current state and to forecast its future performance and thus devise appropriate measures of intervention.

This chapter attempts a definition of the boundaries and methodology of conservation engineering, a framework shared with the authors of subsequent chapters. Below is a very brief history of attitudes to structural intervention in historic buildings from our present perspective mainly based on the evolution of architectural conservation in Europe. There follows a description of the current approach to structural conservation on the basis of the two guiding, but sometimes conflicting, concepts of safety and authenticity. Specific reference is made to official international documents and guidelines. The relevance of the 'time' parameter in any conservation strategy is then discussed and the chapter concludes with a brief review of the book's contents.

A very brief history of structural intervention in historic buildings

A keen interest in the repair and restoration of ancient buildings was expressed as early as the sixth century AD by the emperor Theodoric the Great, who appointed an *architectus publicorum* to oversee the restoration of all important civil structures in Rome, such as the city walls and aqueducts and the Colosseum, already the object of spoil and pillage (Jokilehto, 1999).

A more systematic interest in historic buildings can be traced back to Renaissance architects' studies and drawings of Roman ruins. Particularly interesting examples are the plan and elevation drawings and detail sketches of the Colosseum produced by Giuliano da Sangallo (*Codex Barberini*). While the elevation realistically depicts the state of ruin of the external wall, the plan is drawn as a circle rather than an ellipse, in a sort of idealised interpretation of the real shape. Renaissance architects, however, were interested not only in the proportions and decorative apparatus of Roman buildings but also in the materials and technologies used to erect them. These indeed had been proven successful in ensuring the survival for centuries of the feats of Roman engineering, notwithstanding the effects of war, abandon and natural hazard.

Further proofs of this interest in Roman technology are the wide popularity in the Renaissance of construction treatises such as Vitruvius's *De Architectura* and the fact that Roman construction practices were used in contemporary buildings. The accurate depiction of ruins in the drawings of engravers such as Maarten van Heemskerck and Giovanni Antonio Dosio allow us today to reconstruct the condition of important buildings in the sixteenth century and to formulate hypotheses on the causes and modes of their damage and destruction.

The first to write technically about the maintenance, restoration and consolidation of ancient buildings, using the same form of Vitruvian treatise, was Leon Battista Alberti in the last two chapters of his tenth book (Alberti, 1485, English translation published 1988). He used the medical analogy so popular today and advocated a thorough investigation of the causes of damage and decay before deciding on a course of action. However, it is only with Leonardo da Vinci at the beginning of the sixteenth century that the first accurate mechanical interpretation of structural work is presented, together with structural repairs and preventive measures.

Alberti and other contemporaries stressed the essential importance of continued use and maintenance for the preservation and good upkeep of even the best-constructed buildings. Alongside the development of these new ideas, common construction practice was to use the larger abandoned ancient buildings as quarries and reclamation grounds, either using architectural elements such as columns and capitals in new buildings, as documented by Serlio, or using raw materials such as travertine, for instance from the Colosseum, in the production of lime.

At the beginning of the sixteenth century concern about the destruction of Roman heritage and antiquities resulted in the appointment of Raphael as Commissioner of Monuments, with the role of overseeing all activities connected to ancient ruins. This can be considered as the first step towards the modern involvement of the state in the protection of monuments. The interest in antiquities and historic buildings was exported to the rest of Europe, especially by the engravers and vedutists of the seventeenth century, and fascination with classical architecture was strengthened by the new ideas developed by the Enlightenment that led culture and science to become independent of religious beliefs.

In England the societies of Antiquaries and Dilettanti were formed around this time; these became forums for discussing the experiences and knowledge acquired during the Grand Tour, the journey through Europe lasting several years that travellers took to acquaint themselves with the architectural and artistic marvels of classical Italy and Greece.

Changes in Christian doctrines and liturgies, introduced by Lutheran reform and the Vatican counter-reform, had already led to substantial manipulation of both external and internal medieval church architecture throughout Europe. Architectural changes often revealed or highlighted structural problems, which were often recurrent and needed engineering solutions. One case in point is the celebrated report by Giovanni Poleni on cracks in the dome of St Peter's, Rome, in 1748. This is today considered to be the first attempt to apply rational analysis and an engineering method to explain the causes of an observed damaged state in an existing structure and to propose the least obtrusive intervention (Heyman, 1976).

In the United Kingdom the architectural alteration of churches often took the form of introducing classical architectural elements into Gothic structures, and the conservation movement evolved from the debate between the Neoclassical style and the Gothic Revival, crystallised in the repair campaigns carried out at Durham and Salisbury cathedrals at the end of the eighteenth century by James Wyatt and fiercely opposed by John Carter in the pages of the *Gentleman's Magazine*.

The concepts of reversibility and respectful treatment of works of art, and the importance of authenticity in the original piece as an embodiment of history, were first introduced during the eighteenth century in sculpture and painting repairs by Johann Joachim Winckelmann and Giovanni Pietro Bellori respectively. In Italy these concepts were also at the base of the approach to the restoration of architectural monuments, as demonstrated, for instance, in the work carried out by Raffaele Stern to stabilise the eastern end of the outer wall of the Colosseum in 1806. In this work all original parts, even those threatening collapse, were preserved and supported by a more modest, clearly different material that had a purely structural function, without any attempt to disguise the intervention, so that it should not be mistaken for part of the original. The result was very dramatic. However, just twenty years later this purist approach to structural repair was already diluted, mainly as a result of aesthetic criticism, as can be seen in the second buttress at the western end of the external wall of the Colosseum, inserted by Giuseppe Valadier in 1825. Although fulfilling the same structural function, the two buttresses could not be more different in underlying conceptual approach to structural conservation (D'Ayala et al., 1992).

In the United Kingdom, William Atkinson had an approach similar to Stern's. Realising the weathering vulnerability of the sandstone at Durham, he was the first to propose carrying out repair by using mortar mixes rather than substituting failed stone with new cut. He recommended the use of Parker's cement, a hydraulic lime obtained from the calcination of Bath stone and today better known as Roman cement. This approach to consolidation work was later retained in both the RIBA guidelines and the SPAB manifesto.

The two approaches outlined above were to a certain extent coexistent, and while very often guidelines and writings about the care of historic buildings in the early nineteenth century advocated a 'scientific' methodology respectful of the historic and archaeological value of the monument, actual practice entailed substantial demolition and reconstruction aimed at the glorification of a certain historic period and architectural style. In France especially, the style of choice was Gothic, which was considered the principal architectural heritage of the nation. Substantial work was undertaken on churches and castles, either because of the genuine need of remedial work or to remove additions from other periods, following the lines of 'stylistic restoration' historically associated with the figure of Viollet-le-Duc. While it is impossible to justify the relevance of Viollet-le-Duc's work in conservation policies and practice today, it is fair to say that his activity in France and his writings crystallised a certain ideal of restoration work, which, in his own words, consisted of 'reinstating a building to a condition of completeness which might never have existed at any given time' (Viollet-le-Duc, 1858–68) – that is to say, the restorer was allowed to create a historic falsehood in the name of stylistic unity. This falsehood was so much the greater for Gothic churches and cathedrals which had evolved through two or three centuries, from early Romanesque to late Renaissance, in terms of both style and construction.

From the point of view of structural conservation, the major contribution of Viollet-le-Duc is certainly his interest in and detailed study of medieval construction techniques and materials, and the recognition that architectural forms were a logical consequence of structural principles that depended, in turn, on the behaviour of the construction materials. In reintegration and repair Viollet-le-Duc advocated the use of the same material; however, new stone blocks were inserted in place of weathered ones, and in his later interventions he approved the use of steel in place of the original timber, with the same structural form and function.

In England during the same period, John Ruskin led a strong critical movement against stylistic restoration. More than anyone before him, Ruskin was concerned with the sense of history embedded in a weathered surface as the principal value of a historic building, together with its architectural composition and finishes; these he considered testament to the process of creativity and hence to the authenticity of a particular building. Restoration therefore could only be seen as alteration to either the fabric or the architecture, and in any case was misleading. Much of his work was in defence of Gothic architecture, against the prevailing Neoclassical movement. However, in his later years he also had to speak against the deception produced by the Gothic Revival movement. As for structural intervention, he was in favour of introducing ties and anchors in buildings to stop cracks and the effects of movement, and to minimise intervention he was even in favour of permanent shoring as an alternative to rebuilding a part of a historic building or monument that was threatening collapse. The main objection of Ruskin's contemporaries was to his far too radical attitude, which if assumed as a rule would have led to many existing buildings becoming eventually unusable.

Eventually, it was Sir George Gilbert Scott's approach to historic buildings, as highlighted in a paper of 1862, that became the set of practical rules published by the RIBA in 1865 with the title *Conservation of Ancient Monuments and Remains*. This document not only provided the basic methodological and ethical approach to conservation but also established practice in terms of institutional and private involvement and the roles of the various professionals. Scott's paper was very influential in England and it still informs much of today's conservation practice.

A decade later, in 1877, William Morris founded the Society for the Protection of Ancient Buildings (SPAB) and issued a manifesto which declared maintenance and conservative repair to be fundamental conservation principles. Most importantly, it identified authenticity in a historic building as the original in situ material of any period and style over which the life of the building had spanned. Consequently, any substitution of old with new – or restoration – was clearly associated with loss of authenticity and value, and hence was banned. The SPAB was influential not only in the United Kingdom but across Europe, where its members engaged themselves in debate or denounced restoration work on major international landmarks.

Safety and conservation: a dichotomy?

In the present day, while different approaches are still predominant in different countries, the preservation of historic buildings is regulated worldwide by the Venice Charter issued in 1964. This was underwritten by representatives from sixteen countries forming the International Council on Monuments and Sites (ICOMOS). Since then many other charters have been published and many more countries have joined in. ICOMOS is funded by UNESCO, the organisation of the United Nations involved in education and cultural development across the world.

Current conservation engineering practice in the UK developed from several landmark projects carried out in the late twentieth century, including Ely Cathedral, York Minster and St Paul's Cathedral, and more recently Windsor Castle. It was the critical assessment of these projects and the observation of their performance over several decades that led to the current paradigm; most importantly, there is recognition of the need for alternative analytical and assessment models which acknowledge the substantial difference in behaviour between traditional and engineered materials – masonry and timber as opposed to steel and reinforced concrete. The other strong influence on structural conservation is the increasing awareness of the vulnerability of historic buildings to natural hazards – earthquakes, fire and flood – and the need for damage mitigation strategies and strengthening interventions which will be respectful of the historic fabric.

All structural intervention should be governed by the four maxims of conservation first proposed by SPAB: *conserve as found, minimum intervention, like-for-like repairs* and *interventions should be reversible*. These also represent the current position of English Heritage and are at the core of British Standard 7913: 1998 *A Guide to the Principles of the Conservation of Historic Buildings*. In addition to the four maxims, this recommends that attention be paid to the effects of localised repairs on the overall structure, from both a physical and an aesthetic point of view, and draws attention to the question of whether it is acceptable that they should be seen and how easy it should be to identify them clearly. Similar principles to these form the basis of most historic buildings legislation in the western world.

Conservation engineering can be defined as the process of understanding, interpreting and managing the architectural heritage in order to *safely* deliver it to posterity. The term 'safely' is broadly taken to embody the concept that the bodies and individuals responsible for the care of historic buildings will work towards ensuring maximum private or public usability balanced against minimum loss of fabric and value. The safe use of the built environment is regulated by standards and codes of practice drawn up by competent institutions that assume as a point of reference a certain level of risk in society that is generally considered acceptable. The structural stability and robustness of a building is, however, only one of the elements defining its safe use.

The conflict between safety standards and conservation philosophy usually stems from the fact that not just the standards themselves but also the practice of achieving the standards are based on and refer to modern materials, technology and process. A historic building is considered of value not only because of its age but, most importantly, because of its uniqueness, its deviation from the norm and hence, to a certain extent, from what is standard. This constitutes the building's significance or authenticity, a quality that it is vital to conserve.

Hence it would appear that the philosophical approaches at the basis of the two processes – ensuring safety and conserving a building – are at odds. This, however, is not entirely true, as construction historically was also regulated by standards and rules of practice, even if to a lesser extent and from a different knowledge base.

The task is to redefine the level of risk associated with the use of historic buildings that society is ready to accept in a trade-off for conservation, and to develop a different set of standards and processes to evaluate and ensure a building's compliance. The development of a different set of standards is clearly an operation that requires various elements of society and expertise to come together.

The process of assessing existing structures and buildings – not necessarily of heritage value – is a well-developed branch of civil engineering. This is called upon every time a change of use is proposed for a building or when an unexpected event occurs that may affect its structural stability and capability. However, the procedures and technologies developed for this purpose are in general designed to deliver compliance to the same standards that apply to new buildings.

The issue becomes a matter of whether the procedures and assumptions formulated by structural engineers for existing buildings can be successfully extended to historic buildings of heritage value, in the effort to ensure both safety and protection of the fabric. In these terms conservation engineering can be defined as the application of analysis and design techniques to the assessment of the structural capacity of elements or entire structures which may be archaic, obsolete or originally non-engineered (see also Friedman, 2001).

A 'safe' structure may be defined as one that will withstand the designed loads without becoming unfit for use, the judgement of safety being based on expected performance versus expected environmental and human actions. Most pre-nineteenth-century buildings were not designed to given structural standards, but rather to rules of thumb and general geometric criteria drawn from experience of collapses. This accumulated experience was ultimately based on past performance and its extrapolation to future behaviour for a given use. In this sense the present-day approach to structural design differs from the past only in so far as the evidence from experience has been codified, parameterised, rationalised – in short, it has been provided with a scientific basis.

The two design approaches – the traditional and the modern – differ not so much in their underlying process as in the method followed. This means that in principle modern codes are applicable to structures that pre-date codes, but that in practice, in order to really assess a historic building, the structural engineer needs to travel over the same path that led to the traditional accumulated experience; the engineer thus needs to possess both traditional building knowledge and current engineering knowledge. For this to be professionally practical, a robust method of acquiring that traditional knowledge needs to be devised which is applicable on a project-by-project basis and produces transferable know-how.

Formulating the safety judgement

In most cases a structural intervention serves either to repair so as to restore the original structural capacity, or to add strength to the existing capacity, or to provide an additional structural behaviour – for instance, lateral stability and strength to systems that might not have it. It is then reasonable to assume that the choice of materials, level of alteration, reversibility, even level of safety, should be guided by the type of intervention – that is, whether it is repairing so as to restore or strengthening so as to add. This conceptual distinction between repair and strengthening can provide a robust framework of guidelines for enforcing compliance with present-day standards or, more appropriately, for defining a separate set of standards based on the concept of improvement of performance rather than compliance with the existing codes for new build.

The two issues outlined above – robust acquisition of knowledge and robust measurement of performance – have been thoroughly debated by professionals and academics over the past thirty years. A good example of the agreed body of knowledge and approach so far reached, at least as far as western culture is concerned, is contained in the document of recommendations produced by the ICOMOS International Scientific Committee for the Analysis and Restoration of Structures of Architectural Heritage (ISCARSAH).

The ISCARSAH principles identify a process – of anamnesis, diagnosis, therapy and control – that leads to a robust assessment of safety while safeguarding the fabric. This involves the collection of all relevant data, the identification of the relation between cause and effect, remedial measures and the monitoring of their effects. The approach is not dissimilar to that used in the assessment of existing modern buildings. What is different is the source of information, its interpretation and specifically how the final judgement on safety is arrived at. For historic buildings much of the information will be qualitative and anecdotal rather than quantitative and systematic. Can a judgement of safety be based on such data, and can such data be treated with the same tools with which engineers treat systematic quantitative data? In general, the present-day approach to safety involves an accepted level of uncertainty associated with any information on materials or structural performance; indeed, data is collected and processed so as to provide information with a given level of uncertainty which society assumes to be acceptable.

In the case of a historic or non-engineered building, the uncertainty of any data is variable and may depend on expert opinion. In other words, it will depend on how reliable the structural engineer considers that particular data to be and how confident he or she is in using it. The level of confidence will depend on the knowledge base available to the professional for the particular form of construction. This can be supplemented, when appropriate, with various non-destructive or semi-destructive diagnostic techniques, which will help to locate and identify pathologies and correlate them to plausible causes, but also assist the acquisition of information on the mechanical characteristics of the in situ materials.

On the basis of the information gathered, the engineer needs to consider, first, all feasible structural models with an explicit statement of how conservative each particular scheme is. Nowadays this activity can be aided by computer programs that allow relatively quick and synthetic results to be obtained for a relatively large number of initial hypotheses. In this way, different feasible structural behaviours can be investigated and corresponding safety factors estimated. However, it should be considered that to a certain extent the more complex the model, the less reliable are the results, unless the model complexity is accompanied by a substantial reduction in the uncertainty of the initial data. Hence at each stage of the assessment the analysis should always be carried out by considering the simplest, most conservative model first, moving to more refined or complex ones only if there is not sufficient safety margin associated with it.

For structural models and analytical results to be of value to the conservation process, they need to include all the information associated with the structure that is not numerical or mechanical in nature. Hence the question arises of how qualitative knowledge can be translated into data fit for calculation. General guidelines for relatively simple conditions can be provided as follows:

- presence of cracks: reduction of redundancy; take into account that there is no transmission of forces along cracks
- presence of defects: reduction of capacity locally, for instance reduction of available cross section
- relative rotation between members: acknowledgement of type of connection, working of the joint

However, ultimately the use of qualitative information relies entirely on the capacity of the professional to interpret it correctly and translate it in structural terms.

Choosing an appropriate time frame

Once the phenomena affecting the historic building under assessment have been identified and possibly quantified, the final judgement on how safe the current conditions are and what is required to improve or extend that safety depends entirely on the engineer's perception of the evolution in time of such phenomena. Hence the time parameter, which has not been mentioned so far, is an essential variable of the problem of defining the interventions, both qualitatively and quantitatively. The time parameter affects all aspects of the conservation project:

- First of all, the expected remaining life of the structure.
- The expected interval of time until the next appraisal. Typically for churches and cathedrals this occurs every five years. This is also usually the case for public Grade I listed buildings, but not necessarily for minor architectural heritage, which typically gets reassessed every ten to twenty-five years depending on location and economic value.
- The expected life span of the intervention. Typically engineers design for a life span of fifty years for new buildings – both expected loading conditions and materials characteristics are defined for this life span.
- The variability in time of external loads and the risk associated with the occurrence of natural hazards. For ordinary construction, usually the design values chosen for natural hazards correspond to a given probability (typically 10%) of their not being overcome in the life span of the building (fifty years). For heritage buildings, especially those of great

importance, the tendency is to consider the worst possible scenario, usually determined by the worst event ever to have occurred in the region.

- Finally, the time frame of the project. Depending on what lead-up time to the intervention is available, monitoring of various time-dependent phenomena can be put in place, from which valuable information may be obtained. If the phenomena are highly important, the project schedule will probably need to be altered in order to allow for appropriate monitoring. Monitoring is also important during and after intervention, especially if this is to repair a defect, in order to assess the outcome of the intervention itself. Monitoring over time can also be used to gauge the magnitude and extent of any intervention.

Most importantly, the time parameter affects the whole concept of reversibility, and indeed reversibility is a fundamental principle of conservation. This is based on the observation that our present knowledge of structural behaviour and that of materials may be limited and that in the future, with further research and technological developments, better solutions might be found. At the same time, any intervention has to be durable; that is to say, its structural performance over the expected life span of the intervention should be more or less constant and reliable. Most durable materials usually lead to interventions that have limited reversibility. In this respect, the concept of retractability – falling just short of total reversal – may be more appropriate.

References and further reading

Alberti, Leon Battista, *On the Art of Building in Ten Books* (MIT Press, Cambridge MA, 1988).

Beckmann, Poul and Bowles, Robert, *Structural Aspects of Building Conservation*, 2nd edn (Butterworth-Heinemann, London, 2004).

British Standard, BS 7913:1998. *Guide to the Principles of the Conservation of Historic Buildings*, BSI, London, 1998.

D'Ayala, Dina and Croci, G., 'Recent developments in the safety assessment of the Colosseum', *IABSE Symposium on Structural Preservation of the Architectural Heritage*, Rome, 1993, pp. 425–32.

D'Ayala, Dina, Croci, G. and Conforto, M.L., 'Studies to evaluate the origin of cracks and failure in the history of Colosseum in Rome', *1st International Congress on Restoration of the Architectural Heritage and Building*, Islas Canarias, 1992, pp. 214–19.

Feilden, Bernard M., *Conservation of Historic Buildings*, 3rd edn (Butterworth Heinemann, London, 2003).

Friedman, D., 'Methodology of conservation engineering', *Journal of Architectural Conservation*, 2001, no. 2, 49–63.

Heyman, Jacques, *The Stone Skeleton* (Cambridge University Press, Cambridge, 1995).

Heyman, Jacques, 'The strengthening of the west tower of Ely cathedral', *Proceedings of the Institution of Civil Engineers*, pt.1 (ICE, London, 1976), pp.123–47.

ICOMOS ISCARSAH, *Recommendations for the Analysis, Conservation, and Structural Restoration of Architectural Heritage*, ratified in 2003.

ICOMOS, 1996. *The Venice Charter*, International Charter for the Conservation and Restoration of Monuments and Sites (Paris, 1996).

Jokilehto, Jukka, *A History of Architectural Conservation* (Butterworth Heinemann, London, 1999).

Morris, William, *Manifesto for the Society for the Protection of Ancient Buildings* (SPAB, London, 1877).

Ruskin, John, *The Seven Lamps of Architecture* (London, 1849, re-published 1990 by Dover Publications Inc.).

Viollet-le-Duc, Eugène Emmanuel, *Dictionnaire Raisonné de l'Architecture Française du XIe au XVIe Siecle*, 10 vols (Paris, 1858/1868).

Vitruvius, translation by Ingrid D. Rowland, *Ten Books on Architecture* (Cambridge University Press, Cambridge, 1999).

Warren, J., 'Conservation of structure in historic buildings', *Journal of Architectural Conservation*, 2004, no. 2, 39–49.

Yeomans, David, 'Saving structures', *Journal of Architectural Conservation*, 2004, no. 3, 59–72.

2 The philosophy of conservation engineering

Ian Hume

We all know it is the force of gravity that makes apples fall off trees and makes old structures eventually fall down. Those who have been involved with historic structures for any length of time will have discovered that there is, apparently, the opposite and very often equal force of habit, which keeps many old structures standing – or so it seems. But as, in truth, there is no 'force of habit', what is it that really keeps these decaying structures standing when our theories tell us that they should have long since collapsed?

The first and most important point in dealing with old structures is that they must be understood. The problem is that, initially at least, we do not understand what is happening to the structures we are dealing with; we do not know where the loads are going; we do not know what stresses the structures are capable of carrying; we do not know what effects the various forms of distress and decay are having.

Our approach to old structures is determined by our approach to new construction, as it is usually in new forms of construction that we are educated. We are not able, at least until we have a considerable base of experience, to approach old structures in any other way. Calculations and theory can deafen us to what the structure is saying. The structure must be the primary source of evidence. Saying 'that's OK, leave it alone, don't do anything' or 'don't do very much' should not be seen as taking a risk. Those responsible for historic structural conservation are not in the business of taking risks; they must always be convinced of what they are doing. They must be able to accept the fact that a structure leans and has out-of-level floors, and not be blinkered by training that tells them that all structures should be vertical and all floors precisely level.

The appraisal and assessment of historic buildings and structures has as much to do with art as with science.

Calculations and historic structures

Experience suggests that the condition of an old structure almost always contradicts the results of calculations. Calculations often show that a structure is very weak or that it should have collapsed during erection, while the fact that it has stood happily for many a long year and survived every-thing that the weather and alterations can throw at it proves the calculations to be in error.

There are a number of reasons for this:

- The stress and modulus of elasticity used are too low, often much too low, for the material which actually exists in the structure. The current codes of practice advise values based on new materials which may be very different from those used originally. Timber certainly falls into this category. Old timber has seasoned well over the years, is of higher quality, being slower grown and having fewer knots, and was often better selected.
- The structure has made use of load paths and fixities that may not be anticipated in the calculations and that are often too complex to be introduced into calculations.
- Design live loads (particularly office loads) as recommended by codes of practice have not been realised in real life, and therefore the structure has never been called upon to carry the loads that the codes advise.
- The decay and distress may not be as significant as at first thought.

Calculations should come second to inspection. Engineers and others must learn to listen to what the structure is telling them. All their training relates to new works, and engineers should not necessarily expect old structures to conform to the same standards. We must not take risks, but just because a wall is leaning or a floor is bouncy does not mean that it has to be condemned.

One example of the shortcomings of calculations with regard to historic structures relates to the deflection of timber floors. The modern limits for deflection are laid down with modern inflexible finishes in mind. If the ceiling is of an old flexible lime plaster, or indeed if there is no ceiling at all, as is often the case with old buildings, then the deflection limit might well be exceeded with no adverse effect. A second example relates to foundations. Many old buildings do not have foundations that fit current building requirements. If the current state of the structure indicates that there have been no problems as a result of this lack of conformance to current regulations, or that any such problems ceased many years ago, there may well be no reason to improve the foundations. If calculations bear out the fact that the structure is satisfactory then so well and good, but if they do not the engineer needs to delve much deeper and to be prepared to go outside the normal rules of new structures.

Past good behaviour, load testing and upward revision of allowable stresses and so forth should all be looked at as ways of justifying a structure. It is suggested that it is often not necessary to spend huge amounts of time doing calculations on the structural capacity of old structures. It is much better to spend scarce resources on examining the structure and understanding why it stands up happily without any new intervention.

Structural flexibility

One of the saving graces of historic structures is their flexibility. It is the flexible nature of historic structures that enables them to accommodate so well the movements that all structures suffer. Lime mortars and buildings constructed from a multiplicity of small elements are often able to move to quite a considerable degree without becoming dangerous. The structure's flexibility allows it to sustain the strains applied to it by ground movement, roof spread or whatever.

Light, airy structures with delicate architecture are the most vulnerable to damage from structural movements. The low, solid and stocky type of structure will obviously be less susceptible to damage.

Beam bearings in some old structures are sometimes minimal. Often, skimpy bearing distances are further infringed by decay and there will always be the potential problem that structural movement of walls will cause a beam to slip off its bearings or at least reduce bearing lengths significantly.

Conserving or altering structures

The best chance for a historic structure to survive is for it to be put to a practical and economic use with a minimum of change. However, repairs and some changes to layout and construction may be unavoidable. Conservation engineering aims to ensure that those repairs and changes are carried out in a sensible and sensitive way.

The most successful conservation schemes are those which have involved the structure in the minimum of change. When there are plans for considerable alterations to historic structures, the structural and historic integrity of those structures is put in jeopardy. Removal of walls and floors not only causes loss of valuable historic fabric but risks damage, possibly even collapse, of the structure. Structures do not respond well, either historically or structurally, to attempts to turn them into open-plan offices or shops with minimal supports at ground floor level. Many old structures have, in the past, been subject to changes, often ill-considered changes, and further disruption should be avoided.

It is worth questioning the need to create extensive open areas of floor. Will the layout work as it is? Will satisfactory improvements to circulation be achieved if a few extra door openings are made rather than a full-scale removal of walls?

As soon as possible changes are being considered, advice should be sought from architects, historians and engineers who are experienced in dealing with historic structures, and early advice should also be sought from local authority conservation officers and/or English Heritage.

Demands for unnecessarily heavy floor loadings are often made. But are these necessary? Chapter 5 discusses this topic further.

By and large, historic structures that have stood the test of time are capable, if well maintained, of having a long future life and can be put to good use. Rather than being a liability to its owner, a historic structure, in a state as near as possible to its original condition, should be looked upon as a good, long-term capital asset.

The involvement of the engineer

Conservation engineering includes the structural engineering aspects of repair, refurbishment, rehabilitation and renovation but goes further than these terms suggest. It is actively involved with the conservation of both the hidden and the visible structure of listed buildings, scheduled ancient monuments and structures within conservation areas. It is not always looking for the cheapest option, although conservation need not always be the more expensive option either.

It is important that the conservation engineer becomes involved in the planning of any changes at a very early stage. The future of many listed buildings relies on the amount of damage caused by proposed works. The insertion of new windows and doors can damage walls beyond repair, and the addition of extra floors almost always means that the structure will need strengthening. Usually such strengthening cannot be done without causing great damage to the structure, usually at great expense. It is very difficult to retain a facade if its lower storey is to be removed totally and even more difficult to retain a structure where the ground floor is to be completely removed in order that it can be opened up for shop development. The future of many listed structures relies on the amount of damage caused by proposed works. All too often the layout of a listed structure is replanned without a proper understanding of its construction and structural condition, thus condemning it to unwarranted disfigurement.

Conservation philosophy

When a structure is listed, everything within the curtilage (usually the boundary) of that structure is deemed to be listed. A structure is not usually listed for one particular feature but is listed as a whole, all parts being considered important.

While it is easy to understand that the exterior appearance of a structure is of historic and aesthetic importance and that the principal rooms are highly valued, it is often not appreciated that the hidden structure is also considered important. Floor joists and beams, for example, cannot be destroyed without listed building consent being given. They are an integral part of the history of the structure, as is roof construction, although neither is likely to be readily visible.

The best situation from a conservation viewpoint is to have the original structure, in its original location and in its original condition, serving its original purpose. Many structures fall into this category, but many more change their use and their condition demands repairs – listed building consent may well be needed for such repairs. Conservation engineers have to temper their philosophy of conserving as found and minimum intervention with their responsibility for structural integrity of the structure and the safety of its users.

The principles of conservation

- **Conserve as found.** Structures should ideally be conserved as they are found. They should not be taken back to the condition that it is supposed they might have been in at some period in their history; neither should they be 'improved' without good cause. Part of the value of a historic structure is that it contains a record of the changes that have taken place during its history. A little decay or a slight distortion should not necessarily result in renewal.
- **Minimal intervention.** In many instances it is, of course, necessary to make changes either because of excessive decay or distortion resulting in a threat to the structural stability or because changes are necessary to ensure that the structure has a viable future. Whenever changes are made, these should be kept to a minimum. The first question to be asked of any technique proposed for the consolidation of historic fabric is whether it is tried and tested. Tried and tested techniques are preferable to new methods that may have an unforeseen detrimental effect on the structure at some time in the future.
- **Like-for-like repairs.** If repairs are to be made, the ideal is that they are made using the same materials as are found in the original construction. Ideally a timber beam should be repaired with timber and a brick wall with a similar type of brick. However, there are times when to do this would cause a great loss of fabric and consequent loss of detail and history. For instance, a timber beam may only be decayed at its bearing on the wall. To carry out a like-for-like repair would necessarily mean some loss of good timber so that a structurally sound splice could be made. It might be less intrusive to retain the decayed timber and to effect a repair using a steel shoe. Such a shoe might be fixed to the sides of the beam or it might be partially or totally hidden.
- **Repairs should be reversible.** If repairs have to be made, these should be designed and carried out with subsequent removal in mind. Ideally, it should be possible to remove repairs from a structure, should it later prove possible to make better repairs or should, for some reason, the repairs become redundant. Of all the principles of conservation, this is the most difficult to achieve. Indeed, in many cases it will not be possible to make sensibly reversible repairs.
- **Repairs should be sympathetic.** Repairs need to be in character with the structure. This is not to say that they have to be made to look old (this is not to be recommended at all) or that they have to copy slavishly the original details of the structure. If it is decided to use modern materials for the repair then it is good if the design fits the general style of the original structure. Occasionally repairs that are plainly

modern in design are needed, but these can still be designed to sit happily with the original fabric.

Conservation engineering repair techniques

Additional questions regarding the suitability of any proposed repair techniques include the following:

- Are the repairs really required or will the structure survive without them?
- Does the proposed work improve the overall stability of the structure?
- What damage will be caused if these repairs are carried out?
- Will the repairs be seen?
- If they are seen, are they to blend in with the existing fabric or are they to contrast while still being in harmony?
- Will future historians be able to date the repairs?
- If there is a need to mix materials, what effects might this have?
- Will the structure lose its inherent flexibility? Will it cope with climatic changes without distress?
- How does the proposed method meet the principles of conservation?

The art of conservation engineering

Structural engineering for conservation is an art as well as a science. It takes little effort to design a major and intrusive scheme to deal with a perceived problem. It takes considerable expertise and experience to evolve a scheme that improves the condition of the structure and is unobtrusive and sympathetic to the historic fabric but ensures that it has a sound future. Expertise and experience are also needed to decide whether a structure that is distorted actually has a current problem or if the distortion is a result of movements which took place a long time ago and are not likely to recur. It takes experience and an understanding of traditional structures to carry out sympathetic repairs to historic fabric, not just an ability with numbers.

It is not at all easy to decide to do nothing to the structure, but very easy to advise demolition.

The process of conservation engineering

Load testing can be of great help in determining the structural adequacy of something that defies proof by calculation, and it gives a deeper insight into how old structures work.

Structural monitoring is sometimes carried out to help in the diagnosis of problems, but more often it is done to prove beyond doubt that fractured structures showing signs of distress are in fact stable. Structural monitoring can be complex and expensive, but a great deal of use can be made of straightforward and inexpensive techniques. The simpler methods are underused but have considerable potential, and these topics are discussed in later chapters.

It is with regard to the safety of the structure that conservation engineers most often find themselves at the centre of the argument. Some may consider that a certain structure is dangerous and should be demolished forthwith, while the purist conservationist wishes to retain everything that can possibly be retained. It is of no use whatever retaining a building or structure that is dangerous, but very often a structure is by no means as dangerous as it at first appears.

The philosophy of conservative repairs to structures can be considered as a sliding scale of desirability:

(1) Do nothing.
(2) Add extra members in similar material.
(3) Add extra members in foreign materials.
(4) Carry out traditional repairs.
(5) Insert new materials into the existing materials.
(6) Replace isolated members.
(7) Replace whole elements of the structure.
(8) Replace the entire fabric behind the facade (facadism).
(9) Rebuild in facsimile.

However, life is rarely simple and many cases will be a combination of two or more of these levels of desirability. They are further compounded by the use of materials such as resins in timbers, which could occur at a number of places in the levels of desirability according to the occasion and according to the size of the problem.

While it is sometimes, of course, necessary to repair or strengthen structures and to cause some damage in order that the structure as a whole can be preserved, the last two items in the above list – facadism and facsimile structures – are not deemed to be conservation and are not discussed further.

3 The Building Regulations and related legislation

Peter Norris

When discussing legislation such as the Building Regulations, one is very conscious that by the time of publication what one has said is likely to be already out of date. Therefore any reference to legislation included here should be checked against the current Acts, Regulations or approved codes of practice to ensure that the latest information is being referred to.

The main purpose of the Building Regulations is to ensure the health and safety of people in or about a building. They also address certain aspects of the welfare and convenience of building users, energy conservation, and access and facilities that will accommodate the needs of all, including those with disabilities.

The significant milestones in the evolution of 'modern' construction legislation came initially with the move from the building byelaws to the Building Regulations 1965. The Regulations were from then on regularly amended and updated. The next significant change was the re-casting of the Regulations in 1985, when the functional requirements were supported by the publication of Approved Documents. That year was also significant for the introduction of the Building (Approved Inspectors etc.) Regulations 1985, which opened up the control of development under the Building Regulations to private sector Approved Inspectors.

The Approved Documents, which accompany the present Regulations, give practical guidance about some of the ways of meeting the functional requirements of the Regulations.

The present related legislation consists of

- Building Regulations 2000 (as amended) and Approved Documents
- Part II of the Building Act 1984, which made provisions for privatised building control by Approved Inspectors
- Building (Approved Inspectors etc.) Regulations 2000 (as amended)

The Building Regulations 2000 (as amended): Schedule 1

Current Regulations and Approved Documents cover the following:

Part A   *Structure*
               A1   Loading
               A2   Ground movement
               A3   Disproportionate collapse

Part B	*Fire safety*
	B1 Means of warning and escape
	B2 Internal fire spread (linings)
	B3 Internal fire spread (structure)
	B4 External fire spread
	B5 Access and facilities for the fire service

Volume 1 – Dwellinghouses
Volume 2 – Buildings other than dwellinghouses

Part C	*Site preparation and resistance to contaminants and moisture*
	C1 Site preparation and resistance to contaminants
	C2 Resistance to moisture

Part D	*Toxic substances*
	D1 Cavity insulation

Part E	*Resistance to the passage of sound*
	E1 Protection against sound from other parts of the building and adjoining buildings
	E2 Protection against sound within a dwellinghouse etc.
	E3 Reverberation in the common internal parts of buildings containing flats or rooms for residential purposes
	E4 Acoustic conditions in schools

Part F	*Ventilation*
	F1 Means of ventilation

Part G	*Hygiene*
	G1 Sanitary conveniences and washing facilities
	G2 Bathrooms
	G3 Hot water storage

Part H	*Drainage and waste disposal*
	H1 Foul water drainage
	H2 Wastewater treatment systems and cesspools
	H3 Rainwater drainage
	H4 Building over sewers
	H5 Separate systems of drainage
	H6 Solid waste storage

Part J	*Combustion appliances and fuel storage systems*
	J1 Air supply
	J2 Discharge of products of combustion
	J3 Protection of building
	J4 Provision of information
	J5 Protection of liquid fuel storage systems
	J6 Protection against pollution

Part K	Protection from falling, collision and impact
	K1 Stairs, ladders and ramps
	K2 Protection from falling
	K3 Vehicle barriers and loading bays
	K4 Protection from collision with open windows, skylights and ventilators
	K5 Protection against impact from and trapping by doors

Part L	Conservation of fuel and power
	L1A Conservation of fuel and power (new dwellings)
	L1B Conservation of fuel and power (existing dwellings)
	L2A Conservation of fuel and power (new buildings other than dwellings)
	L2B Conservation of fuel and power work (existing buildings other than dwellings)

Part M	Access to and use of buildings
	M1 Access and use
	M2 Access to extensions to buildings other than dwellings
	M3 Sanitary conveniences in extensions to buildings other than dwellings
	M4 Sanitary conveniences in dwellings

Part N	Glazing – safety in relation to impact, opening and cleaning
	N1 Protection against impact
	N2 Manifestation of glazing
	N3 Safe opening and closing of windows, skylights and ventilators
	N4 Safe access for cleaning windows etc.

Part P	Electrical safety
	P1 Design, installation, inspection and testing

Regulation 7	Materials and workmanship

Other important related provisions under the Building Act 1984 are as follows:

Section 21	Provision of drainage
Section 24	Provision of exits
Section 72	Means of escape from fire
Section 77	Dangerous buildings
Section 78	Dangerous buildings – emergency measures

Control of building work generally applying to historic buildings

In the Regulations, 'building work' means

(a)   the erection or extension of a building

(b)   the provision or extension of a controlled service or fitting in or in connection with a building (relating to Part G, H, J, L or P)

(c)   the material alteration of a building, or a controlled service or fitting, as mentioned in paragraph (2)

(d)   work required by Regulation 6 relating to material change of use

(e)   the insertion of insulating material into the cavity wall of a building

(f)   work involving the underpinning of a building

(g)   work relating to thermal elements, a change of energy status or consequential improvements to energy performance (the requirements relating to Part L, where the Approved Document allows for a more flexible approach with historic buildings, are discussed later)

The provision or extension of a controlled service or fitting in (b) above relates to elements such as drainage, combustion appliances, domestic electrical installations and so on, and for Part L purposes also includes the provision of a window, rooflight, roof window, a door that together with its frame has more than 50% of its surface area glazed, a space heating or hot water service boiler, or a hot water vessel.

An alteration is 'material' for the purposes of the Regulations if the work, or any part of it, would at any stage result in

- a building or controlled service or fitting not complying with a relevant requirement where previously it did

- a building or controlled service or fitting, which before the work commenced did not comply with a relevant requirement, being more unsatisfactory in relation to such a requirement

In the Regulations, 'relevant requirement' means any of the following applicable requirements of Schedule 1:

Part A	(Structure)
	Paragraph B1 (means of warning and escape)
	Paragraph B3 (internal fire spread – structure)
	Paragraph B4 (external fire spread)
	Paragraph B5 (access and facilities for the fire service)
Part M	(Access to and use of buildings)

Meaning of material change of use (Regulation 5)

For the purposes of paragraph 8(1)(e) of Schedule 1 to the Act and for the purpose of these Regulations, there is a material change of use where there is a change in the purposes for which or the circumstances in which a building is used, so that after that change

(a)   the building is used as a dwelling, where previously it was not

(b)   the building contains a flat, where previously it did not

(c)   the building is used as a hotel or boarding house, where previously it was not

(d)   the building is used as an institution, where previously it was not

(e)   the building is used as a public building, where previously it was not

(f)   the building is not a building described in Classes I to VI in Schedule 2, where previously it was

(g)   the building, which contains at least one dwelling, contains a greater or lesser number of dwellings than it did previously

(h)   the building contains a room for residential purposes, where previously it did not

(i)   the building, which contains at least one room for residential purposes, contains a greater or lesser number of such rooms than it did previously

(j)   the building is used as a shop, where previously it was not

Requirements relating to material change of use (Regulation 6) are as follows:

(1)   Where there is a material change of use of the whole of a building, such work, if any, shall be carried out as is necessary to ensure that the building complies with the relevant requirements of the following paragraphs of Schedule 1:

    (a)   in all cases
           B1 (means of warning and escape)
           B2 (internal fire spread – linings)
           B3 (internal fire spread – structure)
           B4(2) (external fire spread – roofs)
           B5 (access and facilities for the fire service)
           C2(c) (interstitial and surface condensation)
           F1 (ventilation)
           G1 (sanitary conveniences and washing facilities)
           G2 (bathrooms)
           H1 (foul water drainage)
           H6 (solid waste storage)
           J1 to J3 (combustion appliances)
           L1 (conservation of fuel and power)
           P1 (electrical safety – design, installation, inspection and testing)

    (b)   in the case of a material change of use described in Regulation 5(c), (d), (e) and (f), A1 to A3 (structure)

    (c)   in the case of a building exceeding 15 metres in height, B4(1) (external fire spread – walls)

    (cc)   in the case of a material change of use described in Regulation 5 (a), (b), (c), (d), (g), (h), (i) or, where the material change provides new residential accommodation, (f), C1(2) resistance to contaminants

    (d)   in the case of a material change of use described in Regulation 5(a), C2 (resistance to moisture)

    (e)   in the case of a material change of use described in Regulation 5(a), (b), (c), (g), (h) or (i), E1 to E3 (resistance to the passage of sound)

(f)   in the case of a material change of use described in Regulation 5(e), where the public building consists of or contains a school, E4 (acoustic conditions in schools)

(g)   in the case of a material change of use described in Regulation 5(c), (d), (e) or (j), M1 (access and use)

(h)   in the case of a material change of use described in Regulation 5(a), (b), (c), (d), (f) – if it provides new residential accommodation, (g), (h) or (i), C1(2) (resistance to contaminants)

(2)   Where there is a material change of use of part only of a building, such work, if any, shall be carried out as is necessary to ensure that

(a)   that part complies in all cases with any relevant requirement referred to in paragraph (1)(a)

(b)   in a case to which sub-paragraphs (b), (d), (e) or (f) of paragraph (1) apply, that part complies with the requirements referred to in the relevant sub-paragraph

(c)   in a case to which sub-paragraph (c) of paragraph (1) applies, the whole building complies with the requirement referred to in that sub-paragraph

(d)   in the case to which sub-paragraph (1) applies

(i)   the part of any sanitary convenience provided in or in connection with that part complies with the requirements referred to in that sub-paragraph; and

(ii)   the building complies with requirement M1(a) of Schedule 1 to the extent that reasonable provision is made to provide either suitable independent access to that part or suitable access through the building to that part

(e)   in the case to which sub-paragraph (g) or paragraph (1) applies, the whole building complies with the requirement referred to in the sub-paragraph

Summary of building work

In the case of **extensions**, the Building Regulations will not normally apply to the existing building (except for Part L) unless some aspect of the extension in some way causes a contravention within the existing building to a greater extent than was the case before. An example would be under Part M where an existing access was being built over so the extension should be accessible in accordance with the Approved Document. Alternatively in this situation, where the extension does not have a compliant access the existing building would need to be altered to make access provisions.

Material alterations are those changes which could effectively downgrade any existing provisions (relating to structural stability, means of escape, fire spread, fire service access, Part L requirements and access and use), whether or not they currently comply with the Building Regulations.

Material change of use is specifically the conversion of any building to a single dwelling, a number of dwellings, a flat, or an increase or decrease in the number of dwellings or residential rooms; a hotel or boarding house;

an institutional or public building or a shop. It applies to any new use of any 'exempt' buildings. Falling within this category are buildings controlled under other legislation; buildings not frequented by people; temporary and ancillary buildings; certain small detached buildings; and conservatories and porches of less than 30 m² floor area.

Justifying departures from the Regulations and Approved Documents

It is important that where departures from the Approved Documents supporting the Building Regulations are proposed for historic buildings these should be set out in a justification statement and submitted to the building control body as part of the building control application. The document should contain the requirement of the Regulation or recommendation of the Approved Document and should identify the philosophy, rationale and approach and justify any departures resulting from any constraints in the existing building. Any supporting documentation should also be included. This is necessary as, increasingly, Approved Documents provide one solution to a great many building situations and they need to be made bespoke to a particular design and justified accordingly.

The Building Regulations and their impact on historic buildings

For the purposes of the Building Regulations, historic buildings include

- listed buildings
- buildings situated in conservation areas
- buildings which are of architectural and historic interest and which are referred to as a material consideration in a local authority's development plan
- buildings of architectural and historic interest within national parks, areas of outstanding natural beauty and world heritage sites

Part A: *Structure*

The Building Regulations Part A: *Structure* generally applies to historic buildings where structural alterations, an extension or underpinning works are being carried out.

Structural alterations should not have an adverse effect upon existing structure; therefore, in addition to any new structural elements being installed, the existing supporting structure should be checked to ensure that any change of load path is adequately supported. The existing structure should be checked for stability where additional loading is being applied, for example from internal partitions and fittings such as baths. If required, strengthening works should be carried out to accommodate the additional load.

For changes of use which involve applying a greater imposed loading, guidance on **assessing the existing structure** can be obtained from BRE Digest 366: *Structural Appraisal of Existing Buildings for Change of Use*. The guidance may be summarised as follows.

The structural criteria and behaviour have to be discovered from the building itself and such relevant design material and other sources as may have survived. For historic buildings, it is less likely that original design information would have survived. Opening-up work will generally be involved to ensure that any increase in load can be safely transferred to the ground. Fortunately, many older and traditional structures have some of their basic structure, such as timber floors, masonry walls and cast iron columns, exposed. The amount of opening up will be dependent upon the extent of the increased loading and proposed changes to the load paths.

Typically an investigation of a building would consist of

- establishing materials (weights, strength, etc.), construction details, structural elements and connections, finishes, etc.
- excavating trial holes to examine existing foundations and safe bearing capacity of the founding subsoil
- establishing weights of any existing and new services
- identifying any structural defects

It may be appropriate to appoint a specialist consultant to investigate specific areas such as

- visual stress grading of timber
- diagnosis of timber infestation

Having analysed the structure and its stability in its present form, it is then necessary to concentrate on the effects of alterations for the proposed change of use, including

- increased loading on structure and foundations
- alterations to load paths
- alterations to existing stability systems
- changes in fire exposure and fire rating

The outcome of the assessment will determine whether the structure is judged satisfactory for the proposal or, if inadequate, what general, local or specific strengthening works would be required.

Another situation where a change in loading takes place and can have structural implications is with **roof coverings**. Where the work involves a significant change in the applied loading, the structural integrity of the roof structure and the supporting structure should be checked to ensure that the building is not less compliant with Regulation A1 than it was before it was changed. A significant change in roof loading is when the loading upon the roof is increased by more than 15%. Where strengthening works or replacement of roof members is required as a result of the increase in loading, the works are classed as a material alteration.

Where work will significantly decrease the roof dead loading, the roof structure and its anchorage to the supporting structure should be checked to ensure that an adequate factor of safety is maintained against uplift of the roof under imposed wind loading.

In the case of either a substantial increase or a substantial decrease of the dead loading to a roof, the following procedure is recommended:

- Compare the loading imposed by the proposed roof covering with the original roof loading. (In calculating, the loading allowance should include the increase in load due to water absorption, e.g. 0.3% for oven dry slates and up to 10.5% for clay plain tiles and concrete tiles based on dry mass per unit area of roof coverings.)
- Arrange for inspection of the existing roof structure and check whether the roof structure is capable of sustaining the increased load; whether roof spread could push out the tops of the walls; and whether the vertical restraints are adequate for the wind uplift that may result due to the use of lighter roof material and/or the provision of new underlay.
- Provide appropriate strengthening measures such as replacement of defective members, fixings (including nails) and vertical restraints; provision of additional structural members, for example trusses, rafters, bracing, purlins, etc., as may be required to sustain the increased loads; provision of restraining straps, additional ties and fixings to the walls, as may be required to resist the wind uplift or prevent roof spread.

Strengthening works to distressed historic building elements are frequent tasks for architects, surveyors and engineers. These may not always require building regulations approval (as they may not have any adverse structural effect) but will require careful thought and consideration. Intervention will be necessary, and the challenge for the designer is the discreet placement of additional structure, the methods adopted and any alteration to the appearance that may result. A badly deflected timber beam, for instance, potentially could fail, causing further damage to the fabric, and remedial measures to arrest any further movement may be to cut a vertical slot in the top of the beam (access permitting) and secure a steel plate surrounded in resin and bolted in position through the side of the beam. The resultant flitched beam will sustain the applied load where previously it was overstressed. The deflection could be taken out of the beam by propping prior to the upgrade but this may disturb the 'settled' fabric, and the deflection may be considered part of the character of the building – a question, perhaps, for the conservation officer!

Repair works are not normally covered by the Regulations, and repair is not defined in the Regulations but is usually taken to mean replacement, redecoration, routine maintenance and making good, but not new work or alteration. When in doubt about whether or not work is covered by the Regulations, a building control body, the local authority or an Approved Inspector can advise. The BRE Good Repair Guides and Good Building Guides, too, give good practical guidance.

Temporary works during construction are not controlled by the Building Regulations. However, where they are supporting the structure during the construction operation, the temporary works need to be designed to ensure that they provide adequate support. This is important not only under the CDM Regulations for health and safety purposes, but also to ensure that no damage is caused to the historic fabric as a result of inadequate support.

Part B: *Fire safety*

PPG15: *Planning and the Historic Environment* relates to 'Building and fire legislation; access for disabled people; house renovation grants'. With regard to the planning process, the document states:

> In exercising their responsibilities for the safety of buildings under the building and fire legislation, local planning authorities should deal sympathetically with proposals for the repair or conversion of historic buildings. The Building Regulations should be operated in a way which avoids removal of features which contribute to the character of a listed building and are part of the reason for its being listed. Sufficient flexibility exists within the Building Regulations and Fire Precautions Act systems for authorities to have regard to the possible impact of proposals on the historical or architectural value of a building, and authorities should consult their own conservation officers, or seek expert advice from other sources, when handling difficult situations. It is particularly important that there should be a flexible approach to structural matters, to ensure that any changes are in character with the rest of the building and that there is no unacceptable damage to the fabric. In order to ensure that requirements which are unacceptable in terms of a historic building can be considered as part of a listed building consent application, the precise Building and Fire Regulations requirements should be made explicit *before* an application has been determined. A successful outcome is more likely to be negotiated if the authorities have been consulted from the outset.

The document encourages early consultation between the design team, planning, conservation and building control body to ensure that fire safety matters, in particular, are resolved at the outset.

Approved Document B also allows for a flexible approach, stating:

> Some variation of the provisions set out in this document may also be appropriate where Part B applies to existing buildings, and particularly in buildings of special architectural or historic interest, where adherence to the guidance in this document might prove unduly restrictive. In such cases it would be appropriate to take into account a range of fire safety features, some of which are dealt with in this document, and some of which are not addressed in any detail, and to set these against an assessment of the hazard and risk peculiar to the particular case.

This part of the document indicates that a fire safety engineering approach can provide an alternative approach to fire safety. It goes on to indicate that the factors that should be taken into account include

- the anticipated probability of a fire occurring
- the anticipated fire severity

- the ability of a structure to resist the spread of fire and smoke
- the consequential danger to people in and around the building

A variety of measures could be incorporated to a greater or lesser extent, as appropriate to the circumstances, including

- the adequacy of means to prevent fire
- early fire warning by an automatic detection and warning system
- the standard of means of escape
- provision of smoke control
- control of the rate of growth of a fire
- the adequacy of the structure to resist the effects of a fire
- the degree of fire containment
- fire separation between buildings or parts of buildings
- the standard of active measures for fire extinguishment or control
- facilities to assist the fire and rescue service
- the availability of powers to require staff training in fire safety and fire routines
- consideration of the availability of any continuing control under other legislation that could ensure continued maintenance of such systems
- management

Fire protection measures to historic buildings should be seen as positive conservation of our heritage and are considered in detail in Chapter 12.

Part C: *Site preparation and resistance to contaminants and moisture*

Historic buildings may undergo material change of use or alteration, and the Approved Document recognises the need to conserve their character with the aim of improving resistance to contaminants and moisture where practical, provided that the work does not prejudice the character of the historic building or increase the long-term deterioration of the building fabric or fittings.

The Approved Document further recognises that particular issues relating to work in historic buildings warrant sympathetic treatment and perhaps further advice, including avoiding excessively intrusive gas protective measures and ensuring that moisture ingress to the roof structure is limited and that the roof can breathe. Where it is not possible to provide dedicated ventilation to pitched roofs, it is important to seal existing service penetrations in the ceiling and to provide draughtproofing to any loft hatches. Any new loft insulation should be kept sufficiently clear of the eaves that adventitious ventilation is not reduced.

Change of use of an existing non-residential building to a dwelling will attract the requirement to ensure that the passage of moisture is resisted. This will generally involve the installation of a horizontal damp-proof course (dpc) in the form of a proprietary waterproofing agent, possibly silicone-based. The thickness of the wall has to be sufficient to resist the passage of moisture or suitably modified by external treatment or internal lining. The roof covering needs to resist water penetration and generally involves re-roofing and providing roofing felt, which it may not have previously had. The ground floor needs to resist rising damp, which would generally involve replacement to include a damp-proof membrane. Care needs to be exercised in window and door reveals where the exposed area has limited thickness in relation to the outer face of the wall.

Where a historic landscape is being altered near to buildings, care should be exercised to ensure that land drainage diverts groundwater away from the properties.

Regulation C2 relates to ventilation of roof spaces to prevent condensation, and considering the measures from the Approved Document mentioned above and depending on the roof covering at ridge and the detailing at eaves, the introduction of ventilation systems could look obtrusive. An alternative, depending upon use (generation of humidity), could be to use a breather membrane, thus eliminating the necessity for eaves and ridge ventilation. The breather membrane allows vapour to pass through, and dew point (the point at which condensation is produced) takes place outside the roof construction, thus avoiding interstitial condensation, which could have an adverse affect on the timber work and finishes.

Part E: *Resistance to the passage of sound*

The Building Regulations 1991 required from June 1992 onwards that flat conversions should comply with the requirements of Approved Document E: *Resistance to the passage of sound*. This document allows for flexibility when it comes to historic buildings, in respect not only of sound resistance to elements of the building but also of flanking transmission.

Some form of intervention to increase the sound insulation performance of a floor for airborne and structure-borne sound is inevitable. With regard to floors, to reduce the impact on hearths, skirting, doors, stairs and such like there is a tendency to favour the proprietary systems which cover the existing floor with a comparatively thin hardboard/resilient layer. These products allow for minimal disturbance to the existing floor, generally only requiring the occasional board to be lifted to allow for the installation of the sound-deadening quilt.

The performance of separating walls in Georgian terraced properties is something of an unknown quantity, and for this reason flat conversions are likely to create a particular problem. With comparatively thin ashlar party walls that would not come up to the mass requirements of Part E, there is a need to justify the sound insulation performance by a field test. Two adjacent properties in Great Pulteney Street, Bath, presented an opportunity for such a test. In June 1992 Bristol Polytechnic was commissioned by the then Bath City Council to carry out performance testing for airborne sound insulation to a separating wall and a separating floor. These properties were selected as typical Georgian terraced houses. One property was to be returned to a single dwellinghouse from a house in multiple occupation, and the other had been converted to two maisonettes. The instructions to the polytechnic were to test the separating wall between the properties on at least two levels and to test the floor between maisonettes, which had recently undergone an upgrade with Reduc Micro 17 system.

The measurements were carried out in accordance with British Standard BS 2750:1980: *Measurement of Sound Insulation in Buildings and of Building Elements*. The results have been processed in accordance with BS 5821:1980: *Rating Sound Insulation in Buildings and of Building Elements*, as required by the Building Regulations 1991, Approved Document E: *Sound*. A building acoustics analyser, Nortronic type 823 with rotating microphones, was used.

At the floor levels tested (first and second), as far as can be ascertained the separating wall consisted of Bath stone (ashlar) about 150 mm thick, plastered both sides. The compartment floor between maisonettes (ground to first) was of traditional construction, with floor joists (probably 250 × 50 mm softwood) with 25 mm lath and plaster ceiling lining and ex. 25 mm square-edge boarding overlaid with a Reduc Micro 17 system.

The current Building Regulations Approved Document E, Section 6: *Field and laboratory tests for conversions*, requires the weighted standardised level difference, D^1nT,w, to be at least 49 dB for separating walls and at least 48 dB for separating floors. According to the results of the test, the unmodified separating wall between the two properties easily met this required standard, having a D^1nT,w, of about 60 dB.

The compartment floor between the maisonettes, which had been modified using a Reduc Micro 17 system, should according to the manufacturer's literature give a D^1nT,w, of 51 dB. This modification consists of an additional composite layer installed over the existing wooden floor plus a 100 mm 'sound slab' laid between the joists, supported by wire mesh, just above a 25 mm plasterboard ceiling. As the property is a listed building, the original 25 mm lath and plaster ceiling has been retained. According to the measurements, the modified floor has a D^1nT,w, of 46 dB for the large front living room and a D^1nT,w, of 58 dB for the smaller rear living room. This difference of 12 dB between the two floors with supposedly similar modification may be explained by two effects. First, the large area of floor in the front room may be the cause of a reduction in performance owing to the loss of stiffness, whereas the rear floor has an increased stiffness owing to the vertical offset of internal partition walls. The most likely cause of the loss of performance from the manufacturer's figure of 51 dB to the measured value of 46 dB is the reduction in ceiling mass, and this could be rectified in future conversions by inserting a layer of plasterboard between the joists, just above the existing ceiling and supported by the wire mesh, and with the 'sound slab' installed above the plasterboard.

The fact that Reduc was used on this conversion and was chosen for the test was purely coincidental and is not an endorsement of the product. It is, however, a widely used system for upgrading floors but it is by no means the only acceptable method. Indeed, Gyproc SI Floor System has similar qualities with regard to airborne and impact sound insulation. In situations where the existing floorboards need to be retained as a feature, British Gypsum's SI Floor System is one option. Here the boards are attached to a light-gauge galvanised steel channel that sits over the existing joists on a resilient layer, allowing for impact absorption. The inclusion of a layer of plasterboard compensates for the use of square-edge boarding acting as a smoke stop. Perhaps the only disadvantage is the visible screw heads securing the boards.

The Approved Document 2003 edition also recognises the need for a sensitive approach to historic buildings. Section 0, paragraph 0.7 states:

> In the case of some historic buildings undergoing a material change of use, it may not be practical to improve the sound insulation to the standards set out in Tables 1a and 1b. The need to conserve the special characteristics of such historic buildings needs to be recognised, and in such work, the aim should be to improve sound insulation to the extent that it is practically possible, always provided that the work does not prejudice the character of the historic building, or increase the risk of long-term deterioration to the building fabric or fittings.

The Approved Document suggests that the appropriate balance between historic building conservation and improving sound insulation should be achieved in consultation with the local planning authority's conservation officer. In such cases the building control bodies should be satisfied that everything reasonable has been done to improve the sound insulation.

The Approved Document does require historic buildings to be tested to demonstrate an improvement in the sound insulation as much as is practical, and the results should be displayed in accordance with Regulation 20A or 12A, in a conspicuous place inside the building. In order to demonstrate improvement, tests would need to be carried out prior to works commencing and on pre-completion.

The level of the performance for separating walls, separating floors and stairs for both airborne and impact sound insulation for dwellinghouses and flats, and rooms for residential purposes is contained in Tables 1a and 1b of Approved Document E as summarised below:

	Airborne	Impact
New build dwellinghouse and flats		
Walls	45 DnT,w + Ctr dB	
Floors and stairs	45 DnT,w + Ctr dB	62 $L'nT,w$ dB
Dwellinghouse and flats by conversion		
Walls	43 DnT,w + Ctr dB	
Floors and stairs	43 DnT,w + Ctr dB	64 $L'nT,w$ dB
New build rooms for residential purposes		
Walls	43 DnT,w + Ctr dB	
Floors and stairs	45 DnT,w + Ctr dB	62 $L'nT,w$ dB
Rooms for residential purposes by conversion		
Walls	43 DnT,w + Ctr dB	
Floors and stairs	43 DnT,w + Ctr dB	64 $L'nT,w$ dB

'Room(s) for residential purposes' means a room, or suite of rooms, which is not a dwellinghouse or flat and which is used by one or more persons to live and sleep in. This includes rooms in hotels, hostels, boarding houses, halls of residence and residential homes but not rooms in hospitals or other similar establishments used for patient accommodation.

With any sound insulation system that adds load to the structure, the floor joists, beams and so forth should be checked for adequacy.

Part F: *Ventilation*

The Approved Document (2006 edition) recognises the importance of historic buildings under Section 3 of the Approved Document. The approach is stated thus:

> Conserving the special characteristics of historic buildings needs to be recognised: see BS 7913. In such work the aim should be to improve ventilation to the extent that is necessary, taking into account the need not to prejudice the character of the historic building, or increase the risk of long-term deterioration to the fabric or fittings. It may be that the fabric of the historic building is leakier than a modern building, and this can be established by pressure testing. In arriving at a balance between historic building conservation and ventilation, it would be appropriate to take into account the advice of the local planning authority's conservation officer . . . Particular issues relating to work in historic buildings that warrant sympathetic treatment and where advice from others could therefore be beneficial include
>
> - restoring the historic character of a building that had been subject to previous inappropriate alteration, e.g. replacement windows, doors and roof-lights
> - rebuilding a former historic building (e.g. following a fire or filling in a gap site in a terrace)
> - making provisions enabling the fabric to 'breathe' to control moisture and potential long term decay problems: see SPAB Information Sheet No. 4 *The need for old buildings to breathe*, 1986.

New build or the creation of a new dwelling requires habitable rooms and kitchens to have purge, background and/or extract ventilation provision. Background (or trickle) ventilation should be provided in replacement windows and is normally accommodated in the heads of casements or sashes. In historic buildings, however, trickle vents could look out of place, and an equivalent alternative background ventilation opening should be provided in the same room. The previous edition of the Approved Document allowed trickle ventilation in the form of securing the sash in a partially open position. For top-hung casements, a similar arrangement of securing in the partially open position is allowed but only above the ground storey, for security reasons. Locating the ventilation opening more than 1.75 metres above floor level is recommended to avoid cold draughts. A similar background ventilation arrangement could be adopted for casements that can be locked in the partially open position, but cold draughts may cause discomfort and for this reason the arrangement is not recognised by Part F. However, provided it is adopted above the ground storey and draughts are not likely to cause discomfort, it would perform as a top-hung casement and thus fulfil the functional requirements of the Regulation. Security risks for ground floor situations could be compensated for with intruder alarms.

Mechanical extract ducts serving bathrooms, kitchens and utility rooms have to discharge to open air. The terminal would need to be accommodated either in the external wall or the roof, though vents on a ridge or on the roof slope could be obtrusive.

Part H: *Drainage and waste disposal*

The installation of both below- and above-ground drainage systems can involve serious intervention into the fabric of an existing historic building. For underground drainage within the building, a trench cut into the ground floor will be required and the drain will need to pass through the substructure walls. Above-ground drainage will need to pass through floors and roofs and be accommodated internally. This will generally involve an intrusion into a room with a pipe casing. The system needs to be ventilated to external air or fitted with an air admittance valve. Trimming to floors, ceilings and roofs involves structural alterations, and if compartment floors are penetrated then fire-stopping will be required to maintain fire separation.

Part J: *Combustion appliances and fuel storage systems*

In historic buildings, particularly those converted to flats, the method of heating can have an effect not only on energy conservation but also on the external appearance of the building. Many external walls have been peppered with unsightly balanced flue terminals serving gas boilers. While gas is generally the preferred method of heating, where available, there is an alternative which addresses both the above issues. Condensing boilers have greater efficiency than those served by a balanced or conventional flue and some are served by a 40 or 50 mm diameter muPVC flue/air intake, thus eliminating the necessity for obtrusive flue terminals. Keston produce a room-sealed condensing boiler that has a unique and versatile flue/air intake system, allowing it to be situated practically anywhere and in the most convenient position. The small-diameter flue/air intake can be extended up to 10 or 15 metres in length from the appliance.

Parts L1A, L1B, L2A and L2B: *Conservation of fuel and power*

The primary purpose of Parts L1A (*New dwellings*), L1B (*Existing dwellings*), L2A (*New buildings other than dwellings*) and L2B (*Existing buildings other than dwellings*) is to make reasonable provision for the conservation of fuel and power in buildings. The Approved Documents give technical guidance on methods to achieve this by insulation of walls, windows, roofs, floors, heating vessels, pipes and ductwork, by limiting air leakage, by control of heating systems and by guidance on efficiency of heating and lighting systems. Replacement windows and boilers are also covered, requiring that the same standards be achieved as for new work.

With regard to historic buildings, Part L2B (work in existing buildings that are not dwellings) applies to

- consequential improvements
- extensions
- material change of use
- material alteration
- provision/extension of a controlled service/fitting
- provision/renovation of a thermal element

With regard to historic buildings, Part L1B (work in existing dwellings) applies to

- extensions
- creating dwellings through change of use
- material alteration to existing dwellings
- provision of a controlled fitting
- provision/extension of a controlled service
- provision/renovation of a thermal element
- providing information

Both documents require that commissioning certification for heating and ventilation systems be provided to the building control body, along with operating and maintenance instructions for the building occupier. For buildings other than dwellings, a building log book is required for the occupier, together with the provision of energy meters.

Parts L1B and L2B recognise the importance of historic buildings and give special consideration to where energy efficiency requirements would unacceptably alter the character or appearance. To this end, where compliance with the energy efficiency requirements would unacceptably alter their character or appearance, Regulation 9 of both Approved Documents exempts buildings which are

- listed in accordance with section 1 of the Planning (Listed Buildings and Conservation Areas) Act 1990
- in a conservation area designated in accordance with section 69 of that Act
- included in the Schedule of Monuments maintained under section 1 of the Ancient Monuments and Archaeological Areas Act 1979
- primarily or solely used as places of worship

Clearly, the aim should be to improve energy efficiency where and to the extent that it is practically possible, always provided that the work does not prejudice the character of the historic building, or increase the risk of long-term deterioration to the building fabric or fittings. In arriving at an appropriate balance between historic building conservation and energy conservation, it would be appropriate to take into account the advice of the local planning authority's conservation officer.

Particular issues relating to work in historic buildings that warrant sympathetic treatment, and where advice from others could therefore be beneficial, include

- restoring the historic character of a building that has been subject to previous inappropriate alteration, such as replacement windows, doors and roof lights
- rebuilding a former historic building (e.g. following a fire) or filling in a gap site in a terrace
- making provisions enabling the fabric of historic buildings to 'breathe' in order to control moisture and potential long-term decay problems (see SPAB Information Sheet No. 4)

Government may well amend Regulations L1B and L2B for consistency so that historic buildings include

- listed buildings
- buildings of local architectural and historical interest which are referred to as a material consideration in the local planning authority's development plan
- buildings situated in conservation areas, national parks, areas of outstanding natural beauty and world heritage sites where the local planning authority's conservation officer has advised that special consideration should apply in the particular case

To assist arrival at an appropriate balance between historic building conservation and energy efficiency, English Heritage, in wide consultation, produced a series of guidance notes entitled *Energy Efficiency in Traditional Buildings* to ensure that due respect is paid to the historic or architectural fabric of the building. The *Guide to Building Services for Historic Buildings*, published by the Chartered Institution of Building Services Engineers, is a similarly invaluable related publication.

As suggested in the Approved Documents, consultation with the local authority conservation officer is an essential part of the development and evaluation process. However, a detailed survey of the fabric and an initial assessment for a strategy for energy efficiency for the building should be prepared as part of those discussions. The resultant documentation would then form the basis for a justification strategy for submission as part of the building control approval process.

There are various ways of upgrading the building envelope, but also various difficulties:

Windows/glazing

For double-glazing units to be installed in accordance with BS 8000 Part 7: 1990, they would need to be secured with beading and not putty. Also, the glazing bars would need to be bigger than those in traditional Georgian-style box-framed windows. With windows being a highly sensitive aspect of a historic building, double glazing is therefore not normally considered an appropriate option. Comparing an existing mid-eighteenth-century sliding sash window detail with a detail accommodating double glazing illustrates the size of members and method of glazing required. Clearly, considerable bulk is added to the member sizes when strictly adhering to BS 8000 Part 7: *Code of Practice for Glazing* and to the Glass and Glazing Federation's Technical Manual, to the extent that the character of the window changes significantly.

Secondary double-glazing units may obstruct shutters and would need to be readily openable (or removable) for ventilation and/or escape purposes. The effect of this system on existing window details is often unacceptable to conservation architects. The same is likely to apply to draughtproofing strips mounted on the surface of sashes or linings, although it is possible to provide a partial draughtproofing strip discreetly located within the sash assembly.

Insulating external walls

Unless any of the external walls or linings are being replaced, insulated dry lining would not be practicable in listed buildings as it would have an adverse effect on plaster ceiling cornices, window and door linings, skirting, architraves, dado rails and so on. Also, this form of insulation often makes fixing to the wall difficult.

Roof insulation

Where possible, roof insulation should be introduced or increased in thickness; however, care should be taken when changing the environment of the roof space. The risk of condensation would need to be reduced by introducing ventilation to the roof space; with additional insulation and the introduction of ventilation, water pipes and cisterns above the insulation layer would need to be protected from freezing, and there is an increased risk of frost damage to the roof covering.

Floor insulation

If the ground floor structure is being substantially replaced or repaired it should be insulated to the same standard as is required for new work. For timber floors, adequate under-floor ventilation should be provided to avoid decay.

Services

Clearly, options for improving the thermal insulation of the building envelope of listed buildings are limited. There are, however, improvements that can be made to general energy conservation from the building services, and these improvements can have a significant positive effect on the SAP rating. These include high-efficiency heating systems such as condensing boilers (condensing boilers are required in domestic situations following the L1 Amendment of April 2005); high-efficiency electrical heating systems comprising a heat pump; and mechanical ventilation systems with heat recovery.

Access and the historic environment

Legislation requiring buildings to be accessible is comparatively recent. In construction legislation, Part T: *Facilities for the disabled* was first introduced in the Building (Fourth Amendment) Regulations 1985 and later as Part M: *Access and facilities for disabled people* when the Regulations were recast as the Building Regulations 1985. Subsequently, the content and scope of the accompanying Approved Document has increased; however, the requirements cannot be applied retrospectively. The latest edition of Part M: *Access to and use of buildings* is clear in not exempting historic buildings from the requirements, but again suggests that improvements rather than full compliance would be acceptable. For existing historic buildings requirements, guidance and 'encouragement' comes from elsewhere, most notably the Disability Discrimination Act 1995 (DDA) and the design code BS 8300: 2001 *Design of Buildings and Their Approaches to Meet the Needs of Disabled People*. The DDA will certainly have an impact on historic buildings where the service provider has to take reasonable steps to provide access where it is unreasonably difficult or impossible for disabled people to make use of their service.

The 2004 edition of Part M suggests the concept of the designer producing an Access Statement. This should identify the philosophy and approach and justify any departures from the Approved Document resulting from any constraints in the existing building. This is particularly important as Part M now applies to material alterations, extensions to buildings other than dwellings and certain changes of use. The Approved Document now has a wider range of recommendations, which are broadly based on BS 8300: 2001. Where Part M is being applied to historic buildings, it needs to be used flexibly and sensitively as the implications could have detrimental effects. The importance of setting out these implications in the Access Statement, therefore, cannot be overstressed.

PPG15 recognises the difficulties which people with disabilities face in the built environment. Paragraph 3.28 states:

> It is important in principle that disabled people should have dignified easy access to and within historic buildings. If it is treated as part of an integrated review of access requirements for all visitors or users, and a flexible and pragmatic approach is taken, it should normally be possible to plan suitable access for disabled people without compromising a building's special interest. Alternative routes or re-organising the use of spaces may achieve the desired result without the need for damaging alterations.

PPG15 encourages designers to seek a dignified alternative to gaining access to a building where the main access has features which present an insurmountable barrier to a person with mobility impairment. Sensitive signage should be located at the main entrance giving directions to the accessible alternative. If any further assistance should be required, it is advisable to have a doorbell which summons help from within the establishment. It is of course preferable to have full and independent access, as would be expected for new buildings, but in reality this will not always prove possible.

The discreet placement of a platform lift to accommodate a change in level at an entrance can avoid significant alteration to a building. This can be located within an area containing railings so that the platform lift is unobtrusive – though sufficiently conspicuous to be identifiable.

The designer will be faced with three approaches to providing access and facilities:

- **additive** – where physical construction is added to the fabric of the building (such as the construction of a ramp)
- **subtractive** – where fabric is physically removed (such as to accommodate a ramp)
- **management** – where the historic fabric does not allow additive or subtractive alteration people with mobility difficulties may have to be provided with a visual alternative to an inaccessible feature

Health and safety

Employers have a responsibility to ensure that the workplace is conducive to the well-being of employees. The risk assessment carried out to this end would need to examine the general health and safety aspects of the internal environment, including the performance of the building. Construction professionals could well be involved in providing such a risk assessment, which would check for statutory non-compliance. Historic buildings are more likely to have elements which could be viewed as hazardous such as guarding to stairs, landings and balconies. Is the guarding high enough? Is it secure in sustaining horizontal forces? Increasing the height for safety purposes may involve re-assessing the stability, as an increase in height increases the leverage.

Where adding to the height of a balustrade on a landing is likely to have listed building implications, consider restricting access to the balustrade: for example, the judicial placement of a piece of furniture (hard surface or non-combustible, as it may be in a protected staircase enclosure), plants or similar objects to physically prevent direct access, thus reducing the risk. Such solutions should be recorded in the risk assessment to alert the responsible person to the function of the object; should it be removed in the future, other measures will be required.

Other elements to check would be glazing in critical locations, trip hazards, lighting levels, stairs (steepness etc.) and electrical hazards. Paragraph 3(1) of the Management of Health and Safety at Work Regulations 1999 requires a risk assessment to be carried out:

> Every employer shall make a suitable and sufficient assessment of (a) the risk to the health and safety of his employees to which they are exposed while they are at work; and (b) the risk to the health and safety of persons not in his employ arising out of or in connection with the conduct by him of his undertaking.

Paragraph 4(1) of the Workplace (Health, Safety and Welfare) Regulations 1992 requires:

Every employer shall ensure that every workplace, modification, extension or conversion which is under his control and where any of his employees works complies with any of these regulations which (a) applies to that workplace or, as the case may be, to the workplace which contains that modification, extension or conversion, and (b) is in force in respect of the workplace, modification, extension or conversion.

Other requirements relate to

- maintenance of workplace, and of equipment, devices and systems
- ventilation
- temperature in indoor workplaces
- lighting
- cleanliness and waste materials
- room dimensions and space
- workstations and seating
- condition of floors and traffic routes
- falls and falling objects
- windows, and transparent or translucent doors, gates and walls
- windows, skylights and ventilators
- ability to clean windows etc. safely
- organisation etc. of traffic routes
- doors and gates
- escalators and moving walkways
- sanitary conveniences
- washing facilities
- drinking water
- accommodation for clothing
- facilities for changing clothing
- facilities for rest and to eat meals
- exemption certificates

Conclusion

The requirements of the Building Regulations need to be balanced against the guidance contained in BS 7913: 1998 *The Principles of the Conservation of Historic Buildings* and PPG15 Annex C. Clearly, professional experience and judgement will be required by all parties involved. This will include the architect/designer in their approach and justification of the building proposals, the building control body in applying the requirements of the Building Regulations, the local planning authority conservation officer in seeking to preserve the nation's heritage in relation to historic buildings and architecture, and other related construction professionals.

4 Metric survey techniques for historic buildings

Bill Blake

Introduction: informing conservation by metric survey

'Metric survey' simply means that a system of measurement has been used in the preparation of a record, whether it be a drawing, a photograph or a model. The metric element can be inherent to the technique or in support of other methods, graphic or photographic. If a survey is to be used by others, it is important to establish the expectations of those who will be using it. For example, if a sketch survey is passed to an archaeologist at 1:20 scale, the sketch will be rejected as imprecise by those who work at a larger scale. If a project demands a consistent data set on a building or site, the use of metric survey is the key to getting the best out of all those working with drawings.

It is quite possible to collect critical information without invoking a metric element into the work. A good set of sketches, photographs and a written description are all vital to understanding a structure or site; valuable opinions can be formed, theories tested and diagnostic details recorded without taking any measurement. But when the record is required for architects, archaeologists, engineers, quantity surveyors and fabric analysts, **measurement** and **scale drawing** provide for the combined skills of the conservation team.

Control systems

If several survey techniques are to be used together on a site, a common **control system** should be put in place to produce an integrated survey. It is a false economy not to map a whole site during a project's initial phase, which may involve only part of the site. Using CAD from the outset is advisable as this will make the best of the survey products available; the assembly of data from imagery, EDM (electromagnetic distance measurement), GPS (Global Positioning System) and photogrammetry (stereo photography) can be achieved easily if all the parts are in a common CAD format and a common coordinate system.

When selecting a measurement method it is necessary to balance the cost, available skills and required degree of precision. In metric survey, the greater the need for precision, the greater the cost will be. For example, **photogrammetry** (for all its shortcomings) will deliver the most *consistently* reliable work across many facades, both interior and exterior, compared with any other method. The photogrammetric process is safe; failures of draughtsmanship in photogrammetry can be recovered by reference to the photographic originals and there is always an option to use 3D output. Photogrammetry is a relatively high-cost process but the cost and other disadvantages are often outweighed by consistency, precision and reliability.

Surveys carried out supported by precise measurement methods such as **EDM (electromagnetic distance measurement)**, sometimes known as **TST (total station theodolite)** and **REDM (reflectorless EDM)** can appear to reduce costs in comparison with photogrammetry, but they require skilled operation and a surveyor who is aware of the data-selection demands of the project. For example, simply tracing around windows is insufficient, and the joinery, lintel details and so on all have to be understood to make best use of the EDM data. At worst, EDM surveys can produce results that need so much 'join-up-the-dots' editing that without good sketching and photography the work is almost worthless. Realtime CAD such as TheoLt can increase the effectiveness of close-range EDM survey by allowing drawing production on site and increasing observational accuracy. When combined with CAD on site, EDM becomes a powerful 3D drawing tool that can place traditional draughting skills at the heart of the metric survey process.

The observational skills of architectural draughtspeople and the value of **drawing on site** should never be overlooked. If a key detail has been noticed, examined and sketched, it can be brought to the surveyor's attention and included in the metric mapping of the whole structure or site. To rely on metric survey to reveal all there is to know about a structure is to ignore the principal focus of the metric process: measurement above observation. The survey brief should identify key features to be mapped. On a large project, metric survey drawings can form a 'base map' so that details can be added to produce enhanced plots showing, for example, petrology, repair history, tooling, masons' and carpenters' marks or fabric condition.

Photography, in survey terms, should be considered either as **metric** or **narrative**. Metric photography will have some form of control so that measurement can be taken from the image; this can be a simple scale in the photograph, or points controlled by observation, or a 2D or 3D coordinate system. Where photography is controlled, taken square on and then printed to scale, it is described as **rectified**. Rectified photographs are a useful (and relatively cheap) tool for recording elevational detail. However, they should be treated with caution as they are usually only rectified to a single plane: trace with care! Narrative imagery is photography that tells the 'story' of the subject. Many details are best seen obliquely or close up; such photography cannot be used easily for measurement but is invaluable as a record of key details as it is often driven by thematic observational selection rather than metric considerations.

Photogrammetric photography can be used to produce high-definition scale-corrected imagery which can be used for an elevation or plan drawing; the process can be costly, but the ability to use a large-scale colour image free from scale distortion should be considered as an alternative to photo-mosaics for large-scale site imagery (Figure 4.1). **Orthophotographs** have been used to map large ceilings, large expanses of flint or rubble wall and buckled mosaic floors. Orthophotography is costlier than rectified photography but is more precise and cheaper than vector-plotted photogrammetric drawings. Orthophotographs have the advantages of being image-based (can be used as photographs) and reliably scaleable.

As to when to commission metric survey, the principal constraints on metric survey are cost and time. Many projects will not need highly precise survey, but as soon as design work begins measurement will be needed.

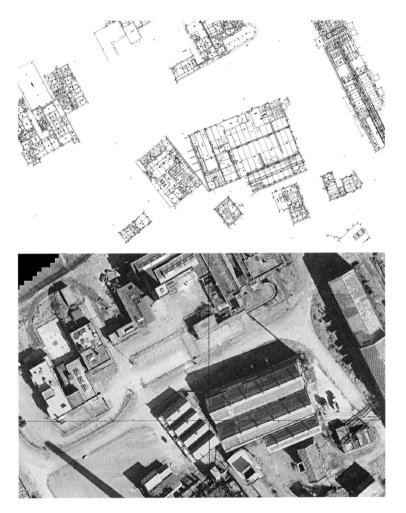

Figure 4.1 Metric survey at Chatterly Whitfield Colliery, Staffordshire: orthophotograph and building plans, originally at 1:200 and 1:50 scale respectively. The survey work was carried out on a common control so composites are possible in CAD without problems of differing scale and orientation.

Metric record should be undertaken to generate the base map for analysis, investigation, interpretation and dissemination. It is often difficult to convince project managers that getting surveyors on site early will reduce the recording costs in the long run and increase the effectiveness of conservation specialists preparing documentation. A carefully prepared brief for the survey should make clear reference to the interests of all those who will be using the survey. It should anticipate specialists' different demands so that there is an acceptance of the technical constraints of meeting different user requirements and clarity over what is expected of the survey.

Control methods

The guidance offered in this chapter is based on the practical experience of the English Heritage Metric Survey Team; the practical outcomes from survey have a theoretical basis, but it should be remembered that survey is a practical art and has long been recognised as such:

> The geometer, how excellent so ever he be, leaning only on to discourse of reason, without practice (yea and that sundry ways made) shall fall into manifold error, or inextricable Laberinthes.
>
> (Leonard and Thomas Digges, *Pantometria*, London, 1571)

Control measurements underpin the precision of the whole survey, so control data will be determined to a higher order of precision than that used for detail. Most control for building survey is undertaken using an EDM, although taped triangulation is still used, especially for small internal spaces; GPS can supply OSNG data to high orders of precision for larger sites. EDM control methods use multiple observations to generate statistical precision to ameliorate instrument and observation error. Control methods are often specific to survey types, scale and speed of work. The control methods described here are

- taped triangulation
- simple linear control: baseline and end over end
- traverse
- resection from 3D detail points
- wireframe fitting (graphical control)
- grids and setting out
- adding to an existing CAD survey
- GPS

Metric survey is the process of positioning objects by measurement. **Coordinate systems** are the standard positioning descriptor in survey, mapping and CAD. Position can be expressed in two ways on a map: as a Cartesian coordinate or as a vector. A vector uses direction and distance, whereas coordinates describe positions using relative distances along three axes by distance. Coordinate systems can be local, national or global and use *easting*, *northing* and *height* to determine the axes. Vectors are common to local and navigation systems where handling angular data is important.

Determination of position in the coordinate system is solved by the measurement of triangles, or **triangulation**. This is the basis of measurement. The legs of an EDM traverse are essentially interlocking triangles and even satellite surveying by GPS is based on resolving triangles. The position of an object can be defined by the distances to it from the two ends of a fixed baseline. Circles of appropriate radius can be drawn around each end of the baseline to plot the point where they intersect, forming a triangle with measured sides. In practice there are two possible solutions to such an equation, on either side of the baseline, but careful notation can eliminate any ambiguity.

Site grids can be laid out through triangulation. When laying out a grid using only tapes, right-angled triangles (those with a 90° corner) are employed to set out the axes of the grid. As with all survey control techniques, rigorous measurement is required to gain adequate precision. The diagonals of the grid should be checked independently of the set-out process, and the survey notes should state the method and likely precision of the control points (Figure 4.2).

Although as a control technique measured drawing has been largely superseded by EDM techniques, it is still a primary technique for confined spaces and detail measurement. Construction of the plan to scale requires all the measured lines to be level and at a common height.

Building plans are commonly constructed by taped diagonals and side lengths of rooms matched together by intersection of compass arcs. Measuring plans by this method works well with other measured-drawing techniques but can be unreliable when variations of height or complexity of

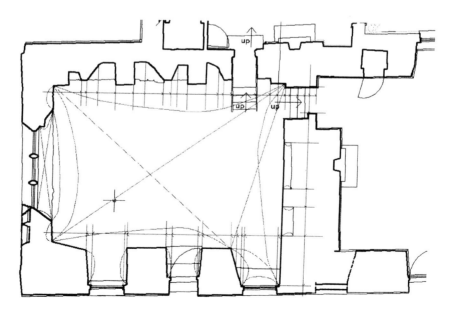

Figure 4.2 Taped triangulation used to control measured drawing. A building floor plan, with baselines, ties for triangulation and chain-lines and 90° offsets, is shown prior to measurement. The principal diagonals and braces are shown as loop lines.

shape require the fitting of many triangles without overall control. If each triangle is formed by using a side of a previous one, errors are easily propagated. For plans of a large building comprising many rooms on several floors, it is essential to have a series of reliable control points linked together by a traverse; the measurement from these control points is often carried out by triangulation or radial observation by REDM.

It is possible to use a distance-only EDM (such as Leica's Disto) rather than a tape. A single operator can use these devices but care should be taken over corrupted distances caused by measurement to internal corners and poor edge targeting. All handheld EDM should be checked carefully to find the effective performance range and target footprint.

Simple linear control with EDM

It is often desirable to record a subject without reference to a coordinate system other than that needed to control a small area; a drawing of a single wall or window may not need an elaborate and costly control. A simple level **baseline** of known length and height can be used. Two stations at either end of a measured line can be matched to triangulated distances for reference to the subject surveyed.

Whole drawings can be made from a single baseline where the precision requirement is less than for a fully controlled framework. Baseline survey with REDM is particularly applicable to room plans and to drawings of single elevations. A random point at the opposite end of the room is chosen as the reference object, and the reference line is used as the baseline from which the observations are taken. The instrument sits at one end of the baseline, and the target point is determined by measurement of angle and distance rather than by two distances from the baseline. The survey notes should include adequate witness diagrams and photographs of the ends of the baseline, since there will be no traverse from which to set out the end points again at a later date.

It is possible to proceed through a small building by linking baselines together by EDM observation without the full rigour of a traverse; this is not without risk as unless a loop is closed there is no check on the work. The procedure is similar to traversing, but the data is of a lower order of precision as it is not applying formal adjustment or checks. A station is occupied, a second is set out and the instrument and target positions are reversed; a new station is set out, and so forth. The only check is the compared distance and height from one end of the set-out line to the other, hence the term **end over end**. Realtime CAD can capture a visual check on overlapping detail from one station position to the next.

Traverse

A traverse is a method of fixing the location of a series of station points by means of distance and bearing measurements. Misclosure can be detected and appropriate adjustment applied. The technique depends upon the precise measurement of distances and angles.

Traversing has early origins. The development of robust angular measurement techniques in the sixteenth century, notably by Leonard and Thomas Digges (*Pantometria*, London, 1571), established the practice of measuring a precise framework of linked lines from which smaller measurements to detail could be made. The mathematician and navigator Nathaniel Bowditch (1773–1838) investigated the method of dead reckoning used for marine navigation, and he published in 1799 a revised edition of *Moore's Practical Navigator*, which described the mathematics used to this day for the adjustment of traverses. The correction of a series of linked vectors is an empirical problem for mapping; the distribution of error can be achieved by many methods. Bowditch gives us a method that is sensitive to weaknesses in distance measurement; by converting polar vectors to Cartesian values, relative positions can be determined. A simple proportional distribution of the errors is achieved by the application of adjustments to both angles and distances.

A traverse consists of a number of points known as stations linked by lines known as legs (Figure 4.3). To undertake a traverse, at least three

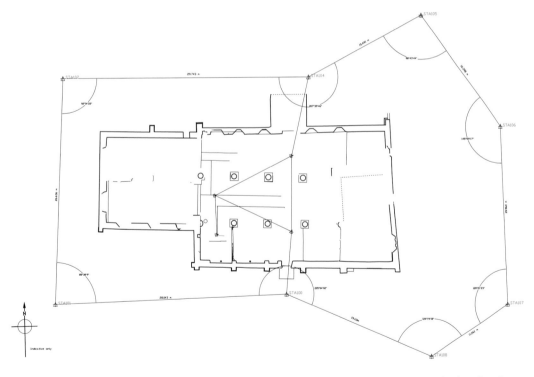

Figure 4.3 Traverse at St Giles' Church, Oxford. The four stations inside the church are tied to the closed loop. The stations on the loop are adjusted and the plan is prepared by polar observation from them. Further interior control is achieved by resection, end over end or spur legs; checks are possible by linking back to the loop. The plan is in progress; wall thickness, window reveals, nave arcade and overhead detail will be recorded from further stations and hand measurement.

tripods are required. The theodolite is set up on a tripod at the second point and used to measure the angle between targets set up on tripods at the first and third points. At the same time, the EDM is used to measure the distances (i.e. the lengths of the legs) between the first and second and the second and third points. To proceed around the site, the theodolite is moved to the third tripod and another tripod is set up on a fourth point. The angle between the second and fourth points is then measured along with the corresponding distances. The surveyor proceeds in this way until all the required ground is covered. If the traverse returns to its starting point it is called a **closed traverse**; if not, it is known as an **open traverse**. Traverses can be used to link two points of known value, and these are known as **link traverses**. Traverses are useful because they generate control points of a high order of precision that enables detail mapping to fit to a wider scheme when needed.

The precision of a traverse depends on the reliability of **instrument observations**. By repeated observation the statistical precision of the results is improved, and errors can be balanced, reduced and distributed proportionally within the network of the traverse.

The cost of precision is a careful field procedure; this will include taking precautions against instrument and observational error by use of multiple observations as well as considering the following points:

- Ensure that equipment and personnel are in good order – calibration status known, and appropriately trained.
- Agree the traverse design and route with those using the control.
- Select station positions so that they are well placed for later detail work, and the angles between stations are well conditioned.
- Ensure unattended stations for backsight and foresight are safe from unwanted attention.
- Always make a careful note of instrument and target heights at each set-up.
- Keep station (witnessing) diagrams up to date as you go.
- Do not expect untrained operators to conduct a traverse.
- Have a plan of action for changes in weather – equipment and person-nel will need protection.
- Understand the limitations of both the geometry attempted and the means of measurement.

Surveyors should be aware of the likely performance of tribrachs and be able to carry out a set-up with confidence in the required constraints of verticality, horizontal stage and centring.

Multiple observation substantially improves reliability. The observations are taken with the telescope in the normal position and *transited* (rotated through 180° of the horizontal axis), thus allowing the reading of opposite angles and distances to the target. This is known as reading from face 1 (f1) and face 2 (f2), also known as face left and face right. The results of the observations are averaged between f1 and f2 and a precise value for the recorded angle can be used for the control geometry.

Observations of angles and distances using *both* faces of the instrument will improve the reliability of the observation set by

- distribution of instrument vertical index error between the two faces
- distribution of instrument horizontal index error between the two faces
- improvement by distribution of error of EDM centre of distance measurement

A typical traversing set will comprise the following **equipment**:

- three tripods with adjustable legs
- three tribrachs; interchangeable, fitted with optical or laser plummets
- two prism reflectors and carriers
- one EDM instrument
- one data recorder/logger batteries/on-site power

The measurement axes of the instrument and prisms must occupy the same height above the tribrach to achieve a common height of collimation for both target and instrument when set up over the same tribrach. Using equipment from the same manufacturer can ensure this.

Control points will need to be re-occupied as reference positions for detail work, using a discreet but durable marker such as a road nail or detail point. This should be combined with a carefully drawn and measured sketch (known as a **witnessing** or **station diagram**) of the station location. The diagram should list the reduced (adjusted) coordinates, the reference stations, description of the mark and date of setting out.

Resection from 3D detail points

When setting out station positions with obscured sight lines, such as on staircases, in roof spaces and cellars, resection from 3D detail points is a useful technique (Figure 4.4). A set of reference marks can be placed on a wall in the area to be surveyed and observed from the current instrument position. These can then be used to determine a new station position. If an REDM is used, effective control can be applied without the use of a second tripod.

Resections work well provided that

- targets are carefully chosen for reflectance
- angles are well conditioned
- reference positions are clearly marked
- obliqueness (especially in Z) is avoided

Wireframe fitting (graphical control)

When using photography in the recording of detail, EDM can fix the position of detail in the photograph. Tracing from photographs is unreliable as

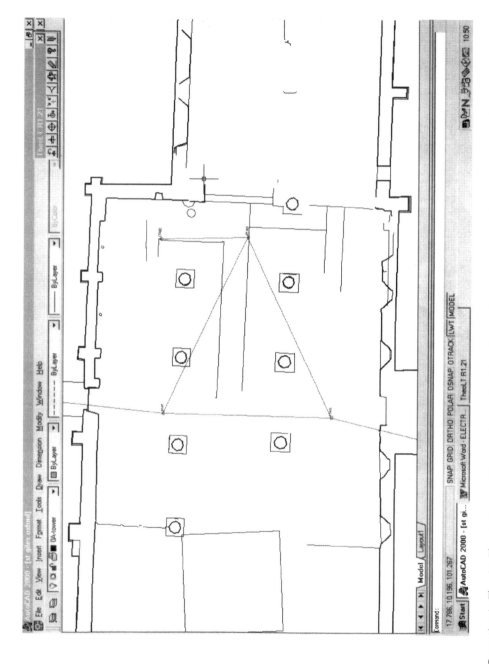

Figure 4.4 Resection in TheoLt. The station position can be resolved by observation to two or more known positions; the station on the centre of the nave has been located by observation to the stations on the loop. A spur has placed a station in front of the north wall from the resected position. Resection is useful with REDM when sight lines are blocked or when a prism cannot be placed at the target easily.

the photograph will not be true to scale and contains perspective distortion. If an EDM trace is made of key features, the wireframe can be used in CAD to resize the image to fit. REDM is well suited to this work as the number of observations can be increased from single points to lines, drawing the outline detail in real time using TheoLt (Figure 4.5).

The following points should be observed when using a wireframe for the tracing of detail from photography:

- Use field CAD to get the wireframe to match the image area.
- Ensure that the planes of the subject are adequately covered by the wireframe.
- Check overlapping data from adjacent images.
- Test the image scale against the wireframe to check for obliqueness.
- Keep the range between instrument and subject as short as possible.
- Take photography as square on as possible, and overlap the image area.

The effectiveness of photography undertaken in this way is limited by ability to control the image area; if a large area across several images is to be mapped, serious consideration should be given to alternative techniques such as photogrammetry or orthophotography.

Measured drawing can be effectively controlled in much the same way as photography. The drawing should be annotated to include the EDM observed outline (usually by marking the lines in red on the drawing) so that the plot can fit to the control.

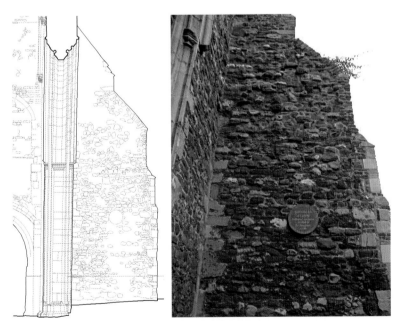

Figure 4.5 Using an REDM CAD trace to control photography of detail. Note the effect of camera tilt in the photograph, corrected on the REDM trace by 3D rotation of the image to fit the wireframe in CAD. The rubble infill was traced off the photograph.

Where hand survey is used to plan a site, it can employ control techniques similar to those of instrument surveys as described above. The main difference is the use of taped distance measurements and triangulation to establish right angles in circumstances where an EDM might otherwise be used. Hand-laid control grids of pegs or other markers are limited to intervals that fit a pattern of 3:4:5 triangles or similar Pythagorean ratios, and each point is rarely accurate to more than +/−10mm in any direction owing to tape sag and stretch. Also, unless the markers are levelled with a dumpy level or similar tool their heights will be random and unknown, requiring a separate marker to serve as a temporary benchmark (TBM) for independent height measurements.

Hand survey on building elevations requires, as a minimum, a level line across the elevation to serve as a baseline from which all other measurements can be taken. Two nails (one at each end of the elevation) are driven into the pointing at the same height, with a string stretched between them and a measuring tape alongside, its end on the left-hand nail. This allows for offset measurements either above or below the level line. Where necessary, the nails can be replaced by self-adhesive targets and masking tape to avoid damage to historic fabric. To speed the control and recording process, a rigid frame of 1 × 1 metre internal dimensions can be held against the wall with one edge aligned with the baseline. The frame marks out a 1 × 1 metre square, which is subdivided by strings into 0.20 × 0.20 metre squares. The frame can be 'flipped' along the baseline to provide a temporary control grid for each square metre of wall above and below the baseline. In this way, baselines across the elevation are only needed at height intervals of 2 metres.

While the baseline method provides survey control for a single elevation, the elevation as a whole will not be related to any other survey of the site. To relate separate elevation grids together, at least three control points on each elevation will need to be surveyed on a single site grid using an EDM to get 3D coordinates.

Adding to an existing CAD survey

Where a CAD-based survey exists for a wall, it can be used as the basis for later survey work. The wireframe outline from photogrammetry can be used to identify control points for resection, and in hand survey as a framework for detail infill. In this way an outline plot from photogrammetry or from a rapid REDM survey can be enhanced at a later date with detail that might only be visible from scaffolding, or after removal of an obstruction that existed at the time of the first survey.

Global Positioning System (GPS)

The use of Global Positioning System (GPS) equipment allows for rapid creation of survey stations in open fields without the need for lengthy traverses from Ordnance Survey control points. The GPS equipment receives signals from a minimum of four satellites, and calculates its position based on these signals. Owing to atmospheric interference and mathematical uncertainty, a precise position suitable for detailed survey work requires a system that compares the 'solutions' of positions of one 'roving' receiver with those of a second 'base' receiver that remains stationary on a tripod during the survey. The Ordnance Survey also maintains a web-based service where base receiver data can be downloaded for post-fieldwork processing without the need for a base receiver on site. When the roving and base data are processed, the resulting data is typically accurate to +/−10 mm in the horizontal plane and +/−20 mm in height. While this affects every point collected, the relative accuracy between points remains close over large distances without the risks of angular error that overshadow theodolite-based surveys. Longer observations can allow for more precise results where needed.

Survey stations are simply created by placing a marker in the ground and then setting the roving receiver over it for a few moments to gather positional data. Two such points are needed in order to provide a baseline, and these must be intervisible. The limitations are the precision, which is sufficient for most landscape survey but is not as accurate as a good instrument traverse, and the need to have a clear view of the sky in order to receive satellite signals. GPS will not work indoors, under tree cover, or near the north side of buildings, since most of the satellite orbits lie in the southern half of the sky. GPS also cannot be used to apply control points directly to an elevation, so it must be supplemented by traditional EDM equipment for building survey. Processing the data requires specialist training, and collecting reliable data requires both survey skill and common sense.

It should also be borne in mind that GPS does not provide any angular or distance data by which the average surveyor might assess the quality of the readings, so results must be taken at face value. It is therefore very important to ensure that any control installed with GPS is designed to be easily verified by other means.

Where the site covers a large area or is to be recorded as part of a wider area, project coordinate values need to respect the projection used to map the wider area. The OSNG uses a projection of a plane to transfer the curvature of the earth and the effects of variation in height. A **scale factor** is used to correct for the projection used; this can be applied at the point of capture or as a post-process adjustment.

It is important to ensure that, if a scale factor is to be applied, all in the recording team are aware so that the mismatch between adjusted and unadjusted work can be anticipated.

Control points derived from GPS survey should be supplied with a statement of the projection used and a local scale factor.

In summary, the precision and accuracy of control will directly affect the quality of detail data recorded. Control will underpin the performance of the entire survey. It is often a matter of common sense when a survey is prepared to anticipate the control requirement for the subject; provided the survey is well briefed, control can work as a backbone of precision not only for the immediate work but also for future surveys.

53

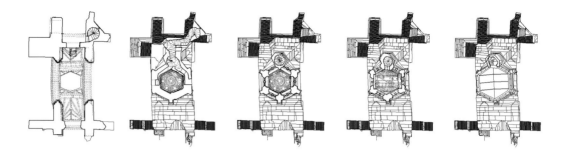

Figure 4.6 Stacked plans to record displacement at Greyfriars Tower, Kings Lynn, Norfolk. The common control used required a traverse to place stations at high level on the floors for consistency of detail position.

Selection of the appropriate control technique is a matter of matching the demands of the subject, the required scale and the future use of the survey; if survey is to be carried out on a site by different teams at different times, the control should be safeguarded accordingly.

Prior to putting control onto any site, it is important to undertake a site reconnaissance. This will enable the surveyor to obtain an overview of the project and observe where problems are likely to occur and so take steps to overcome them (Figure 4.6).

Detail

Electromagnetic distance measurement (EDM) gives a reliable framework to survey work of all kinds but especially to close-range work (5 to 100 metres). Precision is dependent on the density of recorded points and the method used. The use of EDM is becoming more widespread and its application to close-range detail work is now possible with reliable reflectorless EDM (REDM) and real-time links to CAD from software such as TheoLt. The guidance on technique offered here should be used in conjunction with that of the manufacturers and suppliers of the hardware and software.

As to **technique**, EDM is a line-of-sight measurement method requiring a target to measure to, usually a retro-reflective prism. Data is recorded by measuring the distance and horizontal and vertical angles to a reflector, giving a precise measurement (e.g. 2 mm at 2 ppm at 1.8 km). EDM is rapid and precise but requires the surveyor to select the data to be recorded in the field; it is not a mass data capture method like photogrammetry or laser scanning. Single-face observations are made from fixed points or stations, depending on the precision requirement of the survey; further stations are set out as required or a traverse is used to link sets of polar (or radial) observations together.

Operators of EDM instruments should be familiar with common survey practice so that they can set up over a point and understand

- the expected performance of angular and distance measurement
- the importance of level and plumb axes for measurement

- calibration and verification of instrument error
- the correct sequence of measurement to ensure appropriate precision for both control and detail work
- the appropriate point density for the desired drawing quality at a given scale

EDM units are available with combined EDM and REDM functions; this is very useful for recording buildings. Instruments that use a visible laser as a pointer for reflectorless measurement speed up pointing and increase the density of recorded points.

Reflectorless electromagnetic distance measurement (REDM) uses the same principle as reflector-based methods but will operate over a useful range of 5 to 200 metres. This has two principal benefits – speed of targeting and access to remote targets.

REDM can be operated as a one-person system given the redundancy of placing a prism reflector at the target. In practice, two people are often required as subjects usually require a mix of targeting methods to provide complete coverage. Data captured using an REDM needs careful monitoring so that spurious points can be removed. The following three variables can affect the precision of the reflectorless measurement and can be responsible for spurious points:

- **Range:** the return signal is diminished and the contact area of the measuring beam is increased with long-range observations.
- **Obliqueness:** the ambiguity over the targeted point increases with the obliqueness of the observation, and distances will be corrupted.
- **Reflectance:** the reflective quality and surface texture of the target will affect the ability to measure distances.

Target and station selections are determined by these variables; stations should be close to the subject, and targeting edges with an oblique aspect to the instrument should be avoided.

Four simple steps help get the best data-sets from reflectorless measurement:

- Use TheoLt to monitor the recorded points and lines for verification of the measurement results.
- Use a card target for edges; this will improve precision when measuring to edges as it will resolve split beam ambiguities.
- Keep the range and obliqueness to a minimum.
- Make overlapping observations separated by layer from one instrument set-up to the next as a check against height error.

Data logging methods fall into two groups:

- **Post-process** data logging is typically used for digital terrain models and control work at scales between 1:500 and 1:2500. If rapid capture and field equipment survival are more important than detailed verification, a post-process approach will give the benefit of robust field kit and speed of capture.

- **Real-time CAD** is a method of digitising 3D data from the instrument directly into a CAD environment. The use of real-time CAD capture is of great benefit for large-scale close-range work, such as the recording of detail for historic building survey. When it is used with reflectorless instruments, surveyors can edit and complete data in CAD at the point of capture. Close-range reflectorless work such as internal building survey is best recorded by real-time CAD.

Data loggers for post-fieldwork processing (post process) and real time differ. Real-time data capture requires the use of a field computer to plot the observations in their correct positions in a CAD environment. A laptop can be used but it will be exposed to site conditions. Post-process loggers are tough and require low power but are limited to coding the observation string as a means of data separation and definition.

Real-time survey methods

An EDM can be used directly with AutoCAD using TheoLt; this provides an interface for survey instruments, allowing survey data to be recorded in real time directly into CAD. The method requires the use of a robust computer to run CAD on site, an EDM set-up and the TheoLt software. The surveyor can then draw detail using the EDM to position points and lines in the 3D CAD drawing. The product can be a 3D wireframe to be used as an outline for future hand survey or a complete drawing (Figure 4.7).

Real-time field CAD, tracing with an REDM into CAD, is rapid compared with the slow process of direct drawing in CAD. Edits on site, such as off-setting lines for details, closing shapes using fillet, extend and trim, can be effective but a balance must be made with photographing or sketching detail for later work-up in CAD. Setting up views of sectional elevations from a wireframe can help in the selection of detail to be included and is vital in elevation work. Data can be separated and edited by layer for line weight and type rather than by the alternative coding method. Full-size details can be worked up in CAD off site and then fitted to precise 3D positions from EDM on site.

Hand-held, distance-only EDM devices (such as Leica's Disto) can be used as real-time CAD sensors. 2D geometry can be built up by plotting the intersection of arcs, offsetting and copying lines by distance input from the Disto using TheoLt to interface to AutoCAD.

To get the most out of real-time CAD, a field computer is required. The best are those that use a pen interface and have daylight-readable screens. These are more costly than a standard laptop and may need external power from spare batteries. Weather protection is essential and all cables will need to be of robust quality. Suitably robust computers vary widely in specification and performance; it is important to check carefully details such as data exchange, power supply and screen performance before choosing a field unit. Living with a computer in the field can be demanding on both the user and the hardware; a safe mounting bracket is a wise investment

Figure 4.7 3D data collection for 3D model. The spiral stair has been solid modelled; the outline of all other features are in 3D wireframe. Views of the stair on the sectional elevation.

as it will save a computer from costly damage and will improve the work environment for the surveyor.

When preparing CAD data for site work, field CAD work needs to be separated from other data sources. This can be done by layer so that fitting of blocks is possible if there is a mismatch between the site work and any earlier work. It is a good idea to set up the required views for the job before site work begins; much time can be lost finding your way around a large cumbersome drawing, and it is better to use small drawing files on site.

Complementary techniques

Because EDM data is digital, it readily sits in CAD and can be used to

- construct a wireframe to control hand survey work
- control the digitising of drawings and photographs
- infill and supplement 3D photogrammetric data
- build up CAD drawings directly on site
- infill and supplement 3D laser scans
- infill and supplement GPS data

57

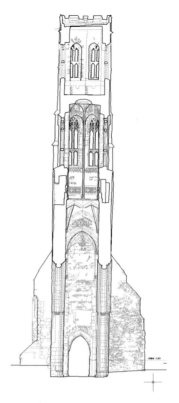

Figure 4.8 Sectional elevation from an REDM survey originally plotted at 1:20 scale. The quatrefoils, tracery and mouldings were drawn up by hand and digitised into position by fitting to the 3D wireframe from TheoLt (see also Figure 4.5).

Because EDM requires a high order of target selection, it is rare (with the notable exception of small-site topographic surveys) for it to be the sole method of data collection; it is common to combine data from EDM with drawings prepared by hand measurement or derived from photography. Detail from photographs and site drawings can be scaled and fitted to the armature of the wireframe from REDM. The record gains metric integrity when details are positioned in 3D (Figure 4.8).

In terms of **skills and resources**, detail survey requires type-specific knowledge; the ability to describe architecture with clarity and understanding and a readiness to draw are still prerequisites for anyone who undertakes work of this kind. It is often effective to deploy a mix of skills on a complex or detailed recording task.

Drawing detail at large scales

It is rare for a mass data capture system like photogrammetry or laser scanning to work at the high resolutions needed to map detail at large architectural scales (1:20, 1:10, 1:5 or full size). It is also rare for detail-recording techniques to work well at mass data capture scales; the quality of the record will be visible in the treatment of detail. If a project requires a crude outline for schematic purposes, it is worth making an assessment of the features that warrant detailed attention and focusing resources onto these significant details rather than attempting to resolve detail from survey carried out by a mass capture system.

There are three techniques used in the preparation of drawn details; each technique has its place in the survey workflow depending on the needs and scale of the survey, the time and resources available, and the desired quality of the outcome. Drawings and photographs are essential adjuncts to metric techniques like REDM or photogrammetry, as they amplify the necessary abstraction needed to characterise historic detail as well as define the quality of the survey as whole. The three methods are as follows:

- **Direct plotting**: plotting measurements to scale on site, usually by use of a string grid placed over the subject. Direct plotting is a common method of archaeological recording.
- **Measured drawing**: the preparation of fair drawn notes with dimension annotation for plotting off site to scale.
- **Sketch diagrams**: explanatory sketches to show key diagnostic details, used to clarify details measured by other means (Figure 4.9).

3D data capture for 3D outputs

If a survey is required to provide 3D data, it is worth carefully considering the exact nature of the requirement; a high-parity 3D model is costly and time-taking, and must have significant project benefits to be justified (Figure 4.10). Many survey techniques are 3D by default, and the retention of the 3D base data for future development of 3D outputs should always be included in the brief for survey.

Laser scanners can capture huge numbers of precise points at great speed. The points are undifferentiated and rarely make a useful contribution to historic building survey practice. In exceptional cases, the point cloud data can be used to record surfaces that defy mapping by traditional edge-driven methods: for example, sculptural details or subjects where the surface is of greater interest than edges.

Survey products and their procurement

Procurement of a metric survey

As discussed in the introduction to this chapter, the selection and application of survey techniques must balance end use, content and technical constraints against resources available. The driving principle is 'fitness for purpose'; the levels of survey deployed should be appropriate to the needs of the project. The most common application of metric survey is not in the

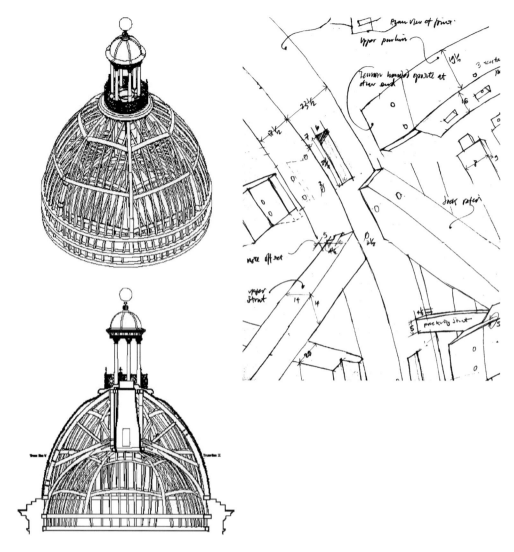

Figure 4.9 The roof space of the Archer Pavilion, Wrest Park, Bedfordshire, recorded by REDM as 3D wireframe. The completion to CAD drawing is impossible without drawing the key details on site, including cross-section measurements of components as they are often absent from wireframes.

area of conservation recording; the precise 3D recording of buildings is an adaptation of general survey practices. It is thus advisable to describe the required service with care to avoid confusion, and the process needs to be carefully overseen for success.

There are three main procurement issues for metric survey:

- Technique or data source – is the proposed method appropriate?
- Practitioner discipline – is the service to be delivered from a provider with the right skills?
- The project brief – it is vital to be clear as to what is expected of the final product: what should the survey look like?

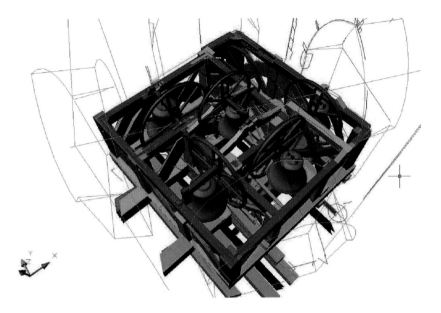

Figure 4.10 A 3D CAD model of the bell frame at St Mary's Church, Attleborough, Norfolk, to help the design of strengthening work and encourage interest in the project, as all the work is hidden from view. The same data was used for traditional plans and sections.

There are six main points that need to be addressed when procuring a metric survey of historic buildings:

- **Specification**: there should be descriptions of the acceptable toler-ances for the task, including the relevant scale tolerances, a method and resource statement, a safety procedure and a requirement for professional indemnity.
- **Brief**: this should describe the extent, scale and intensity of the survey, including a clear, relevant example of the treatment of detail. Variation of detail cover proportional to scale should be shown by example, if needed.
- **Reconnaissance**: the practicalities of power, light, access and personnel contacts should be noted in the brief.
- **Control**: this may require Scheduled Monument Consent (SMC) for station markers, and interested bodies should be encouraged to col-laborate in siting permanent ground markers (PGMs) on sensitive sites. The difficulty of tying into existing site control is often overlooked; it is worth considering the use of GPS to determine Ordnance Survey National Grid (OSNG) values.
- **The method and resource statement**: the surveyor should be able to describe the proposed technique and its likely performance. The resource statement should describe not only equipment and its condi-tion (calibration certification etc.) but also the procedures, skills and personnel to be applied.
- **Survey products**: the specification of the CAD protocols, plot size, line weights, etc. needs to be undertaken with care, particularly where

presentation of drawings is important or if the data is to be used by other recording practitioners. Other necessary considerations are the archive quality of the output material, number of copies and where the final product is to be sent.

Metric survey products

Photographic/image-based

- photogrammetry: field package, 3D CAD products – high cost/high reliability
- digital orthophotography
- rectified photography: field package, 2D CAD products
- scaled photography
- narrative photography

Measured survey/EDM-based

- REDM trace 3D
- CAD drawings 2D and 3D
- laser scans – high cost/high speed/low resolution
- digitised drawings

The Metric Survey Specification for English Heritage

This document is the specification used by English Heritage for the procurement of metric survey. The Metric Survey Specification defines the acquisition and presentation of base data by a repeatable method within a known precision. It describes the technical requirements for metric survey and as such should not be taken as guidance on the application of thematic recording. The specification has proved a valuable and robust control on the provision of base mapping data in conservation and recording projects for and on behalf of English Heritage; however, standard specifications should always be used with care, and the selection of survey products should never be made without careful consideration.

The Metric Survey Specification for English Heritage is available free in pdf format at www.english-heritage.org.uk (viewing this file requires Adobe Acrobat Reader, which can be downloaded free from www.adobe.com).

Conclusion: appropriate application of metric survey

The metric record of historic subjects requires careful attention to both the practice of survey and the drawing standards needed to meet the specific needs of the survey. It is desirable to have a brief for the survey that will leave no doubt as to the outcome. Planning the techniques, their common control and the performance of the products from survey is essential if the survey is to meet both the needs of the record and the precision required.

The practice of metric survey is best undertaken by adhering to the following principles:

- Time spent on reconnaissance is seldom wasted.
- 'Work from the whole to part.' Work from control to architectural detail.
- Match the economy of method to the time and resources available.
- Anticipate the demands of the scale and the end user(s).
- If CAD is to be used, agree a common format at the outset.
- Never expect more from survey data than the method deployed can deliver.
- A picture is worth a thousand words: photograph what you can, and draw what cannot be depicted in a photograph. A photograph with some measurement or control is better than one without.

It is important to understand the potential and limitations of survey techniques. It is essential that the survey technique proposed for a particular building is suitable for the building and fit for its proposed purpose. The correct techniques must be chosen based on the size, complexity and type of structure and the potential end uses of the survey data.

No single technique is likely to provide a complete record of a building, and the need for deploying several complementary techniques should be recognised at an early stage in the project, preferably before issuing any briefs or setting any budgets. Efficient use of complementary techniques requires planning to ensure that a suitable control framework is established for all the work, and that each area of site is assessed for the best use of techniques to avoid repetition and waste of resources.

Adequate site preparation is essential to all of the techniques covered in this chapter, and should be addressed early in the project.

When procuring a survey, the specification will control the quality and content. The Metric Survey Team publishes specifications for English Heritage-commissioned survey products; these can provide a useful guide to the type of product that a project manager can expect from each technique. Additional publications of use include *The Presentation of Historic Building Survey in CAD*, which sets out systems of organising survey data as well as quality standards for products. Further advice can always be sought from English Heritage – from the Metric Survey Team, Historical Analysis and Research Team (HART), Centre for Archaeology (CfA) and Architectural Investigators.

The precise technical processes that define metric survey, if undertaken with care and sensitivity, will provide records that communicate the patinated and irregular character of our historic buildings and monuments. The close contact with a building that metric survey requires generates observation and understanding, which inform the drawing process. The patterns of building use can be revealed by the survey, and these will inform the understanding of the structure in the unique way that only the drawn and measured can.

5 Investigating, monitoring and load testing historic structures

Ian Hume

Investigative work

This chapter outlines the reasons for investigating a structure and suggests ways of minimising damage to historic fabric while endeavouring to ensure that problems are not left undiscovered. Before work to historic fabric is commenced, detailed survey work is vital for a full understanding of the real strengths and weaknesses of the structure. All the major elements of the structure should be examined for decay and for other problems, but too much opening up should be avoided. Floors can be examined by carefully lifting occasional floorboards, leaving ceilings and cornices intact.

Asking questions of the structure

A detailed inspection of the historic structure will provide answers to these and many more questions:

- When was it built?
- How was it built?
- What are the details of its construction?
- What changes have taken place since it was built?
- What is known of its past history?
- What has it been used for?
- Has it survived thus far?
- How has it survived thus far?
- What problems does it have?
- How long has it had these problems?
- Is there ground movement?
- Do the drains work properly?
- Is there roof spread?
- Is there any fungal or beetle decay?
- Are the problems terminal?
- Can a small improvement reap a great increase in strength and life?

General considerations

Before starting work on a historic structure, prudent owners and their professional advisers will want to minimise the scale of unforeseen works. The more problems that are unknown, the more the costs are likely to escalate, because an inadequate schedule of work will result in the need for additional work. Decisions about the repair or alteration of an old structure should be based on an understanding of its original form, its construction and the stages in its subsequent evolution. Many apparent structural defects are the result of modifications to the original structure, and many, having existed for a very long time, may well be problems no longer. Such knowledge can reduce uncertainty about the extent of any necessary repairs.

The following paragraph from the *Guide to Surveys and Inspections of Buildings and Similar Structures*, published by the Institution of Structural Engineers (November 1991), is relevant:

> It should be emphasised that when inspecting an existing structure it is not realistic to assume that each and every defect which exists within that building will be identified and it is important that the client be informed of the limitations of the exercise which is being carried out. The engineer who carries out a survey must exercise the skill and care of a reasonably experienced and competent engineer. The law recognises that perfection is unattainable and hence does not impose liability simply because the engineer fails to make a perfect diagnosis.

Existing records

Drawings of the construction of all or part of the structure and records of any work carried out to the structure, if available, should be examined. Records of former works will give indications of past problems and will indicate where apparent problems have already been dealt with. Geological maps can be useful and construction drawings may survive. The history of a structure can often be built up from looking at old maps, prints and other documents, and records of previous works may survive. In the case of churches, quinquennial inspection reports should exist and so should records of actions taken as a result of those reports. Dating a structure is often looked upon as being purely the role of the historian. However, knowing its approximate date can give vital ideas as to how it might be constructed and what problems it might therefore have.

Opening-up works

In many cases it may be worth investing money on preliminary opening-up work. Clear and specific documentation should be prepared for such work to ensure that there is as much contractual control as possible. Safety must always be considered.

This 'opening up' must be sufficient to enable the professional advisers to have adequate information to proceed with the work with minimal risk of escalation of costs as a result of unforeseen problems and to ensure that they do not put themselves at risk of legal action after the work has been completed. However, the opening up must not be so extensive and so damaging that the historic value of the structure is lost.

Most local authorities have conservation officers and it is advisable, where opening up is likely to be considered, to consult with them or, where appropriate, with English Heritage, at an early stage. If English Heritage has grant-aided the repair of the structure in the past, it is particularly important that they are consulted. The conservation officer's views are likely to be of value from both a practical and a procedural point of view. In the case of ecclesiastical buildings, it is important to make early contact with the Church of England Diocesan Advisory Committee or with the relevant denominational committee. The destruction of important finishes is not likely to be seen as acceptable and it should be borne in mind that wall paintings or stencilling sometimes exist under later finishes, especially in older structures. The cost of reinstatement of historic finishes can be high, and the repair bill resulting from over-enthusiastic opening up can be as undesirable as the destruction of historic fabric.

It is a criminal offence to carry out demolition or alteration that would affect the character (both external and internal) of any ancient monument or listed building (including Grade II) unless those works have been authorised. In many cases it will be enough, after consultation with the local authority about simple exploratory work, to exchange letters confirming an agreed sensible course of action, with sketches showing opening-up proposals. In less straightforward cases, formal applications for listed building consent may be required.

The churches and chapels (and their accompanying buildings) of the Church of England, Church of Wales, Roman Catholic Church, Methodist Church and United Reformed Church and churches belonging to the Baptist Union of Great Britain (and of Wales) are exempt from normal listed building control. However, the Church of England has its own system of faculty jurisdiction and the other exempt denominations have control systems that must be used. Other denominations need listed building consent in the normal way.

The investigation

A preliminary investigation should be made to establish whether there are any unsafe areas in the structure. A considerable amount of information can be gained from a detailed examination of the structure prior to any opening up being undertaken. Structural deformities should be closely examined for signs of recent movement as there is little value in 'repairing' a fracture that has not moved for many years. Likewise, there is dubious value in underpinning a building at great cost, both financially and in terms of loss of historic fabric and archaeology, if the settlement ceased a few years after the completion of construction.

Careful examination of the building can pinpoint the most effective locations for any necessary opening up. A damp-stained patch on a ceiling or mould growth behind a downpipe suggest possible problems with timber decay, and particular attention should be paid to such areas. Defective rainwater services discharging water onto the face of a building or through gutters are indicative of possible problems within and focus attention on areas which are worthy of special attention.

Making a record of the significant cracks and analysing these can often give guidance as to the past behaviour of the structure and will also point to areas of the building finishes which need to be exposed in order to confirm the theory of past behaviour. This work may also include taking levels and plumb-bob readings of sufficient accuracy to assist in the assessment. It is necessary that proper access is made available and that ladders and so on are to hand.

It is unsafe to assume anything about the layout and design of a historic structure without careful checking of dimensions and details. A wall on an upper floor may not be directly above a wall on the floor below, joist spacing may vary and beam sizes may not repeat. Decay may be found in unexpected places and more recent changes, including the insertion of modern services, may have weakened the structure.

The extent of **opening-up work**, including removal of finishes, could vary depending on the nature of the investigation. A general assessment of the state of a building would require less opening up than is required during remedial work where, for example, all floor joists must be examined, particularly where they bear into the wall structure. Methods such as drilling small-diameter holes into the timber should be considered, to check on the presence of rot in the joist ends. Floorboard removal should be minimal. Floorboards are frequently of historic interest, and it may sometimes be more convenient to remove areas of ceiling (where these are of no historic interest) in cases where the floorboards are tongued and grooved and removal would result in their destruction. Excessive removal of floorboards can sometimes destabilise a structure as floorboards provide essential diaphragm plate action to a structure. Where adopted, opening-up works should be kept to a minimum and should be carried out by skilled contractors.

As many historic structures occupy archaeologically sensitive ground, **trial holes** should only be dug if there is a clearly defined reason for doing so. The position and depth of any necessary holes should be agreed beforehand by the appropriate authorities and, where necessary, the relevant consent obtained. Archaeological supervision may be needed during the work. Care should be taken to ensure that foundations are not undermined.

It is useful, often vital, to carry out **structural monitoring** to learn more about the magnitude and direction of the movements of the structure, or indeed to ascertain whether or not the structure is moving at all, to assist in the correct diagnosis of the problem and to help in the production of effective and sympathetic solutions to the problem. A later chapter discusses structural monitoring in more detail.

Load tests are sometimes appropriate in helping to decide whether remedial work is necessary, particularly in cases where calculations are not possible, such as with cantilever staircases built into walls on one side only. (Load testing is discussed further later in this chapter.)

Non-destructive techniques

Non-destructive techniques enable a broad overview to be taken relatively quickly and limit the need for opening up. Many non-destructive techniques, including radar, thermography, radiography and ultrasonics, need specialist operators to use the equipment and to interpret the results. Pulse radar and other sophisticated surveys can be helpful in finding voids in structures, and resistivity surveys can locate pipes and cables in the ground without excavation.

Less sophisticated, but still useful, are optical methods using a **borescope**. This instrument provides views of inaccessible areas such as behind panelling, under floors and in ceilings, and can be used to check the condition of floor joists and brickwork in cavity walls, reducing the need for opening up. Very often there are cracks or open joints into which the borescope can be pushed. At worst, a few 8–10 mm diameter holes are all that is required. **Closed-circuit television** can survey drains and chimneys, and high-quality metal detectors can locate cramps or reinforcement in masonry.

Load tests can sometimes be a useful, non-destructive method of establishing structural adequacy, but such tests need to be carried out with great care and under the supervision of a structural engineer. (Load testing is discussed further later in this chapter.)

There is a range of simple methods that are useful. The **decay-detecting drill** bores 1 mm diameter holes 200 mm long into timber and, without being able to tell the grade or permissible stress of the timber, can determine the location and extent of decay. **Hammer testing** the faces of flint walls to listen for hollow sounds, **looking closely at cracks** to determine which way the structure has moved and taking **level and plumb readings** are all important techniques that can be used to better understand how a structure has moved. Also vitally important is to discover whether or not a distorted and distressed structure is still moving. Structural monitoring is discussed below.

While every attempt should be made to discover the full extent of the **problems of the building** (but without destroying its historic value in the process), it is likely that something unforeseen may be found during the work on site. This risk should not be underestimated, but equally it should not be allowed to become a reason for extensive demolition. Experience, diagnostic skill and flexibility in costing and programming can help to reduce the effects of unforeseen problems.

Monitoring structures

All structures have fractures of one kind or another; the difficulty is to decide how important those cracks are, whether or not they are currently moving, what effect they will have on the life of structure and whether or not remedial works are necessary. The problem is especially acute with historic structures. The simple but accurate monitoring of structural and ground movements is a powerful but much underrated weapon for use in the conservation of the built environment. It is useful, often vital, to monitor accurately in order to learn more about the magnitude and direction of the movements, and so to assist in the correct diagnosis and help in the production of effective and sympathetic solutions to the problem.

Movements in structures fall into three categories. They may be **current**, in which case some action needs to be taken, or they may be past movements which have either **ceased permanently** or are only **dormant**. In each of these cases monitoring can have a role to play. If there is current movement, monitoring is a helpful diagnostic tool where directions, speed and magnitude of movement are not clear. In the case of past movements, monitoring can be utilised to confirm that cracks and other signs of distress have reached a point of stability.

Accurate monitoring has a number of advantages. First, it can help in the correct diagnosis of structural ills; this means that an effective and sympathetic treatment is more likely to be implemented. Before remedial works are commenced, a careful survey of cracks and other damage should be made and accurate monitoring commenced to learn more about the magnitude, direction and speed of the movements. Surveys and monitoring procedures can often avoid costly but incorrect solutions. For example, the building will not be underpinned when it is the roof that is at fault.

Secondly, it can be a source of reassurance and an invaluable aid in convincing others that the decision to take no action to remedy an apparent problem was correct because the structure, having once moved, is now stable. Deciding to do nothing is often much more difficult than spending sums of money on remedial schemes which may not be necessary. Monitoring can provide the peace of mind which may be needed and can be used to show that the professional responsible for the structure is taking a proper attitude and is not being negligent.

Thirdly, it can prove that cracks which have been repaired but which have reappeared are due to seasonal and/or climatic variations and are therefore subject to opening and closing cycles rather than progressively opening. In such cases it is often not necessary to carry out any further remedial works; sometimes remedial works in these situations can be counterproductive.

The long-term view

Monitoring is the most effective, indeed often the only way of proving satisfactorily and without doubt that apparently distressed structures are in fact stable, and therefore no major remedial works need be undertaken. It is very rare for structures to collapse without warning, and even large cracks can often prove benign or to need only minimal intervention.

It is often wise to establish a system to monitor movements and to keep a close watch for some length of time, possibly over a period of years, before coming to a definite conclusion. It is important to take readings regularly rather than erratically and to take them frequently to begin with, increasing the period between readings as time passes if it appears reasonable to do so.

To maintain a thorough check on structural or ground movements, it is often necessary to employ more than one technique and to consider the results obtained over a period of several months in the light of experience gained from work of a similar nature, and to take account of matters such as temperature, rainfall, soil conditions, state of structure and so on.

The importance of having good monitoring points that will not become dislodged or corroded, detailed, orderly and duplicated results, and easy-to-understand charts cannot be overemphasised.

Crack monitoring

Movements in structures can make themselves apparent in a number of ways. The most obvious sign, and usually the earliest, is cracking. Settlement of fill and washing out of joints can lead to bulging. Ground movements can result in differential settlement, tilting and other movements within the superstructure. In more extreme cases, cracking of the ground can occur.

Is that crack getting wider?

Cracks appear to get wider the longer they are studied. This may be due to the crack getting dirtier and therefore more noticeable, it may be psychological, or it may actually be a fact that the crack is widening as a result of movement. The only sure way of discovering the true nature and speed of the apparent widening is to accurately monitor the fracture.

Movements of cracks in structures can be monitored using a **demountable mechanical strain gauge**, the DEMEC, together with suitable locating points fitted to the structure adjacent to the cracks. The locating points are 6 mm diameter stainless steel discs with a small hole drilled at the centre for accurate positioning of the conical points of the gauge. These steel discs can be fixed to the structure with either sealing wax or glue. An alternative method of fixing locating points is to drill 5 mm diameter holes 2 mm deep into the structure and to insert into these a hammer-in fixing consisting of a flanged expansion sleeve and a nail. The nail is driven flush with the surface and drilled with a BS1 centre drill in order to receive the conical gauge point.

For monitoring movement in **timber structures**, brass screws can be inserted at suitable locations. The head of the screw can be drilled to receive the conical gauge point. Some cross-head screws provide a good seating for the gauge but others allow the conical point to move around excessively. The type of locating point used is dependent upon the material to which the fixing is being made, the degree of exposure to the weather and the location in relation to possible vandalism. For a **soft wall material** the drilled-in fixing is advisable, while for a hard material sticking on discs is easier and quite satisfactory. Avoid drilling into mortar joints, as the fixings will eventually work loose and the readings will become unreliable.

Movements of 0.025 mm are easily traceable and with care greater accuracy can be achieved. The only visible signs of this form of monitoring are three small discs at each monitoring point. The DEMEC strain gauge, although easy to use and robust, is rather expensive for occasional use.

If a DEMEC gauge is more expensive than desired, a good **vernier gauge** can be almost as effective. These can be purchased from any supplier of engineering tools and can be used to measure accurately (to at least 0.1 mm) between the shanks of brass screws set in plastic plugs in a triangular pattern around a crack. Cheap verniers can be obtained from do-it-yourself shops, but the better quality engineers' verniers are much more reliable. A good vernier usually incorporates a depth gauge – a useful facility for monitoring fractures in corners of walls.

The use of **glass telltales** cannot be recommended at all. These are susceptible to breaking by frost or vandalism, and are difficult to fix adequately, often becoming detached at one end and suggesting, because they are still intact, that no movement has taken place. No record of progressive or climatic movement can be kept and they are unsightly. Modern **plastic telltales** using two overlapping plastic plates, one marked with cross hairs and the other in a grid pattern, are accurate only to 1.0 mm, which may well not be good enough to detect thermal and climatic movement. These can be unreliable in their fixings and suffer the same unsightly characteristics as glass telltales. Although their cost is small per unit, it is better and cheaper to invest in a vernier gauge than in a dozen or so plastic telltales.

On a 'consumer guide' basis, the best value for money is the vernier gauge and brass screw system, although the DEMEC is to be recommended if much accurate monitoring is foreseen.

Recording results

Experience has shown that it is vital to keep good, neat records of monitoring results on pre-printed charts. This reduces the risk of forgetting to note the date (important when considering seasonal movements) and missing out some locations that are perhaps out of the way.

A site plan indicating the location of the various monitoring points and a sheet of notes indicating precise location – for example, 'Point 5: on outside of window sill, west end' – are vital for finding monitoring points. Such detailed recording is very much worth the time spent initially, as a lot of time can be wasted searching for two small screws 'somewhere up the east wall (I think)' – as often happens when monitoring is done infrequently. Also, of course, good records are invaluable when staff changes occur and for people trying to check for movements in the future. All records should be kept in duplicate, at least. Separate office copies and site copies are needed, as the latter, particularly in bad weather conditions, can easily become illegible and vital information can be lost.

It is useful, especially when explaining movements to non-technical people, to have the results of monitoring shown in graphic form rather than in columns of unintelligible numbers. It is necessary to exaggerate movements 10 or 100 times in order that patterns of movement can be seen, and fitting movements to a timescale helps with understanding seasonal variations, which are often significant.

Is it leaning more than it used to?

To maintain a thorough check on any structural or ground movements, it is often necessary to employ an accurate crack-monitoring method, possibly in conjunction with techniques for monitoring level and plumb. It is often necessary to consider the results obtained over a period of several months in the light of experience gained from similar work and to take account of matters such as temperature, rainfall, soil conditions and state of structure. Changes in the out-of-plumb state of structures can be measured by any one of several methods.

The **Autoplumb** is a sophisticated optical form of plumb bob that can be used over heights of between 2 and 150 metres. Because it is an optical instrument, it does not have the problems of bob swing and wind drag on the line. This instrument can read down to better than 0.5 mm in 10 metres. At some high point on the structure a target must be attached, and a small reference point is also necessary at ground level. This instrument is used at ground level and thus only one high-level 'visit' need be made. It is often possible to use a brass screw or a small bracket as the high-level target.

A **theodolite** can be used to check the out-of-vertical movements of structures to a degree of accuracy similar to that of the Autoplumb but without the need to gain access at high level. There are a number of restrictions that limit the use of the theodolite for vertical checks and that make the Autoplumb the better instrument for this purpose. The modern electronic distance reading (EDM) theodolite is capable of measuring distances (and therefore can measure stretching and shortening of structures) to an accuracy of 1 mm, and this is a much more useful instrument for monitoring than the older type of manually operated theodolite. For structural monitoring purposes, a target has to be attached to the structure under observation and a base station for the theodolite set-up. The target can be a small white reflector (rather like a bicycle reflector), 24 mm in diameter.

The traditional method for checking out-of-plumb conditions is, of course, the **plumb bob**. While this is perfectly satisfactory for building walls, fitting doorframes and hanging wallpaper, its value as an accurate means of monitoring structural movement is limited. However, as the Autoplumb and theodolite cost several thousand pounds each, the plumb bob must be considered as a monitoring method, particularly over heights of just a few metres.

It is vital that the locating positions for the top of the plumb line and the rest position of the plumb bob are accurately defined. This can easily be arranged using brass screws or (for the top) a brass rod with a notch in which to seat the line. The plumb line should be of good quality and of a type that will not unravel itself under the weight of the plumb bob. The plumb bob should be heavy, with a well-defined point on the bottom. Bob swing is always a problem; suspending the bob in a bucket of water or oil may help to dampen this. Wind drag on the line is almost impossible to stop, and a calm day may well be the only solution when plumbing out of doors. A heavy plumb bob such as a window sash weight can help to reduce the wind drag problem. Clearly, the accuracy of such methods is limited and too much reliance on readings should be avoided.

Is there any settlement?

Vertical levels of the ground or of structures can be taken with a high degree of accuracy (0.2 mm) by the use of a precise level with a **parallel plate micrometer**. Periodic checks can be made to detect movement. The levelling staff used is constructed from Invar, a thermally stable alloy. Again, this equipment is expensive and use may be made of levels of a lesser standard. To place any reliability on the results obtained, the level needs to be of a high standard and kept in good order with frequent checks on its adjustment. A builder's level, in dirty condition, which has been standing in a corner unused for years, is clearly not likely to give reliable results.

English Heritage engineers generally use levelling points that are manu-factured to the design of and standards set up by the Building Research Establishment. These are not necessary for use with a normal level and staff, but it is vital, even in these cases, to ensure that the staff is returned to exactly the same point each time monitoring levels are taken. The 'left-hand side of the door step' is clearly not good enough, as dirt may accu-mulate and the step may even be lifted and reset. A very heavy gauge brass screw will provide a good location point, although if left projecting horizontally from a wall face continued dropping of the staff on it may cause it to bend, thus giving a false reading.

Changes in distance

Where ground movements are known or suspected, a line of targets can be buried in the ground and checked for position periodically by the use of an optical or EDM theodolite. Again, targets can be unobtrusive or indeed totally hidden and made visible only when required.

Horizontal changes can also be detected by accurate measurements with a **steel tape** held under constant tension by use of a tape extensometer. Rigid eyes must be fixed in the structure to enable the tape extensometer to be attached and tensioned properly. It is possible to use purpose-made demountable eyes that can be accurately repositioned each time a set of readings is taken. Adjustments to the readings have to be made to allow for temperature variations. The tape should be held under constant tension using a spring balance and a special clip that allows a handle to be attached to the spool end of the tape. Fabric and plastic tapes should not be used for monitoring as these are liable to stretch slightly with use.

Photographic monitoring

The use of old photographs when looking for changes in the condition of a structure is widespread but can be rather unreliable and is also often not conclusive, certainly where a degree of accuracy is required. However, it is a useful method of discovering how long a structure has been distorted and for getting a general 'feel' of past movements.

For future monitoring purposes such photographs are best taken square on to the fracture to reduce distortion and to produce a clear rather than an attractive photograph. They are also best taken with this purpose specifically in mind rather than selected from more or less suitable photographs taken for other purposes.

Load testing

Load testing is another powerful weapon that the structural engineer can use as a means of justifying the structural adequacy of historic structures that cannot be proven by calculation and can be a way of proving a structure satisfactory without recourse to expensive and disruptive but unnecessary strengthening schemes. If the structure has behaved satisfactorily for many years then its whole life will have been a long-term load test.

Perhaps the best form of load test is the examination of the past history of the building or structure. The following matters should be addressed:

- What loads did it have to carry?
- What distress have these loads caused?
- Has there indeed been any serious distress at all?
- Is its continued existence a better justification for its future life than the evidence produced by calculations that only prove that it should have collapsed already?
- What loads should the structure carry in the future?
- If these loads are similar to or less than past loading, are any strengthening works really necessary?

Consideration of these questions, together with perhaps some repairs to local areas of weakness caused by the effects of time, weather, beetle and corrosion, can often be used as a long-term load test to justify confidence in the future use of a historic structure.

Structures and structural components can be load tested both for serviceability and ultimate capacity. Clearly, only the first of these can apply to a historic structure. Tests to destruction, although capable of giving research data, do not, of course, fit in with conservation philosophy. The load applied during a test for serviceability should be representative of the real-life situation of the structure.

Case study 1: A timber-roofed barn

Neglect, weather and death-watch beetle had caused some decay to the barn, and this had resulted in a partial collapse in the central section of the roof. A mixture of traditional carpentry repairs, steel plating and replacement timber, together with a little resin repair work, had resulted in the successful conservation of the principal framework. However, there was doubt as to the adequacy of the rafters, which had been attacked by beetle and which in some instances had new ends scarfed on.

It was therefore decided to load test a number of the borderline rafters. Clearly, some rafters were beyond redemption while others were largely unaffected by beetle, but a large number were in the grey area between these two extremes.

The load test was simple. Two plasterers' trestles provided end bearings and two-gallon buckets full of water provided the load. A scaffold tube was fixed between the trestles to carry a number of dial gauges to record deflections, and screws drilled with a small hole to accept the point of a DEMEC strain gauge allowed strain to be recorded. All rafters were tested to their design working loads and to a 25% overload.

Several conclusions were drawn:

- In all cases, except for a rafter with a damaged scarf, the actual deflection was considerably less than that predicted by calculation using the actual measured sizes but not taking account of waney edge or minor beetle decay.
- The original rafters, both repaired and unrepaired, behaved satisfactorily, and this gave confidence to replace them as necessary in the reconstructed structure.
- The rafters behaved considerably better than their apparently decayed state suggested they would.
- Simple tests can be of great value both in saving historic fabric and on economic grounds.

Case study 2: A cantilever stone staircase

The lower flights of this stair are frequently used by large numbers of people attending functions on the principal floor of the building. This had led to concern over the structural adequacy of the lower flights.

A standard steel tube and fitting scaffold was used with screw jacks to allow the support scaffold to be erected to within about 25 to 30 mm below the staircase; 56 pound (25 kg) steel weights were used as kentledge. As the building was in use at the time of the test, the carpet was protected by double-sheeted polythene and a layer of scaffold boards below all scaffolding and underneath the steel weights. The load was applied in stages and the maximum load represented something like one hundred people standing on the staircase. This was close to the value of 4 kilonewtons per square metre, as suggested by BS 6399.

The conclusions drawn from this test were that the staircase was safe for the number of people who used it. Although the maximum recorded deflection of 22 mm was in excess of the BS 5268 permissible value of 10.8 mm, it was not considered excessive as the finishes were of a flexible type not easily damaged.

Case study 3: Medieval vaulting in the ruins of a Cistercian House

This monastery was built largely between 1148 and 1179. The load test was on part of the cellarium vaulting. The intention was to cover the roof with a 100 mm concrete slab and 50 mm thick York stone slabs. Concern was felt that this additional load would overload the construction. The complexity of the structure did not lend itself to accurate analysis, hence the load test was considered to be the most practical method of proving its adequacy to withstand the additional loads.

The proximity of the structure to the river made water the obvious medium for applying load. A contract was let for the supply and erection of a temporary dam constructed from polythene sheeting, scaffolding and timber. A safety scaffold was erected beneath the vaulting and a separate scaffold was erected to enable the engineers to read the strain gauges and dial gauges beneath the vaulting. Theodolite readings were also taken to check spreading of the vaulting in a horizontal direction. Measured deflections were considered to be well within acceptable limits, and after removal of the load it was noted that the recovery of the deflections was in the order of 85%, and therefore only a very small residue of deflections was left. The test was regarded as a success and the proposed work was put in hand.

Particular care must be taken to ensure that damage to the historic fabric is not caused either by the installation or the removal of the test equipment or by a failure during the test itself. In most other aspects the testing of a historic structure or building is similar to the testing of a recent structure. Load tests can be a useful way – perhaps the only way – of proving conclusively that a structure or part of a structure is adequate to carry the loading demanded of it by its future uses.

Floor loadings in historic buildings

If a historic building is to be given a new lease of life, much may need to be done to make it satisfactory for its new task. However, it is not always necessary to gut the building or indeed to make any major changes at all to enable it to have a long and useful future. Changes in use demand that consideration be given to the loads to be carried by the building. It is the aim of this chapter to encourage careful thought about the loading requirements and to avoid blanket use of design loadings taken from British Standards when something less might be equally acceptable with no increase in risk.

It is often claimed that high floor loadings are required to give the client the flexibility that is required and to avoid overloading, excessive deflections or collapse. Attempts to upgrade a historic building to a high load-carrying capacity will almost always result in both massive and expensive intervention into the valuable historic fabric or, in extreme cases, complete loss of the building.

The English Heritage leaflet *Office Floor Loadings in Historic Buildings* (1994) debates at length the problem of accommodating office floor loadings in historic fabric. It suggests that, very often, there are no good reasons for the blanket use of $5.0\,kN/m^2$ (suggested by the British Standard Code of Practice for the 'design loading for buildings' for 'file rooms, filing and storage'), and that $2.5\,kN/m^2$ ('offices for general use') is more than adequate. This chapter takes the topic of floor loadings further by discussing the effect of loading requirements on historic buildings with various other uses.

The **self-weight of existing structures** can be calculated with a high degree of accuracy as floor structure and other elements of the building can be seen and measured and their weight calculated. Therefore in structural check calculations smaller than usual factors of safety can be used with impunity. The factors of safety generally recommended are designed for use in new build work where materials may be heavier or of larger size than that specified.

Considering the new loading: is the designation correct?

The initial, and correct, action when checking a floor for any loading is to look to the British Standard Code of Practice for loading. This document gives advice on what floor loadings should be used in the design and checking of structures.

The information contained in the British Standard for loading, and indeed any other British Standard, is only advice regarding good practice. It is not mandatory. To reinforce this statement, the British Standard Code of Practice BS 7913: 1998 *Guide to the Principles of the Conservation of Historic Buildings* states that 'British Standard and other specifications and codes of practice should not be applied unthinkingly, in the context of building conservation'. If a structural engineer decides to choose a value different from that proposed by the British Standard he is free to do so, although there must be good, sound evidence that the chosen value is adequate.

It is often suggested that engineers and surveyors use high floor loadings in their designs because the clients demand the flexibility to use buildings in any way they wish, while clients frequently say that the higher loadings are necessary because their engineers and surveyors recommend it. There seems to be scope for closer liaison and discussion between clients and their professional advisers as to the realities of the situation.

Are high floor loadings, employed to give flexibility of use, really justified, or can lower values be used without compromising flexibility or structural safety? The British Standard Code of Practice for loadings is designed to give a degree of flexibility that may not be required or even possible in a particular circumstance. It is important that the use of the building is not overly restricted by the loading that the floors are capable of carrying, but equally there is no need to upgrade floors to make them capable of carrying loads that cannot be achieved in use. A few examples may serve to illustrate this point.

The designated loading for a **library** is $4.0\,kN/m^2$ while that for a **reading room** is only $2.5\,kN/m^2$. Is the room in the historic building to be a library in the sense in which one understands the term when searching for a novel in the public library or a technical volume in a professional library, or is it to be a room where people sit to read and which will be furnished with tables, chairs and a few bookcases around the walls? If it is to be the latter then why does the floor need to be upgraded to carry the full library loading?

Major intervention into the historic fabric of one listed building was avoided in just this way. The room marked on the drawing as 'library' was, in reality, to be a reading room and therefore the lower load was used with confidence and conviction that the floor would be safe.

Again, the floor loading designated for a **museum** is $4.0\,kN/m^2$. Museums display a wide variety of artefacts ranging from stamps, coins and other virtually weightless items, displayed in relatively light flat-topped cabinets, to stone sculptures and machines from the early days of mechanical power, which can be extremely heavy. It is suggested that a blanket loading of $4.0\,kN/m^2$ is not suitable for all cases.

Very often, particularly in the case of small local museums that use historic buildings, the use of each room is well known in advance and the precise floor loading can be easily and safely calculated. The weight of the objects to be displayed can be worked out, as can the weight of the display cabinets. An allowance must be made for the visitors, remembering that they may come in groups as well as in ones and twos. It is very often the case that these calculations will prove that there is no way in which the floor can be subjected to $4.0\,kN/m^2$. To upgrade a floor to carry this load is wasteful of scarce resources as well as being destructive of the historic fabric of the building.

Discussions took place concerning one particular museum building that was to display a fine collection of bone china in glass cabinets that were to be fixed to the walls and floors. Even taking account of the fact that the space between cabinets could easily be crowded with visitors, it was shown that the floor loading was less than half the $4.0\,kN/m^2$ suggested by the British Standard. A lower value was used and the amount of structural intervention was dramatically reduced without encroaching on the safety of the visitors or of the building.

Conversely, in another museum there were proposals to display Egyptian sculptures. If the floors had been designed for just $4.0\,kN/m^2$, the sculptures would literally have disappeared through the floor.

Locate heavy items in specific areas and light loads in the centre of floors

If there are known to be requirements for the storage or display of heavy items, can these be located in places where they will have little effect? Can they be restricted to floors with small spans, can filing be stored in the basement and can racking or shelving be fixed to the wall so that it does not apply load to the floor?

It is possible, in places where there are likely to be crowd loadings, to place an obstruction, such as a table or a display, in the centre of the room so as to keep the heavy weight of people towards the edges of the room. This method of avoiding excessive loading is particularly useful where loading can be carefully controlled, such as for one-off events and in museums and galleries where light display cabinets can be screwed to the floor to avoid crowd loading at the position where it will create maximum bending moments and the highest deflections in the floor.

An event was to be held to celebrate the completion of conservation work to a particularly important domestic house where the floors could be shown to be capable of supporting domestic loading but could not be proven to carry crowd loading. The tables for the food were deliberately located at the centre of the room so as to keep the guests away from the area where their weight might cause excessive deflections. It is doubtful that the guests noticed that their whereabouts were being controlled in this way.

Consider past life

Although not directly related to deciding what load to use in the checking procedures on a historic building, it is always wise to consider what loading the building has had to carry in its life to date and how well it has survived its previous uses. If the building has been in use as a warehouse for the storage of grain, do the floors really need to be upgraded when the building is to become flats even though calculations show that excessive deflections might occur? A detailed inspection of the structure of a building may be much more valuable than computer analysis.

It is not uncommon to encounter historic buildings where both common sense and visual inspection demonstrate that a building is sound while calculations indicate that it is substandard and incapable of carrying any live load at all. Calculations of stresses and deflections often show that timber floors are capable of carrying little more than their own weight even where the building has been carrying a substantial load for many years. Are the calculations wrong or is the building wrong? If the building has been working satisfactorily, there must be something amiss with the calculations.

Although not directly related to considerations of design loadings, the load testing of a structure or elements of that structure can prove that the building is satisfactory in spite of theoretical predictions to the contrary.

Conclusion

The purpose of the above advice is to encourage realism in the adoption of floor loadings for use in historic buildings. It is not an attempt to persuade designers to use low loadings to avoid damage to historic fabric at the risk of reducing **safety** and encouraging claims for negligence. It is an attempt to ensure that the worst-case loading is not assumed unless there is a real possibility of its being achieved.

If it is proposed to upgrade a historic building to carry high superimposed loading, this can all too easily, as suggested above, result in major structural intervention, sometimes in virtual gutting of the interior of a building, and the associated high costs that this type of work entails. Are the **costs**, both financial and those associated with the loss of historic fabric, justified by the perceived need for high floor loadings?

This chapter is not suggesting that historic buildings should be capable of only carrying light loads when there is the possibility of overload, damage and possible disaster. To suggest that would be irresponsible and would put both lives and historic fabric at risk. What it is suggesting is that design loads should be thought about carefully. Unrealistic design loads need not be used when it is impossible to generate that load or when, with a little forethought, high loading can be avoided.

Further reading

Generally

There are many useful articles in *Context*, the quarterly journal of the Institute of Historic Building Conservation. Many of these can be found on the IHBC website: www.ihbc.org.uk

The following bibliography is only a beginning.

Structural surveys and appraisals

Bravery, A.F., *Recognising Rot and Insect Damage in Buildings* (Building Research Establishment, 1992).

Bussell, Michael, *Appraisal of Existing Iron and Steel Structures* (Steel Construction Institute, London, 1997).

CIRIA, *Site Safety*, CIRIA special publication (CIRIA, London, 1990).

Heyman, Jacques, *Arches, Vaults and Buttresses* (Ashgate, Aldershot, 1996).

Heyman, Jacques, *The Stone Skeleton* (Cambridge University Press, Cambridge, 1995).

Hinks, John and Cook, Geoff, *The Technology of Building Defects* (Taylor & Francis, London, 1997).

Historic Scotland, *Non-destructive Investigation of Standing Structures* (Historic Scotland: Technical Conservation, Research and Education Division, 2001).

Holland, R., Montgomery-Smith, B.E. and Moore, J.F.A. (eds), *Appraisal and Repair of Building Structures* (Thomas Telford, London, 1992).

Institution of Structural Engineers, *Appraisal of Existing Structures* (ISE, London, 1980).

Institution of Structural Engineers, *Surveys and Inspections of Buildings* (ISE, London, 1991).

Parkinson, G. *et al.*, *Masonry* (Thomas Telford, London, 1996).

Richardson, Barry A., *Defects and Deterioration in Building* (Taylor & Francis, London, 1991).

Richardson, Clive, 'The AJ guide to structural surveys', *Architects' Journal* (1985).

Robson, Patrick, *Structural Appraisal of Traditional Buildings* (Donhead Publishing, Shaftesbury, 2005).

Surveyor's Check-list for Rehabilitation of Traditional Housing (Building Research Establishment, 1990).

Swallow, Peter, Watt, David and Ashton, Robert, *Measurement and Recording of Historic Buildings*, 2nd edn (Donhead, Shaftesbury, 2004).

Structural monitoring

Moore, J.F.A. (ed.), *Monitoring Building Structures* (Routledge, London, 1992).

6 Basic soil mechanics, foundations and repair of settlement damage

David Cook

Fundamental nature of soil deposits

Background

In 1939 an engineer from Vienna presented a keynote lecture to the Institution of Civil Engineers entitled 'A New Chapter in Engineering Science'.[1] The engineering science in question was soil mechanics and the engineer's name was Karl Terzaghi. While this was not the first authoritative presentation of the subject, it made British engineers acutely aware of the shortcomings of their understanding of soil behaviour.

In comparison with other fields of engineering and the physical sciences, soil mechanics was a late starter. The Industrial Revolution in Great Britain saw the establishment of classical applied mechanics, hydraulics, much of physics, chemistry, electrical theory and engineering mathematics in the form in which it is recognised today. By contrast, the first coherent English-language text on soil mechanics did not emerge until 1940,[2] some years after Terzaghi had been obliged to flee his native Austria.

The reason for recalling this landmark point is because virtually all buildings which relate to the subject matter of this book were constructed during a time of little real understanding of soils or foundation behaviour. The subject was without a coherent theory or collected wisdom or language whereby the lessons of experience could be rationalised or expressed. The body of experience remained as a random collection of disconnected fragments.

Despite the shortcomings of any analytical framework, engineers from Roman times through to the Victorian period developed an empirical understanding of soil behaviour and problems relating to groundwater. They developed a 'gut feeling' for what was right, or wrong, and they carried out surprisingly ambitious schemes. Nevertheless, it should come as no surprise that many historic buildings have a legacy of foundation problems. It would be difficult to estimate how many suffered something worse, as there is no accounting for those that collapsed. Buildings we nurture today, like the Tower of Pisa, are the survivors.

Soil mechanics rapidly evolved into a key component of civil engineering. Geotechnical engineering – as it is now more often called – is less a subject than a subject field, embracing not only applied mechanics but also a working knowledge of chemistry, geology and geomorphology. The chief reason is the enormous age span between different natural soils and rocks. Those in place through events of 5000–10 000 years ago are regarded as 'recent'. However, they themselves would have been the product of weathering breakdown, transport and re-formation, through a variety of cyclical processes within the last 5000 million years and back to the beginnings of time.

This 'engineering geology' aspect of the origins of materials contributes to the understanding of soil behaviour; engineering and geology maintain mutual engagement, while the two fields maintain their separate identities; yet on their interface, they merge.

It is not possible to cover this subject within a single chapter of a book. What follows will simply describe the basic make-up of soil materials, a classification system and the fundamental mode of behaviour. By a comparison with the more familiar, traditional structural materials such as steel, brickwork, concrete and timber, it will emphasise those features that matter most and are the cause of common hazards. The explanation contained here can offer only a very basic understanding of the wider field.

First, the reader should note how soils display a much wider range of some basic properties. For example, the spread of particle size extends from gravels, at 20–25 mm size, to clay, where the size is typically 2 microns. The range between extremes is a factor of ten thousand. Likewise, the rates at which water will flow through gravels and clays (permeability) varies by a factor of ten million. This is comparable with differences of heat transmission through materials, or differences in the flow of electrical current (conductivity) between a 'conductor' (say, copper for carrying current) and an 'insulator' (the cable covering)!

Basic composition and character of soil materials

The presently used British Standard soil classification system has been developed over a period of some sixty years. Its purpose is as follows:

- To identify the key characteristics of soil material that bear most on its engineering behaviour – these are its particle size, compressibility, strength and permeability;
- To provide a common language for description and assessment so that previous records, and the experience of others, can be safely relied on and interpreted. The procedures for soil classification occupy a major part of the British Standard BS 5930 *Code of Practice for Site Investigations*.[3] The aim of any such classification is to maintain objectivity as far as is possible.

The majority of soil materials of concern for foundations and building work lie within 10 to 20 metres of ground surface. In nearly all cases they

are of sedimentary origin. The material was at some time part of a rock mass, derived from previous igneous or other sedimentary deposits but now reduced to the point of ultimate chemical and mechanical breakdown. The cyclical process probably took several hundred million years; materials may have been transported by water and then deposited several times to form new sediments. Eventually we are left with an assembly of discrete particles of varying sizes. So while the total number of constituents within the earth's crust is large, only a few minerals survive this process by reason of their relative chemical stability (Figure 6.1). Where soils derive directly from the decomposition of volcanic (igneous) rock material, a residue of slightly less stable minerals may be found. We should not ignore the less common organic deposits (coal, peat) and the most recent domestic and industrial waste.

Despite the many different processes by which these materials have arrived in the place and condition in which they are now, it is quite satisfactory to work to a simplified picture definition – that of an assembly of discrete particles of varying size in point-to-point contact (Figure 6.2a). Larger particle sizes are often 'modelled' as though they were spheres, and their behaviour compared to that of a mass of glass beads or lead shot. But a packing of idealised spheres cannot realistically simulate clay materials (Figure 6.2b), which are made up of flat, plate-shaped particles. Further reference to this and other singular features of clay will follow.

As already mentioned, **particle size** is the most important characteristic governing the engineering behaviour of soils. Typically, cobbles are 60 mm or more in size, while the size of clay mineral particles is generally 2 microns (0.002 mm). The main divisions are as follows:

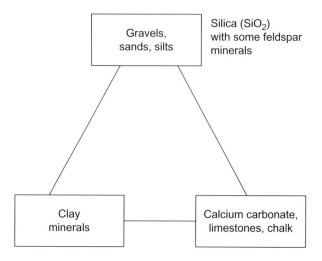

Figure 6.1 Basic constituents of soils and sedimentary rocks. Note also subsidiary deposits of peat and domestic and industrial waste.

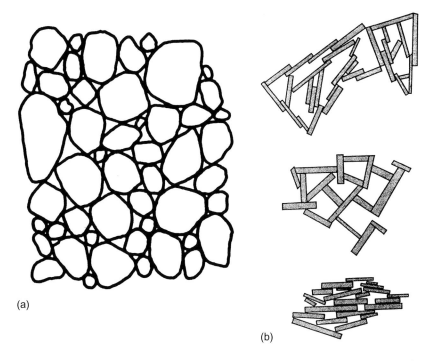

(a)

(b)

Figure 6.2 (a) Typical cut through a granular soil; (b) 'plate'-shaped assemblies of clay particles.

- coarse to fine gravel   60 mm to 2 mm
- coarse to fine sand   2 mm to 0.06 mm
- coarse to fine silt   0.06 mm to 0.002 mm
- clays   less than 0.002 mm (2 microns)

The grading, meaning the variation of soil particle size, is most commonly represented as a grading chart.[4] With the exception of clays, the defined particle size is roughly that of an equivalent sphere. Particle shapes can vary enormously, of course, but the simplification holds quite well over a wide range of properties.

Individual particles of fine sand can just be seen with the naked eye; particles of silt are the size of particles of face powder or cement and can be seen with an ordinary microscope. But the plate-shaped particles of clay can only be examined using an electron microscope. Analysis of the proportions of different sizes in a soil sample follows a routine laboratory procedure, giving results in the form of a grading chart. It plots each key particle size against the percentage of the whole mass that is smaller than that size. Where the grading line runs evenly across a large section of the range it indicates an evenly distributed particle sizing. If it shows a flat zone, it is 'gap' graded, meaning it misses out some intermediate sizes. Where the curve drops steeply, the material is mostly a single size (e.g. wind-blown sand or loess).

A widely or evenly graded material will naturally have a higher density than a single-sized material, because the smaller-sized particles can 'nest' more efficiently within the void spaces of the larger. This is evident, for instance, in concrete mix design. A common concrete mix of four parts gravel, two parts sand and one part cement (which is silt size) crosses the whole range.

Overall you will see the extremes of particle size run from 2 microns (0.002 mm) for clay to gravel size at generally 10–60 mm, so the range between extremes is 30 000 – much greater than the spread between like characteristics of most other common structural materials such as concrete, bricks, timber or steel. Therefore we may expect the performance of different soil types to vary considerably.

The nature of the clay fraction

If we crush down a mineral specimen of quartz to powder consistency and add water, the whole turns to a paste. The paste reflects the so-called property of cohesion, providing some strength or stiffness. It is also seen that the strength (the simple ability to stand up) is sensitive to the amount of water. Even a damp sand retains shape temporarily – how else are sand castles made? It is because the water, at the particle-to-particle contact surfaces around the outside, forms menisci within the spaces, allowing surface tension to pull them together. On drying out, the former fine quartz paste may be left lightly 'caked', but will crumble back to powder easily enough.

While quartz powder mixed with water shows temporary cohesion, unlike clay it does not show **plasticity** – that is, the ability to be rolled into a thread. Clays derive from a complex family of aluminium silicate minerals. The assemblies are plate-shaped, which gives them a high surface area; consequently, the characteristic of an ideal packaging of spheres ceases to be relevant.

There is no 'short' explanation of the chemistry and mineralogy of clays that can offer a simplified picture of properties. Water molecules attracted to the plate surfaces are chemically bonded in what is known as an 'absorbed' layer that has nothing to do with surface tension. This water will not evaporate off at normal drying temperatures of 100–105°C. However, the 'free' water in a clay behaves in the same way as water in the voids space of a sand or gravel.

The soil model

Soil is thus defined as an assembly of (usually) variably shaped particles in point-to-point contact (Figures 6.2a and 6.2b). Although the plate or flaky shapes of micron-sized clay particle structures differ from those of rounded or angular gravels and sands, the same model is accepted. On the initial basis of a unit volume of solid material, it proportions the voids space (e) as a fraction of the solid volume. For calculation purposes, the diagram in Figure 6.3 is universally accepted. The amount of water occupying the voids

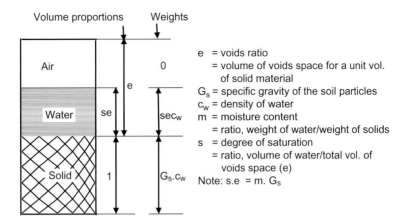

Figure 6.3 Soil model (for calculation).

spaces is proportioned to the solids by their weights. Other terminology is given alongside the figure.

If the entire space is filled with water, it is said to be 'saturated'; without water at all, it is – fairly obviously – defined as 'dry'. In nature, clays will normally maintain a state of water saturation unless there has been some fierce evaporation process, such as a drought. Look at the dried-up bed of a lake or reservoir: the clay or mud is left as a hard 'cake', sometimes broken at the surface by patterns of hexagonal shrinkage cracks. The Giant's Causeway in County Antrim shows basalt rock solidified from a melt, demonstrating the same shrinkage pattern. Continued drying of clay at high temperatures is the way to produce bricks.

Unit weights and densities

Virtually all earth calculations require figures for the gravity weight of the ground itself, and the groundwater component. The parameters in this respect are the soil density and unit weight of the mineral particle constituents. The latter lie conveniently close together and it is usual practice to handle these in terms of their specific gravity (G_s): that is, the ratio of the number of times a unit volume of the solid particle is heavier than water. The measurement of specific gravity is used because soil mechanics calculations involve water exclusively, and water is an integral part of the soil system. The density of the whole is then a multiple of water density.

For clay minerals specific gravity is 2.6–2.8; for quartz, 2.66; for calcite (or limestone), 2.72. Where it is necessary to guess, a value of around 2.65 or 2.70 may be taken without risk of serious error. Be cautious, however, if you happen to have a situation outside the common range. The specific gravity of metal ores may be 4.5–5.0; domestic refuse or power station fuel ash (sold as PFA) reduces to 2.0 or less.

Soil density is the basic parameter required at the outset of a ground profile analysis. This is because densities enter into every calculation for earth pressure, settlement and deformation. Referring to Figure 6.3, we derive terms for saturated density and dry density as follows:

$$\text{dry density} \qquad \psi_d = \frac{G_s \cdot \psi_w}{1+e} \qquad\qquad (6.1)$$

$$\text{saturated density} \quad \psi_{sat} = \frac{(G_s + e)}{(1+e)} \psi_w \qquad\qquad (6.2)$$

It is not possible to measure the voids ratio directly, whereas a simple laboratory drying-out routine quickly measures moisture content. Note also that the term for degree of saturation (s) reduces to zero or 1.0 if the material is bone dry or saturated, respectively.

By substituting $s.e = m \cdot G_s$, the expressions define more conveniently in terms of moisture content. It is important to maintain a 'feel' for what typical values to expect for voids ratios in different soils. If we take a loose single-size material of rounded particles like marbles or lead shot then the loosest packing obtainable would be 0.91, meaning the voids space and volume of the solid material are nearly equal. If the spheres were nested to give the densest packing possible, the voids ratios would reduce to about 0.35.

Lastly, in SI units the unit weight of water is correctly $1000\,\text{kg/m}^3$. However, calculations of pressure work in units of force (newtons or kilonewtons). In this context the gravity weight of 1000 kg, or $1\,\text{m}^3$ of water, exerts a force of $1000 \times (g = 9.81)$ newtons, or 10 kN. Therefore, at 5 metres' depth below a water surface the pressure will be $(5.0\,\text{m} \times 10.0\,\text{kN/m}^3) = 50\,\text{kN/m}^2$ in both horizontal and vertical directions. By the same token, earth pressures in a vertical direction (below a ground surface) calculate in the same way, substituting the *kilonewton* unit of force for the kilogram expression of mass.

Groundwater and groundwater flow

Water is present in virtually all natural soil deposits, depending on location. In the vicinity of rivers, lakes or the sea, the voids space is saturated. As already mentioned, in temperate climates clays generally remain saturated; in deserts, the sands are almost totally dry. Static groundwater exerts normal hydrostatic pressure within any soil mass by reason of the continuous irregular pathways threading through the voids space. Differences of pressure between adjacent zones initiate a flow through this open-cell soil structure, and the resistance to flow varies according to the channel path size dictated by the particle size. The governing equation, known as Darcy's law, states:

water flow (Q) = gross area of flow section × soil permeability coefficient (k) × hydraulic gradient (Δh/L)

where: hydraulic gradient = head pressure loss between two adjacent points, divided by the straight line length of the connecting flow path

Those familiar with expressions for heat flow (conductivity) or Ohm's law (electric current) may be helped to understand water flow by comparing the very similar equation form:

heat flow (Q) = conductivity (K) × temperature gradient . . . or
current flow (amps) = electrical conductivity × voltage gradient

Like a temperature gradient or voltage drop, the hydraulic gradient is the resulting drop of head pressure, or energy loss, by reason of the resistance to flow.

Fine-grained clays and silts have very low permeability (k value); coarse-grained soils (sands, gravels) allow water to pass relatively freely. In practical terms clays are virtually impermeable, while gravel permeability is something of the order of one million times higher than that of clay. Because clay has very low permeability, any recently opened excavation in clay may appear dry. But do not be deceived: the reason is a simple time delay, which may even amount to days, before water fills the hole.

In one other important circumstance water flow in soils cannot compare with an electric current or heat. When water flows through a granular soil, particularly fine sands, the head pressure loss generates a body force which acts in the direction of flow. If the flow is in a vertical or sub-vertically upward direction, it imparts an uplift, which diminishes the effective unit gravity weight of the soil mass. This reduction in overall stability of the mass leads to the situation known as 'quicksand'. It can be very dangerous. In construction works it may occur in a deep excavation, or across a tidal river estuary; the uplift pressure will trap boats and people. A good standard text will provide a fuller understanding of groundwater flow.[5]

Soil compression and natural consolidation (sedimentation)

Changes of soil volume only follow reduction or enlargement of the void space, brought about through changes of confining pressure. This can be visualised diagrammatically (Figure 6.3), or more explicitly (Figure 6.4). If saturated, external pressure causes pore water to be squeezed out. Within the range of loading we need to consider, we may ignore the minute compression of the actual soil grains, and the water, and only consider the particle packing. With increasing pressure there is a progressive volume reduction, so that eventually the voids space could be all but eliminated, reducing the soil to a rock-like consistency. This is different from the more familiar 'elastic' behaviour of most structural materials, within their working range, where any elastic deformation or strain is proportional to change of loading. The volume change of the material is not a significant parameter except where it is caused by change of temperature.

It is helpful to follow the sedimentation process in nature – the way deposits are first formed. We may begin with a soft mud, laid down across a river estuary or shallow sea, at an initial saturated water content of, say, 80%. Some millions of years later the lower sediments become compressed to a soft rock-like consistency, with water contents reduced to perhaps 15%

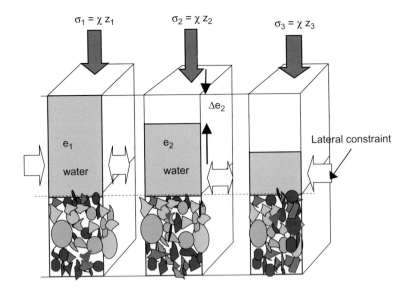

Figure 6.4 One-dimensional sedimentation process. Columns of soil are laterally confined by those adjacent. They can change length or thickness, but not their plan shape.

or less. Figure 6.4 depicts three elements, at increasing depths, in a typical vertical column of a natural sediment. At each level, z_1, z_2, z_3 (z) below the current surface, the accumulation exerts an overburden pressure due to its own gravity weight, which calculates in the same way as a hydrostatic pressure:

$$\sigma_z = (z) \cdot \chi_w \qquad (6.3)$$

Additions of sediment loading (e.g. from σ_1 to σ_2 then σ_3) reduce the voids space by Δe_2 to e_2, then Δe_3 to e_3.

Now, the whole mass of the sediment column is laterally confined at every level by a surrounding assembly of identical columns of similar material, so there can be no lateral movement across a horizontal plane, or change of the unit area within any of them or in the adjacent columns; each one of these infinite numbers of columns is confined within an unalterable plan shape. If free, they would deform laterally, but they cannot.

In this situation, increasing overburden pressure generates a complementary horizontal pressure proportional to the magnitude of the vertical overburden. It is termed the 'at-rest' earth pressure. Most routine calculations do not actually need to measure these in situ horizontal pressures; nevertheless, it is important to remain aware that soils, like fluids, exist under what is termed a biaxial or triaxial stress system. Very approximately, the at-rest earth pressures vary from 0.50 to 1.0 times the vertical pressure (= σ_z). Natural soil consolidation, or sediment accumulating under the boundary conditions described above, is termed 'one-dimensional consolidation'. It is convenient to maintain this as a boundary condition in traditional laboratory apparatus for measurement of soil consolidation characteristics. The soil specimen under test is simply contained within a rigid steel ring.

General relationships: voids ratios, moisture content and confining stresses

The preceding discussion describes the nature of compression of soils in response to their *first time* loading only. In nature, only the most recent post-Ice Age deposits (20 000 years old or less) conform to this characteristic, and in virtually all cases they are soft. Older sedimentary deposits which developed to very considerable depths were then eroded back as a consequence of earth crustal movements. Glance at a geological map of your region of interest. Very old deposits have been folded, faulted, then broken down, and eroded back yet again to a flat land or seabed surface. These in turn are further overlain with new sediment layers. The most recent are inevitably derived from earlier erosion products. Thus, in engineering terms, most surface deposits have been subjected to a whole series of loading and unloading cycles.

To recap, it was explained above how volume compression of soil involves compaction or densification of the solid particle assembly, leaving behind a progressively diminishing voids space within the mass as a whole. Therefore, the load/compression relationship is not a linear one. We may trace this with the graph plots (Figures 6.5a and 6.5b). Voids ratios and corresponding effective confining stresses (σ_v) are shown on the ordinates and abscissa of both figures. While the equivalent moisture content value can substitute for voids ratio ($e = m \cdot G$), the relationship is more usually given in terms of the former. The sequence is as follows:

- As a loosely assembled, laterally confined soil mass is progressively loaded, it will follow its own unique path. The first-time loading will be defined by the line, A–B–F.
- If the sequence is broken at some point B because the deposit is eroded, it 'un-loads' from B, through C to D (Figure 6.5a). Note that the unloading follows a flatter slope; it does not recover its original volume. Point D will now define its *present-day* equilibrium position, below the surface, at an overburden pressure of $\sigma_z = (z) \cdot \chi sat$.
- A reload then returns through E (quite close to C) to rejoin the so-called 'virgin' loading curve just below B. With further loading the line reverts to its original 'first-time' path from B to F. The material retains a memory of its earlier loading.

The important features to note are these:

- Engineers normally draw the relationship to a logarithmic scale (Figure 6.5b), because the first-time loading and unload/reload curves then follow near straight lines. This is how it would be seen in a test result.
- For a specific material defined by the line A–B–F, no point can exist above and to its right-hand side. However, there are an infinite variety of un-load/re-load possibilities to the left. The pattern is the same for

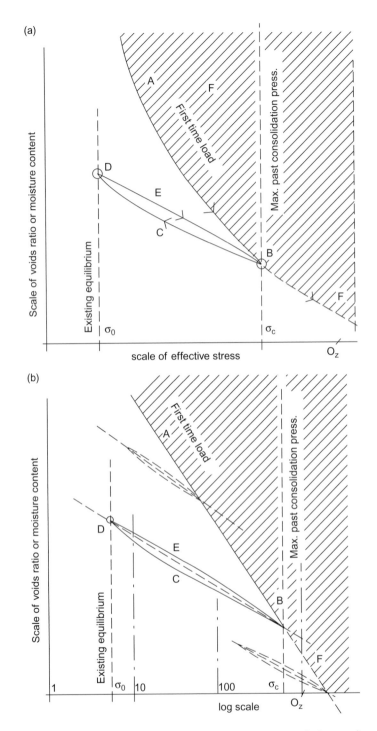

Figure 6.5 (a) and (b) Volume change versus compression during sedimentation. Loading–unloading and re-loading (shown to natural scale and 'log' scale).

all soils although gradients vary considerably. Compressibility increases with decreasing grain size, which is to say that clays are a lot more compressible than sands and gravels. The first-time load lines are steeper, and different clays indicate a relationship to their clay mineralogy.

- Recent soil deposits, still in equilibrium on their first-time loading line A–B–F, are said to be **normally consolidated**. Those with a previous stress history (to B) in excess of their current loading (point D) are said to be **over-consolidated**. The maximum past loading is termed the pre-consolidation pressure. The ratio σ_c / σ_0 is termed the **overconsolidation ratio**.

Soil laboratory tests are able to define point B, indicating the amount of over-consolidation in a clay sample, and the findings are basic to calculations of foundation settlement. It should be evident that normally consolidated clay layers will show high compression, whereas a pre-consolidation cycle improves soil-bearing properties, provided that a new loading can be limited to the range between points D and B. This makes it essential to identify the origins of the ground on which any structure is built.

The model for behaviour of soils described here is not new. It emulates certain patterns of strain hardening in metals and other materials.

Soil strength and deformation under loading

Soil strength is brought into play when existing vertical or horizontal ground equilibrium stresses are increased or diminished by external events. A foundation loading may cause excessive compression; the ground reduces in volume by consolidation and it also distorts if the additional vertical loading is excessive. Similarly, an open excavation removes horizontal support, maybe causing the soil mass to collapse. A land slope which is too steep will adjust to a 'just-stable' equilibrium. These are typical of earthworks problems. Stability in all such cases is governed by soil **shear strength**.

This vital feature can be illustrated by a diagrammatic soil block contained by a vertical stress σ_1 and conjugate stress, σ_3 (Figure 6.6). Consider σ_1 greater than σ_3. It then subdivides the arrangement into an equal all-round compression (like a water pressure), and the residual stress difference ($\sigma_1 - \sigma_3$). The latter causes lateral deformation, in other words a lateral 'spread' with tensile strain. We can best identify the deformation of the right-hand element due to the axial component ($\sigma_1 - \sigma_3$) by connecting the mid-points of the four sides where they are shown dotted. If the initial element in Figure 6.6 were a perfect cube then deformation would change the shape to parallelograms at 45° to the direction of loading.

Internal forces set up by this deformation are shown by the arrows alongside. The whole gives a visual picture of the fact that simple axial loading (taking σ_3 = zero) invokes what is defined as **shear**. In fact, the ultimate criterion of strength in soils, and indeed virtually all materials, rests with a

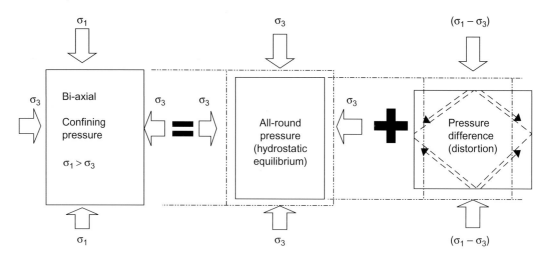

Figure 6.6 Two-dimensional system of pressure subdivision into all-round stress and stress difference.

capability to resist shear. An all-round stress σ_3 does not give rise to material failure except through the possibility of crushing within the material itself; it is only the stress difference $(\sigma_1 - \sigma_3)$. Remember, a fluid can resist the highest pressures but has no shear resistance, which is why pressures at a point are the same in all directions, and fluids distort to the shape of the container. Figure 6.6 applies to all aspects of material strength and deformation. It is saying compression, tension and shear are mutually complementary.

Source of soil strength – friction – shear resistance

The French engineer Charles-Augustin de Coulomb was the first to document a practical understanding of sliding friction in soils in connection with the design of military fortifications.[6] A less romantic but more user-friendly example of sliding friction is a pile of dry sand (Figure 6.7). A sand heap can be built to any height but is limited to a maximum slope angle α. Provided the sand is dry, the surface layers of the heap respond to gravity sliding by friction resistance, performing similarly to the interface between a block of wood and a sloping surface x – x that it is sliding down.

To be stable, resistance to sliding must not be less than the disturbing force, $W \sin \alpha$. The reaction normal to the potential surface of sliding is $W \cos \alpha$. Therefore at the point where it just slips, $W \cos \alpha \times \mu$ (coefft of friction) = $W \sin \tilde{\alpha}$. This gives us the answer for a coefficient of friction, $\mu = \tan \alpha$.

In soil mechanics the coefficient of friction μ is discarded in preference to the use of an **angle of friction** Φ. In the particular case above, the angle of friction Φ is shown by the limiting angle of slope $\tilde{\alpha}$. This may be theo-

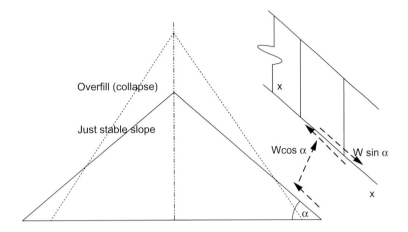

Figure 6.7 Limiting stability of the surface of a sand heap.

retically correct, and useful as a means of demonstrating the concept, but be warned that for a number of reasons it is not recommended as a serious method for the measurement of an angle of friction in sand.

Soil strength – influence of groundwater – definition of effective stress

Figure 6.8 depicts what we could observe if an imaginary separating 'cut' were made across a horizontal surface at depth 'z' below the ground level. Presuming the material is fully saturated and water level at the surface, then, by simple gravity, the gross vertical (compression) force per unit of area must be

$$\sigma_z = \chi_{sat} \times \text{depth z} \tag{6.4}$$

Simultaneously, the water in the voids space exerts a corresponding pressure, $u_z = \chi_{water} \times$ depth z.

In effect, therefore, the soil column has an element of buoyancy, because the water provides an uplift pressure. Below a standing water level, the particle contact stress in the soil, contributing to friction resistance, is a function of its submerged weight.

For simplicity, the water and the soil depths in Figure 6.8 are shown as the same. Where the groundwater table level is below surface, the foregoing still applies on the basis:

effective stress = total overburden pressure – the hydrostatic water pressure

The groundwater table level is observable by its depth as exposed in the ground when an open pit is dug. If the free water surface is lower, it is the level to which water will rise if you insert a standpipe. Because clays are very impermeable it may be necessary to wait several days to get an accurate observation, whereas in sands or gravels this takes only minutes.

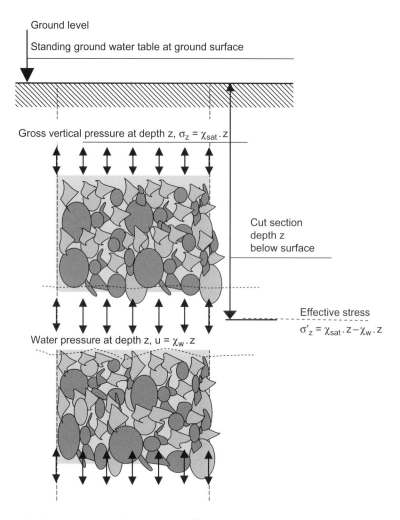

Ground level

Standing ground water table at ground surface

Gross vertical pressure at depth z, $\sigma_z = \chi_{sat} \cdot z$

Cut section depth z below surface

Effective stress
$\sigma'_z = \chi_{sat} \cdot z - \chi_w \cdot z$

Water pressure at depth z, $u = \chi_w \cdot z$

Figure 6.8 Buoyancy. Particle-to-particle effective stress determined by the submerged weight of the soil particles.

The final equation above is probably the most important concept to grasp for understanding soil behaviour, particularly as regards problems of strength and stability. It was a keynote point of Terzaghi's lecture in 1939.

Foundations and underlying ground support

Old building foundations carry with them some good news as well as bad news. The bad news is that, by present-day standards, the majority of older structures were provided with inadequate foundations, and over their life span they, and consequently the superstructure, may well have suffered excessive deformation for one reason or another. Masonry buildings were constructed using a softer lime mortar mix, and the building process itself took a lot longer to complete; indeed, both features worked to the advantage of the buildings' stability. The earlier construction practice carried with it an ability to sustain higher structural deformations and ground settlement than is the case today. Masonry cracking and related damage was dealt with by simple repair. Relatively large distortions of the structural fabric would be stiffened up – without apology – with ranks of tie bars, prominent on an outside wall end by reason of their large circular (300 mm) anchor plates and nuts.

The good news is that the structure is still standing. Established longevity means you do not normally expect to be dealing with an imminent foundation failure. Nonetheless, it is essential that sub-soil conditions are investigated through archival research (most old buildings have a history of significant alteration) and observation, especially of crack patterns (see also Chapter 7). Ignorance of ground conditions can be catastrophic. The Tower of Pisa famously came very close to toppling and was physically pulled back, initially by a complex arrangement of massive lead counterweights![7]

Foundation design – soil reactive pressures under spread foundations

Except in the case of rock, the strength, hardness and related bearing capacity of surface soils is a lot less than that of the corresponding materials of construction. So the superstructure weight and building contents must be spread out, which of course is the basic function of all 'spread' foundations. There are two basic checks to be made.

First, the foundation contact bearing pressures must lie significantly below the level where there is any tendency at all for a soil bearing failure. If you push a stick into the ground, or your heel into mud, you get penetration because of local bearing failure at the pressure point, which causes the soil to yield or flow, and this is a function of ultimate soil strength (Figure 6.9). Such – thankfully rare – events in practice always result in a serious construction failure, undoubtedly indicating a mistake in design. Avoidance requires the unit working bearing pressure, in all situations, to be limited to a defined fraction of the soil's ultimate bearing resistance, assessed from a conservative estimate of the soil strength within the zone

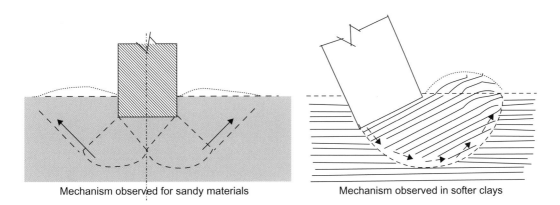

Mechanism observed for sandy materials   Mechanism observed in softer clays

Figure 6.9 Local bearing failure under a strip footing.

or depth of influence of the foundation structure. A strip or spread foundation, or a raft, is normally deemed safe if the 'working' bearing pressure is no greater than about one-third of what would cause such a collapse. This is what is termed the 'overall factor of safety'. It is the collapse load divided by the working load, which in this case would be three. Interestingly, this limit figure of three remains about the same for a wide variety of structural materials such as steel, timber and concrete. It defines a load limit beyond which any deformation will *not* recover itself when the load is removed. Otherwise, common cycles of load–unload–reload promote permanent yield, and the structure becomes unsafe over time.

Secondly, the combination of loading, the load spread and the foundation size must not give rise to soil compression resulting in unacceptable settlement of the structure. This is a feature of soil compressibility, and is a check against deformations as opposed to a general over-stress. Soil compression may exceed acceptable limits even though the loading lies well within a tolerable safety margin in respect of a bearing failure, such as seen in Figure 6.9. These limiting criteria of strength and elastic response to loading apply to most other components of a building. Design normally undertakes both checks; for instance structural beams are routinely checked for deflection. A tolerable settlement limit is usually the determinant for design over clay soils. In normal work, spread foundations over granular materials seldom provide serious problems.

Both calculations require reliable information on soil properties down to the depth to which there is any influence from the foundation loading, with particular attention to any known zones of softer, compressible materials. In this respect, the actual foundation size determines the depth of influence of the foundation loading. Effectively, a larger spread foundation will invoke compression in the ground to a proportionally greater depth. The problem arose in the past where an inadequate site investigation failed to detect the presence of a varying thickness of soft deposits.

Pressure distribution and settlement variation under spread foundations

An appreciation of the mechanism of 'load spread' (Figure 6.10a) starts with the common-sense approximation that a foundation distributes its load through a simple 45° load spread. By looking at the way in which the diagram is drawn, it can be seen that at a depth equal to the foundation width B the average applied pressure to the ground reduces to 0.33 Δp. At a depth of 2B, the load spreads out across five times the foundation contact area and the load intensity reduces to 0.2 Δ.

We could refine this reasoning by dividing up the same foundation width into a series of smaller-sized elements (Figure 6.10b). This is admissible, whether the actual width of the elements is large or small; it simply goes one step further towards advancing the concept of 'load spread'. Now, however, we see adjacent 45° segments overlapping, the more so as the load spread penetrates deeper underground. Without recourse to heavy mathematics, this points to some important facts:

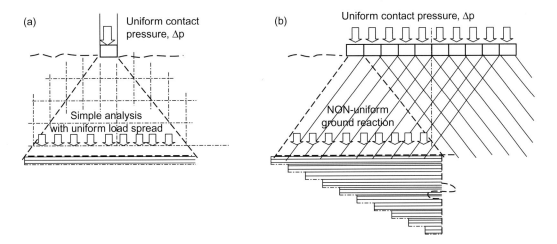

Figure 6.10 (a) Assumption of a simple 45° load spread; (b) 45° load spread pattern divided into a series of small segments. Soil reactive pressures vary across any horizontal plane.

- Soil reactive support pressures, across horizontal planes under the structure, vary across the foundation plan area, although the actual pressures reduce with depth.
- Higher relative pressures are created within the central zone than around the sides. In other words, the reaction from the supporting soil is not uniform.
- The degree of load spread at any particular depth is related to the foundation size shown here as small segments.

The last step in this appraisal must ask the question: 'So what?' The answers are as follows:

- At successively deeper levels, the ground under the centre and edges of a spread foundation experience a variable loading.
- This applies even though the applied building load is uniformly distributed. There is not a uniform soil response; therefore there is a tendency for differential settlement.
- Even if it is not immediately visible, the variation of soil compression creates secondary stresses in the building fabric.

Figure 6.10b illustrates that differential soil pressures will cause the ground profile to dish into the middle while the building as a whole attempts to retain its 'as-built' level. The question is whether the resulting deformations are tolerable (in terms of serviceability) and/or the strains set up in the structural fabric give rise to damage (e.g. cracking).

Even with the latest computer resources available to engineers, a comprehensive analysis combining the ground stiffness with the stiffness of the structure, in all its detail including its cladding components, is an impossibly complex task. The criteria for assessing tolerable settlements of masonry, vis-à-vis the likely onset of crack damage, still fall back on experience gained from patiently compiled case records of the settlement of similar structures. This important adjunct to foundation-related repair is further discussed below.

Ground movements independent of the foundation loading

With new build, the design may proceed from this point – in which respect it is rare for a present-day building scheme to 'trip up' on account of unforeseen settlement. On the other hand, older buildings were quite often built on soft soils, their builders unaware of the future consequences. Nevertheless, if an old or even newish structure escapes pain from poor design early in life, all categories remain vulnerable to settlement or other damage through subsequent ground movements or events independent of the foundation loading. These may be a consequence of mining subsidence, tunnelling, earthquake, changes in local groundwater levels, loads imposed by a new adjacent building, drag-down due to adjacent excavation, swell or shrinkage of clay soils, or heavy flooding, particularly on a sloping site. Other reasons also abound.

In England during the period 1989 to 1993, the problem of soil shrinkage arose through long periods of dry weather, which triggered escalating insurance claims from owners of domestic property. The problem was most acute in southern England where outcrops of fissured and shrinkable London clay (Eocene) and Lias clays (Jurassic) underlie much of the urban landscape. A check on all such possibilities must be carried out before blame for structural damage is attached to historic settlement.

Repairs to an existing foundation

The loading of soil invokes compression and also results in an increase of strength. So soil compression under a foundation leaves this beneficial legacy alongside the building's settlement. Even if that settlement sometime causes excessive deformation, while the foundation maintains a stable equilibrium there are few good reasons to interfere with it; intervention may only be justified if there are real signs of continued movement, or the foundation substructure is clearly degrading. This may be the case with timber piles or grillages, following a lowered groundwater table, perhaps. External changes to the immediate environment, such as those referred to above, form the more likely reasons for any need for intervention below ground level.

Replacement or strengthening of an existing foundation falls under the general umbrella of **underpinning**. If there is no reliable data in the building's record files from previous work on the site, an investigation must be undertaken. On a medium-sized job, two or three inspection pits should typically be opened up using a mechanical excavator, followed by one or possibly two deeper boreholes to a depth appropriate to the size of the building.

The underpinning of strip foundations, under walls and the like, was traditionally done by a series of staged pits hand-dug under the line of the footing strip, followed by their filling with mass concrete. Load transfer could be effected by jacking and wedging, before grouting in the final gap between the foundation piers and masonry courses. Present-day health and safety standards limit the depth of such work to about two metres, and it is only practical if there is actually a suitable ground-bearing stratum within reach. With increased use of construction plant and the development of so-called 'mini-piling', it tends to be more economic now to underpin with piles unless the job is small. Special rigs can access confined spaces and they can angle their piles if necessary. The piling contractors themselves, in many cases, have been party to the development of these specialist techniques.

Piling serves to transfer the building load from ground surface to a deeper level of higher ground strength. They may be driven, which means displacing the ground as penetration proceeds – with the hazard of the possible effect of vibrations – or, preferably, the soil is augered out and replaced with vibrated concrete. Most piling incorporates a steel casing for added strength and to maintain a protected hole free of debris.

The bearing capacity – the integrity of any piling – is very sensitive to the process of installation and the quality of workmanship. For several reasons it is difficult for a supervising engineer to maintain a meaningful control over the step-by-step process of pile installation. As a result, piling contracts are frequently negotiated on the basis of a 'design-and-install' package. In these circumstances the important task, for the engineer or employer, is to carry out a thorough appraisal of the contractor's track record for good work and their indemnity insurance, in particular the form of underwriting, in the event that the company ceases trading.

Settlement deformation of masonry and associated crack damage

Brick and stone masonry is the oldest and most commonly used building material, yet for years it has remained one of the least understood in structural terms. This is less a criticism of engineering analysis than an honest acknowledgement of the very complex behaviour of this apparently 'simple' combination of rigid blocks and softer joint material. Apart from questions of appearance, masonry is seldom remarked on unless it goes wrong, usually with the 'surprise' appearance of cracks, which quite often signal a foundation problem. The process of remedial work thereafter is worthy of some discussion here.

The tolerance of masonry construction in consequence of a foundation movement has been intermittently addressed for nearly a century, although masonry research generally has proceeded for longer than that. Unsurprisingly, however, engineers mainly concerned with new build prefer to direct their energies into new construction and new products.

The assessment of foundation settlement damage, fault-finding and appraisal of cracking leading to repair followed a trend. Field studies of building damage due to ground settlement largely remained within the domain of the geotechnical specialists, still usually the first to be involved in fault-finding whenever foundation subsidence is suspected. Inevitably, their geotechnical interest focused on the subsoil conditions, which tend to be at the root of structural movement, rather than the mechanics of deformation of the masonry structure itself. In this way they accurately diagnosed 'cause', but for the most part they simply observed a crack, or no-crack, situation. However, their careful accumulation of the emerging field settlement records led them to compare the crack damage against their own assessments of its seriousness. This has provided invaluable guidance as to what tolerable deformation limits are acceptable for different forms and types of building structure. It still remains common practice to estimate a safe or tolerable total settlement, or differential settlement, from empirical rules based on experience and settlement records. The early work by Skempton and Macdonald is regarded as a benchmark for what was a tolerable settlement at that time, derived from field measurements under both visibly damaged and undamaged buildings.[8] Their work stimulated others to enlarge the stock of comparative field data.

Definition of modes of building settlement

Following the work of Skempton, and others, common definitions came into use setting out a basic method of classification of modes of settlement deformation. These developed into the basis of present guidelines used for new build. The thinking offers the most convenient vehicle for setting up a logical approach for dealing with repair works as they relate to the building, rather than the foundations.

At the risk of stating the obvious, settlement refers to (usually) movement of the finished building structure. Differential settlement is movement that causes the structure to change shape and therefore introduces strains within the fabric. Figure 6.11 reduces the forms of deformation movement

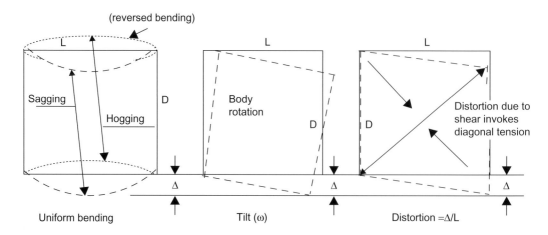

Figure 6.11 Customary definitions of building settlement.

to three, though a structure, in whole or part, will usually be subjected to a combination of all of these.

Uniform bending by **sagging** or **hogging** of the structure is the response of a flexible foundation in cases similar to that discussed in connection with Figure 6.10b. The superstructure is forced into bending because the reactive ground support is high in the middle of the loaded area and less on the edges. If excessive, the result would be seen through an emergence of hair cracking above the damp-proof course. The facade goes into bending like a simple beam. However, the resistance to sliding between the concrete footings and walling, under low-rise buildings in particular, actually tends to suppress the propagation of tension cracking at the base. Tensile cracks in the overlying brickwork, emerging above the damp-proof course level, tend to distribute fairly evenly and they are not normally so prominent.

It is not uncommon, however, to experience settlement under the end property of a long terrace rank. The result is hogging, as structural bending is reversed. The damage here is more severe, because the bending action puts the masonry at eaves/roof level, rather than the base, into tension. In this case the traditional detail, along the top course of masonry at eaves/ roof level, has no built-in resistance to tension. In consequence, once an initial crack develops continued settlement only serves to enlarge that same wound, which splits open, on a single near-vertical crack line, down to the wall base.

Tilt is a body rotation of the entire structure or a part of it. Here there is no distortion of the building fabric and therefore a wall panel can remain immune to potential crack strain, although there is ground settlement.

Distortion due to shear invokes diagonal tension. Therefore diagonal cracks will develop at right angles to the direction of the tension stresses. The distorted parallelogram shape in this case is effectively the same as that given in the right-hand part of the diagram in Figure 6.6.

It is important to bear in mind here that any deforming masonry panel – a whole wall or a part – will always be subjected to combined bending and shear distortion. Whether the 'bending' action invokes sub-vertical cracks at the top or bottom, or whether shear stresses produce cross-diagonal cracks, depends on the geometry of the wall – that is, the ratio of the length to the overall depth of the unit. This will be referred to further in the special context of spandrel walls, which make up the brick/masonry infill above or below window openings or a door. For those interested in a detailed study of the cracking of masonry walls, a landmark analysis of the problem is given by Burland and Wroth.[9] Their analysis makes an analogy between tension strains in the elastic deformation of a deep beam and the action of a masonry wall, up to the point at which cracking occurs.

All buildings will settle and deform during their lifetime, and the engineer's responsibility is to predict whether that movement constitutes **tolerable settlement** in terms of either its effect on the function of the building or visible damage to the fabric. Where the building is of masonry or brickwork, deformations above certain limits cause cracks and, as mentioned, they are a result of tensile strain. It then becomes necessary to establish whether the damage is due to foundation movement or some other cause, as described by Grimm.[10] If the movement is ongoing or very bad then the foundations will need to be repaired, but only as a last resort. Decisions in this respect are mostly made on the basis of the severity of cracking and ease of repair. The case of the Tower of Pisa is exceptional.

The subjectivity of the problem of settlement-related crack damage came under scrutiny as the seriousness of damage became associated with usage and as the public grew more sensitive to cracks in their dwellings, particularly as this affected property values. Bjerrum[11] compiled one of the clearest comparative summaries of acceptable distortion limits (Figure 6.12). Half a century on these rule-of-thumb criteria are still used, although tolerance limits on new build are now more restrictive. The debate on crack damage continues to the present, fuelled by persistently rising costs of house repair. The Building Research Establishment[12] and the Institution of Structural Engineers[13] have promoted wider-ranging discussions on the topic with varied advances on Bjerrum's original work. These compare the extent of crack damage and physical crack sizes against their effect on serviceability (e.g. damp penetration), or the actual risk of instability as a result of very wide cracks.

The engineer or architect engaged in repair should be au fait with up-to-date information and, in particular, current attitudes to acceptable crack tolerance limits in present-day practice.

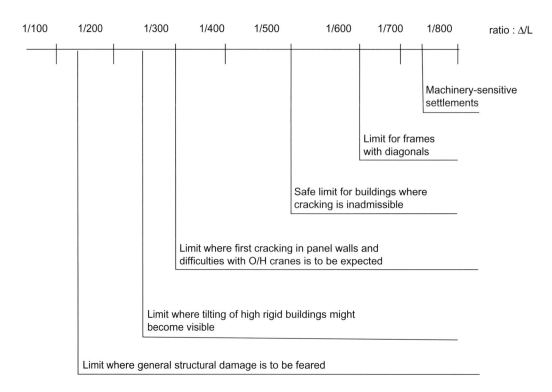

Figure 6.12 Limitations on building settlement (from Bjerrum, 1963).

An approach to the repair of settlement crack damage

The author studied the repair of masonry crack damage in collaboration with the Institut für Tragkonstruktionen, University of Karlsruhe, between 1989 and 1997, and their research remit embraced all aspects of the maintenance and repair of historic buildings. It is informative to take a glimpse at the parallel German philosophy of repair of old structures, which is here summarised from their Sonderforschungsbereich document 315:[14]

> The permanency and present condition of historically significant works of building construction are investigated by a collaborative inter-disciplinary working group of engineers, scientists, and architectural historians together engaged in the field of monument care. With this purpose in view, the decay of the building fabric, and also its causes, are researched in tandem in a careful and cost-conscious manner, in order to develop processes of material restitution and, where necessary, improvement and strengthening. A research methodology sets up, as its priority, the development of specific engineering investigation and safety measures which are targeted sympathetically towards the historic context of the building's background.
>
> The object is to restrict or limit invasive treatment of the material substance, and any additional repair, to what is absolutely necessary, and within such a preservation and repair philosophy embody 'self-help' mechanisms into the construction . . .

The philosophy puts constraints on the approach to masonry repair, indeed all repair, in a manner similar to that of British practice. It emphasises features which cannot be dealt with by current codes of practice, or conventional solutions, which could be invasive or even counterproductive. At the same time that repairs to historic structures impose constraints, they call for an innovative approach, to achieve practical solutions. In short, this entails

- avoidance where possible of any change to the original structural mode of behaviour
- maintenance of original character by the minimum of interference with, or damage to, the original structural fabric
- an ability, where possible, to reverse the repair
- imaginative, high-quality engineering

Historic buildings undergo frequent changes of use during their life, and there is inevitably some compromise between the conservator's 'ideal' and what can be achieved through engineering practice. Conservators approach their buildings rather as a doctor, who will only use surgery where there is no other choice, approaches a patient. All engineering repairs are invasive, but they can be discreet and made to maintain the status quo. In this setting, to eliminate incipient crack damage by ponderous underpinning would be looked on as 'overkill' and preferably avoided unless there is some serious overall instability.

Case study: Crack damage in the spandrel wall element of a masonry facade

One study within the German research programme consisted of careful field surveys of settlement crack damage along a number of long masonry terraces. The terraces offered advantages over shorter structures because of their repetitive patterns of doors and windows. This provided a very useful common denominator for comparisons of cracking, and damage generally, arising from different settlement amounts and reverses of curvature, such as hogging or sagging (Figure 6.11). Three facades selected for study were Georgian terraces in the City of Bath, 15 metres high and between 70 and 90 metres in length.[15]

The nub of the investigation concerned the small area of masonry between window sills and lintels, usually known as the spandrel wall (Figure 6.13a). This element appears to be more susceptible to crack damage than other parts. Some initial common-sense observations explain why:

- If a wall is uniformly plain, without openings of any sort, then stress/ strain paths should flow through smoothly without abrupt change. But window openings, or any discontinuities, are natural 'stress-raisers'. This was made tragically clear to the designers of the first passenger jet aircraft, Comet I, in 1946–49. Localised high stresses caused fatigue failure, leading to disastrous hair-cracking around the 90° corners of the rectangular windows.
- Deformation of the spandrel is usually observable from the distortion of the window frame, or the door frame at ground level. One of the first complaints from a householder is that 'the doors stick'. Figure 6.13a indicates the facade's 'racking' movement through the displaced window lintels.
- A view of the whole facade shows a pattern of alternating columns of solid masonry and columns of windows separated by their spandrels. However, this undoubtedly elegant architecture means that a precise

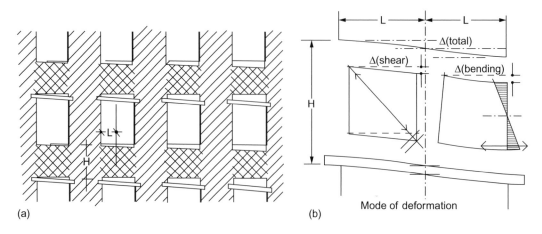

(a)

(b)

Mode of deformation

Figure 6.13 (a) Long facade: regular pattern of columns and windows; (b) Spandrel wall acts as a fixed-end beam in shear and bending.

settlement path will not flow in a smooth curve along the length of the terrace. It will go in a series of small 'steps' across each vertical line of windows. The stiff, continuous vertical columns of masonry may move up or down but otherwise stay intact. Virtually all *differential* changes of level take place within the weaker columns of windows and spandrels.

- Cracks propagate from the window corners initially; if the damage becomes heavier, shear cracks open up on a diagonal line across the body of the spandrel.

Analysis of the spandrel wall elements

The ends of a spandrel are rigidly held in position by their adjacent full-height rigid columns of masonry, and they deform in the manner of a fixed-ended deep beam. The ends translate but do not rotate; by symmetry, each half span acts as a simple deep cantilever with constant shear throughout and zero bending at the centre (Figure 6.13b). Figure 6.13b further sketches the deflection components of deformation caused by the actions of bending and shear respectively.

Burland and Wroth's deep beam analysis[16] applies to a cantilever spandrel element, on the assumption made of masonry's elastic behaviour up to the point of first cracking. A crack develops when the tension strain from either beam bending or diagonal shear reaches a defined critical limit.

The deflection ratio for the twin cantilever halves follows the text book form:

$$\frac{\Delta}{L} = \frac{WL^2}{3EI} + \frac{3W}{2GH} \tag{6.5}$$

where H, L are the proportions of the cantilever, Δ = deflection, E = elastic modulus of brickwork, G = shear modulus, I = beam moment of inertia (= $H^3 / 12$ for unit beam width); the ratio $E / G = 2.4$ (approximately).

In terms of strains, the diagonal tensile strain due to shear remains constant along the half length, while the bending strain varies linearly with the moment. The ratio of maximum bending strain to shear strain is

$$\frac{\varepsilon_{shear}}{\varepsilon_{bending}} = \frac{EH}{8GL} \tag{6.6}$$

It follows that unless the cantilever half span is very deep ($H/L = 3.2$), the element will always reach a limiting bending tensile strain before the shear strain limit. Given the customary proportions of spandrels (ratio: H/L), deformation will inevitably initiate cracks from bending, in advance of shear, propagating in a sub-vertical direction from window corners. This simple prediction is confirmed by observation of damage.

Actual values deflection ratio (Δ/L) can be calculated, due to shear or bending, given an assumed limiting tensile strain in the brickwork. Burland and Wroth's findings had concluded that a value of 0.075% was a reasonable guideline figure as a threshold for initial cracking of brickwork. The

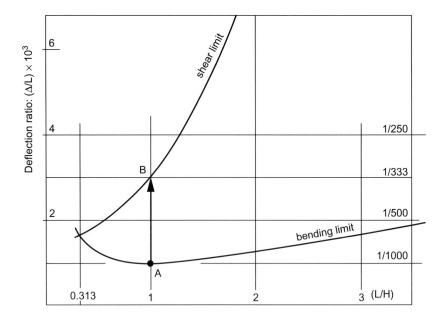

Figure 6.14 Deflection ratio (Δ/L) versus (L/H), for a limiting tensile strain of 0.075% in shear or bending.

range of estimated limits of deflection ratio at this threshold for initial cracking are shown in Figure 6.14.

The graph plot shows the relative decreasing tolerance of a spandrel to bending strains, vis-à-vis the corresponding shear limit. However, this graph plot raises another issue; if the inferior bending effect could be compensated to match the shear limit, then the sustainable deflection would improve by a factor of say two or more, for example from A to B in Figure 6.14.

The veracity of the argument was examined through a series of eleven full-scale wall tests.[17] The tests examined the effectiveness of introducing stainless steel reinforcement into the bed joints above and below the corners of the spandrel after an initial crack situation had emerged. In summary, the key steps in the test were

- to deflect the wall to the observed limit of crack formation, initiated by tensile bending strain (point A, Figure 6.14)
- to repair the wall, by insertion of one or two layers of bed-joint reinforcement in the upper and lower brick courses
- to continue deformation up to the onset of diagonal shear cracking (point B, Figure 6.14)

These tests demonstrated, in a simple, direct way, how reinforcement imparts greater flexibility to damaged masonry – which practising engineers can understand, on the basis of ordinary deep beam theory.

The last two decades have seen the successful introduction of reinforcement, similar to reinforced concrete, into new masonry structures, and its use to improve the properties of brickwork is now commonplace. Bed joint reinforcement of the spandrels to compensate for bending cracking is able to delay the growth of further damage and create a facade able to withstand greater settlement.

Where the context is conservation and repair, the purpose of reinforcement is to increase ductility in order to limit cracking rather than enhance strength as all masonry is inherently weak and the forces involved are large. The ideal repair needs to contain initial corner-cracking caused by bending, up to the limit of diagonal tension due to shear. In practical terms, if a masonry structure develops cracks around a window or door lintel then a minimum bed joint reinforcement repair can contain a significant amount of further movement, at least equal to that causing the damage in the first place. This offers the possibility of extending the life of the building in such a way that its future design life matches its life to the present.

This does not deny that progressive settlement movement caused by landslip, or some other major change in the ground conditions, may require the normal process of foundation repair. However, where further settlement is likely to be limited and quantifiable there is the scope to contain existing damage by simply introducing reinforcement.

In conclusion, settlement of buildings leads to bending and shearing of the facades as well as tilt. It is common to find that multi-windowed facades first manifest deformation damage by the appearance of sub-vertical cracks from the window corners. The introduction of stainless steel bed joint reinforcement can provide an economic means of repair that is discreet, particularly for repair of older buildings. For other repair situations, it offers an economic form of repair. If the onset of bending cracking can be contained up to the tolerance limit to shear cracking, then the result measurably enhances the overall tolerance to further damage.

Endnotes

1 Karl Terzaghi, 'Soil Mechanics – A New Chapter in Engineering Science', James Forrest Lecture, *Journal of the Institution of Civil Engineers*, **12** (1939), 106–42.
2 Karl Terzaghi, *Theoretical Soil Mechanics* (John Wiley & Sons, New York and London, 1943).
3 British Standard 5930: 2002. *Code of Practice for Site Investigations*.
4 Ibid., fig. 32.
5 For example, Malcolm Bolton, *A Guide to Soil Mechanics* (Macmillan, London, 1979).
6 Jacques Heyman, *Coulomb's Memoir on Statics: An Essay in the History of Engineering* (Cambridge University Press, Cambridge, 1972).
7 J.B. Burland, M. Jamiolkowski and C. Viggiani, 'The stabilization of the leaning tower of Pisa', *Soils and Foundations*, **43**, 5 (2004), 63–80.

8 A.W. Skempton, and D.H. Macdonald 'The allowable settlement of buildings', *Proceedings of the Institution of Civil Engineers*, **5**, II (1956), 727–68.

9 J.B. Burland and C.P. Wroth, *Settlement of Buildings and Associated Damage*, BRE. Building Research Series, No CP 73/75 (Construction Press, 1974).

10 C.T. Grimm, op.cit.

11 L. Bjerrum, 'Discussion', *Proceedings of the European Conference on Soil Mechanics and Foundation Engineering*, vol. 2 (Wiesbaden, 1963), pp. 135–7.

12 Building Research Establishment, *Assessment of Damage in Low-rise Buildings*, BRE Digest 251 (revised 1990).

13 Institution of Structural Engineers, *The Real Behaviour of Structures: Soil Structure Interaction* (ISE, London, 1989).

14 *Sonderforschungsbereich 315: Empfehlungen für die Praxis* ('Manuals of recommended practice for the care, maintenance and restoration of historically important buildings') (Ernst & Sohn, Berlin, in press).

15 D.A. Cook, S.L. Ledbetter, S. Ring and F. Wenzel, 'Masonry crack damage, its origins, diagnosis philosophy and a basis for repair', *Proceedings of the Institution of Civil Engineers, Structures & Buildings*, **140** (2000), 39–50.

16 J.B. Burland and C.P. Wroth, 'Settlement of buildings and associated damage' BRE. Building Research Series, No CP 73/75 (Construction Press, 1974).

17 D.A. Cook, M. Harris and W. Fichtner, 'Masonry crack damage repair by bed-joint reinforcement', *Proceedings of the Conference on Large and Full-scale Testing of Structures* (City University, London, 1996), pp. 15.1–15.8.

7 Effects of induced movement

Michael Bussell

This chapter considers the sources of movement that can occur in buildings (and other structures – bridges, towers, gasholders, etc.). It describes their effects, and indicates what remedies might be necessary. However, it should be stressed at the outset that the effects of movements are not always harmful or demanding of remedial action. Instead of rushing towards what could be expensive repair measures, it is important to observe or *monitor* movements so that informed judgement can be made on causes, consequences, and any intervention that might be needed to remedy or mitigate their effects.

A significant source of potential movement comes from inadequate or changed ground conditions and the present chapter should be read in conjunction with Chapter 6, which discusses ground movement.

The inevitability of movement

It may be disconcerting, but it has to be accepted as a fact that every building moves throughout its life. It is of course important that the original design and construction is such that movements are modest, and indeed usually imperceptible, if a serviceable performance is to be achieved. Listed, scheduled and other historic buildings and structures are not exempt from this need, nor from the effects of movements. However, if remedial work is considered necessary then it is essential to apply conservation principles, especially minimal intervention – doing as little as is necessary – which also chimes happily with cost considerations.

Movement occurs in every building component and every material, and typically takes the form of a change in geometry – an increase or decrease in the component dimensions. The movement may be instantaneous, as in the deflection of an iron or steel beam when loaded, or it may be gradual over time, as in the shrinkage or swelling of timber, masonry and other materials as a result of drying or wetting. The movement may be static – once-for-all – as when an iron or steel beam is subject to an additional constant load; it may be slowly cyclic, as in the movement of the tip of a masonry spire in sunlight, which traces out a closed irregular loop as the sun moves across the sky and heats the masonry surfaces differentially; or it may be rapidly cyclic, as when a structure supports vibrating machinery or is exposed to the effects of moving traffic.

Types of movement

The commonest types of movement, sometimes requiring remedial treatment, are

- cracking
- tilt
- out-of-plane movement
- in-plane distortion

Cracking

Cracking can be a very emotive subject, particularly where one's own home is concerned. However, not all cracking is evidence of a serious problem. For example, plasterboard as used in modern ceilings and partitions will shrink as it dries out – particularly where central heating is in use – and this is likely to cause hairline (very narrow) cracking between the sheets. This is easily remedied during redecoration by filling the joints and taping over them. Similarly, cracks at the junctions of new joinery timber are a natural consequence of drying shrinkage, and can be filled and overpainted. Such cracks are not evidence of structural distress!

On the other hand, cracking can also indicate serious problems – particularly when monitoring (see Chapter 5) indicates that it is 'active', that is to say continuing beyond the normal variations to be expected from daily or seasonal changes in temperature and moisture content.

Formally, cracking occurs when the total imposed tensile applied strain on a material exceeds its tensile strain capacity. Materials such as unreinforced masonry and concrete are brittle and have low tensile strain capacity. As a guide, a figure of 0.075% strain (i.e. 0.75 mm per metre) is often used for assessing the effects of ground movements on unreinforced brickwork. Steel, reinforced concrete and, to a lesser extent, timber have significantly higher tensile strain capacities and are ductile, so they are able to accommodate larger movements without cracking or collapse.

Not surprisingly, cracking is most likely to occur where the cross section is weaker, for example at a line of windows in a wall. This is analogous to the effects of perforations in toilet paper, which 'tears along the dotted line'.

The pattern of cracking is a very important pointer to the cause of movement. Table 7.1 shows common typical patterns of overall cracking in a masonry building, indicating the most probable cause(s). It also suggests whether the movements may be structurally significant, but it must be stressed that this is dependent on the circumstances of specific cases and should not be taken as hard-and-fast advice. In particular, if movement continues it is more likely to become structurally significant. Note that the movements and crack widths in Table 7.1 are exaggerated for clarity.

Another valuable pointer is the state of the crack faces. If they are clean and bright, this suggests recent movement; dirty faces with dead spiders and so on indicate that cracking occurred some time ago – but this, of

Table 7.1 Typical crack patterns in masonry walls

Typical elevation with cracking pattern	Probable cause(s) of movement and structural significance
Cracking essentially vertical and of reasonably constant width	Temperature changes and/or drying shrinkage; often not significant
Expansion, then essentially vertical cracking	Irreversible moisture expansion of bricks, followed by expansion in warmer weather and then cracking in cooler weather, as wall tries to contract but is restrained from movement by frictional restraint from weight of wall resting on its thermally more stable base;* often not significant. Can also occur in parapets
Progressive outward movement towards ends of terrace, with associated vertical/diagonal cracking	Progressive outward 'shunting' effect, which has been described as the 'bookend' effect; could be or become significant, e.g. requiring stabilisation work to ends of terrace* (discussed further in relation to in-plane distortion, see below)
Diagonal cracking as right end of building settles or subsides (or as remainder heaves upwards!)	Ground movements such as differential settlement under building, subsidence, or heave (see Chapter 6); could be or become significant
Cracking (vertical and diagonal), wider at top of building, can result in 'lozenging' of openings	Ground movements such as differential settlement, subsidence – building on edge of sinking area; could be or become significant (note cracks increase in width up building)
Cracking (vertical and diagonal), wider at base of building, can result in 'lozenging' of openings	Ground movements such as differential settlement, subsidence – building within sinking area; could be or become significant (note cracks decrease in width up building)
Cracking and disturbance of masonry suggests corrosion of embedded steel frame (shown in broken lines)	Corrosion of embedded steel column, beam, etc.; could be or become significant
Cracking of mortar joints and bricks (and staining of surface) suggests corrosion of wall tie or other embedded iron or steel (also occurs in stonework and terra cotta)	Corrosion of wall ties, cramps or other embedded metal; could reduce lateral restraint to structural members, and also increasing physical damage to masonry units, and staining, over time

*Such cracks often fill with brick or stone dust which then 'jams' the cracks solid; this leads to repeated cycling or 'shunting' of the wall, which gradually moves outward at both ends.

course, does not mean that the movement responsible for the cracking has necessarily stabilised.

The effects of cracking vary. At their least they are purely 'cosmetic' – perhaps unsightly but not affecting performance, although they can affect serviceability by allowing the ingress of water, noise or dirt. At worst they are structurally significant – for example, allowing moisture to reach steel and risk corrosion, or removing restraint to a wall panel that depended on bonding to its neighbour for stability. The width of a crack is not necessarily an indication of seriousness; a wide crack at mid-length of an inherently stable garden wall is structurally unimportant, whereas a narrow crack at the exposed top of a masonry-clad steel-framed building will draw in rain-water by capillary action, which could cause corrosion of the embedded steel (and indeed may indicate that rusting is already occurring).

Tilt

Tilt is a rotational movement of a building, wall or column without any distortion within its surface – that is, with no out-of-plane movement (for which see below). In reality, it is virtually impossible to build anything truly vertical because of the inevitable minor dimensional inaccuracies inherent in the construction process. Modern design codes require provision for such minor inaccuracies.

Figure 7.1 illustrates the effects of tilt in the simple case of a column or wall assumed to be resting on the ground (with thickness much exaggerated in relation to height, for clarity). Its total weight can be represented by an equivalent concentrated load, W, acting at the mid-point of the section (Figure 7.1a); its weight is evenly distributed, so that the base is uniformly compressed and the section is clearly stable. Now if the section tilts a little – for example, owing to softer ground under the left-hand edge – the line of action of its self-weight, which of course is still straight down, moves towards the left-hand edge, and the compressive stress on the section increases towards this edge (Figure 7.1b). It can be shown that if the tilt is such that the line of action passes through a point one-sixth of the base width away from the centre line then the stress at the right-hand edge is zero while the stress on the left-hand edge is twice the uniform stress seen when the section was perfectly upright (Figure 7.1c).

Further tilt increases the stress on this leading edge, while the section starts to lift off the ground from the right-hand edge inwards (Figure 7.1d). This is a common state, not just for a column or wall sitting on the ground but also in unreinforced masonry, where mortar provides little or no 'stiction' between bricks or stone when subject to tension. Once the section has tilted so much that the line of action passes through the left-hand edge, the end is nigh and the section falls over (Figure 7.1e). (In practice, it would have collapsed sooner, as the ground under the left-hand side would have been unable to sustain the rapidly increasing compressive stress.)

The best-known example of a structure showing conspicuous tilt is of course the Leaning Tower of Pisa, recently the subject of a major – and

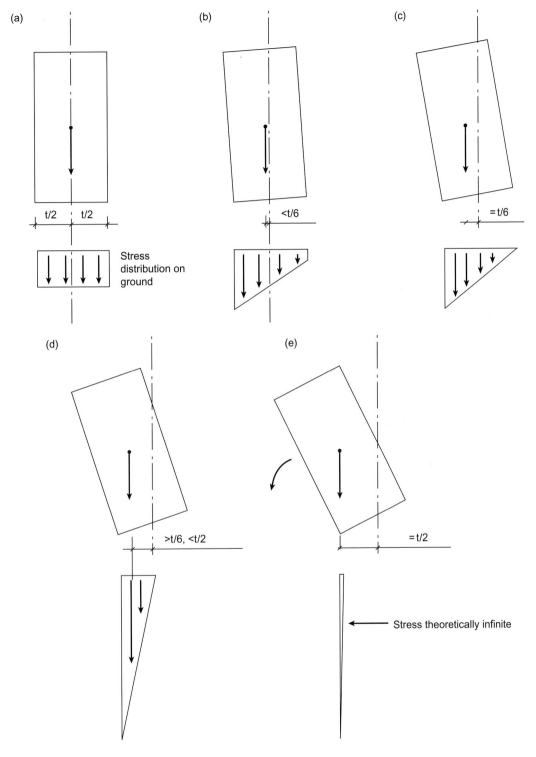

(a)

t/2 | t/2

Stress distribution on ground

(b)

<t/6

(c)

= t/6

(d)

>t/6, <t/2

(e)

= t/2

Stress theoretically infinite

Figure 7.1 Effect of tilt on ground stress distribution and stability.

what appears to have been a successful – attempt to arrest its tilt, which was shown to be increasing year by year. Its movement was a result of variations in the compressible ground strata under the tower, and most cases of tilt are due either to this or to loads that are eccentric to the centre of the building foundation. These have a similar effect on compressible ground, as the figure has illustrated.

In most cases of tilt the angular rotation is of course very much less than at Pisa, but it often requires structural intervention as, once started, the tilt can increase with time until the building, wall or column becomes unstable. At Pisa the tilt was arrested by adding heavy lead weights on the 'rising' side of the tower foundation, and then carefully withdrawing soil through tubes to induce subsidence on this side so that the tilt of the tower was slowly reduced by a controlled amount. More common remedies include local underpinning or installation of supporting piles concentrated on the 'sinking' side. Tilting of flank and party walls in terraces due to the so-called 'bookend' effect is described below.

Out-of-plane movement

The distinctive feature of tilt is that it is a block or 'rigid body' rotation without conspicuous out-of-plane movement. The other movement type that results in an out-of-plumb section is where local out-of-plane movement occurs, with or without tilt. Such out-of-plane movement is a characteristic of columns or walls rather than the structure overall. The principal types of out-of-plane movements are

- bowing – curvature of the member with no change in thickness (Figure 7.2a)
- bulging – unmatched curvature of the member on one or both faces (Figure 7.2b)

Both can threaten the stability of the building overall, or the individual column or wall.

Whether or not tilt occurs in addition depends on the absence or presence of lateral restraint, together with a triggering cause for the tilt such as foundation rotation or eccentric loading, as discussed above. A wall in which the absence of lateral head restraint results in both tilt and bowing owing to foundation rotation is shown in Figure 7.3a (overall tilt is prevented by the vertical restraint provided by the bonded-in cross-walls at either end of the wall panel); a wall where lateral head restraint complements vertical restraint from the cross-walls to confine the form of movement to bowing is shown in Figure 7.3b.

Bowing can arise from a variety of causes, the commonest of which are

- foundation movement (see above)
- eccentric loading on the member or its foundation (see above)
- inadequate lateral restraint (see below)

116

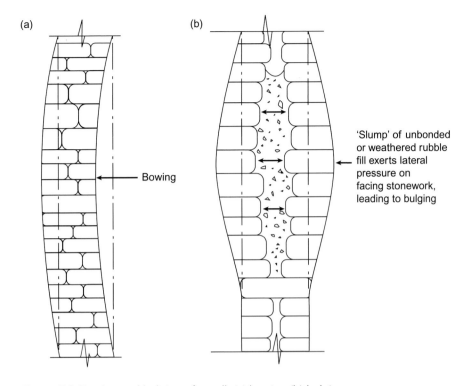

Figure 7.2 Bowing and bulging of a wall: (a) bowing (b) bulging.

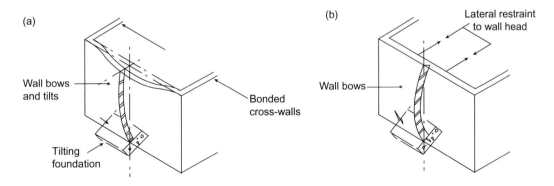

Figure 7.3 (a) Wall both bowing and tilting owing to foundation rotation; (b) tilting of the wall prevented by lateral restraint to head of wall.

- sulphate attack on mortar in masonry (see below)
- decay of bonding timbers (see below)

A further cause can arise from arched floors in brick, stone, or concrete. This form of construction is commonly found in multi-storey mills and similar nineteenth-century industrial and commercial buildings. Customarily the arches were tied or 'jacked' by wrought iron tie rods, which restrained the tendency of the arch springings to spread under gravity loading (Figure 7.4a). If the tie rods are absent or have been mistakenly cut out for some reason, the unbalanced thrust against (usually) an outside wall can produce local bowing (Figure 7.4b). Movement can be arrested by reinstating the tying provision or by replacing the adjacent arch bay with, for example, a reinforced concrete slab. The latter solution is not preferred in conservation terms as it loses original fabric; it is also likely to be more expensive.

Bulging involves distortion of the wall or column cross section. The commonest causes are

- 'slumping' of rubble fill in stone walls due to deterioration or absence of binding mortar (see below)
- absence or corrosion failure of wall ties in cavity wall construction, rendering both individual leaves more slender and hence vulnerable to 'unorchestrated' bowing

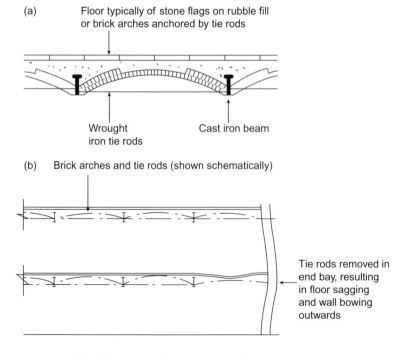

Figure 7.4 (a) Brick 'jack-arches' in floor, restrained from spreading by tie rods; (b) arch spread and distortion of wall arising from omitted or removed tie rods in end bay.

In-plane distortion

A common sight in traditional construction is **racking of timber frames** – the out-of-square doorway and general distortion – arising usually from repeated wear and slop in the pegged joints. It is seldom of structural concern (as adequate stability is assured by the brick or wattle-and-daub frame infill), and indeed is often regarded as an attractive characteristic (although a similar appearance in a new house would cause alarm!).

Another is the **'bookend effect'**. Mention has already been made of the 'shunting' action that can occur in walls as a result of cyclic thermal movements, which can lead to cracking; the wall cools and tries to contract but instead cracks as its tensile strength is less than the force required to draw the wall section back along its damp-proof course. The crack(s) can then become filled with brick or stone dust, which 'jams' them so that further expansion causes the wall to gradually move further outwards.

A particular manifestation of this has been argued to occur in terraces built of brick or stone. These typically comprise solid party walls, and front and rear elevations punctured by door and window openings. Cyclic thermal movements, accompanied by jamming of the consequent vertical cracks through window-lines, may lead to apparent expansion of the elevations; this is greatest at the top of these walls and minimal at ground level, where there is greater lateral restraint to the structure and greater thermal stability. This expansion can also cause the party walls, and in particular the gable walls, to tilt and lean. In extremis, this movement could render the gable walls potentially unstable, and necessitate rebuilding.

The term 'bookend effect' was coined to describe this process by Clive Richardson, a structural engineer with substantial conservation experience. His paper, published in 2000, attracted a variety of reported discussion when presented.[1] He suggested that the rate of movement, at around 1 mm per year, could pose serious problems for Victorian and earlier terraces. It could also raise complicated issues of liability, since the end-of-terrace owners could argue that costs associated with any required rebuilding were in part at least attributable to damage caused by the adjacent buildings! His proposal that further movement should be prevented by cutting vertical movement joints in the front and rear elevations at 12–15 metre spacing (as recommended for new brick wall construction) also raises conservation issues.

Restrained movement

Damage can result from movement, as considered above. However, severe damage can equally result if the movement is fully or partially prevented by physical restraints. The example has already been quoted of the 'shunting' or progressive in-plane movement of masonry walls as a result of cracks becoming filled by brick or stone dust. Other problems with restrained movement have been more common in modern rather than traditional construction, particularly where materials with different movement characteristics have been used together without an awareness of their behaviour when combined.

Two examples associated with reinforced concrete structures and their cladding, one brick and the other mosaic, serve to illustrate the effect of restraint. Both have occurred quite frequently, and have entailed considerable expenditure in remedial work in recent decades.

The wide use of **multi-storey reinforced concrete frames with brick cladding** began in the 1950s. The frame was built first, and while this was proceeding the external non-loadbearing walls were erected, with an inner leaf typically of concrete blockwork and an outer leaf of clay brickwork. Both leaves were typically pinned up tight with mortar to the underside of the concrete slab above, leaving the slab edge either exposed or 'expressed', often smartened up by a render facing (Figure 7.5a) (those were the days before concern about cold-bridging!), or masked by thin brick 'slips' (Figure 7.5b). In both cases it will be seen that the concrete slab did not extend over the full width of the brick leaf.

The concrete columns and walls underwent movement from three sources. First, the increasing loads on them as construction proceeded led to them shortening elastically. Secondly, they underwent drying shrinkage as the concrete lost moisture. And thirdly, over time 'creep' occurred under load. The cumulative effect in each case was that the concrete shortened in height over each storey.

Meanwhile, the bricks – if fresh from the kiln – were undergoing some irreversible expansion, while in warm temperatures the outer brick leaf sought to expand further. However, it was restrained by being pinned between floor slabs, so the only movement it could undergo, with its head only partially restrained by the slab above, was bowing outwards; if there were brick slips present, these were then subject to 'prying' by the rotation of the head of the brick leaf. (See Figures 7.5c and 7.5d, in which movements have been exaggerated for clarity.) The leaf itself was dependent for its stability against collapse on the ties linking it to the inner leaf, so it was to be hoped that these were present and not corroding! Usually the first noticeable sign of distress was when patches of render or one or more brick slips fell off. Investigation would then reveal the bowing of the brick leaf, and remedial work was usually necessary on safety grounds.

The remedial solution had to provide for the inevitable movements and relieve damaging stresses, as is recommended in guidance for new construction nowadays.[2] This meant either rebuilding the outer leaf completely, if badly bowed, or dismantling the top courses, removing loose render and brick slips, and rebuilding the outer leaf with a 'soft' joint (a horizontal mastic-filled gap) immediately under the concrete slab. Missing render or slips could then be replaced (preferably using a bonding additive, and roughening the slab edge to give secure adhesion). Additional metal ties would be installed if the retained inner leaf was judged not to provide adequate lateral restraint to the brickwork. This work was usually costly and disruptive of the use of the building!

Mosaic-clad reinforced concrete was fashionable in the 1950s and 1960s, with the tiling usually attached to the concrete – walls, columns, and

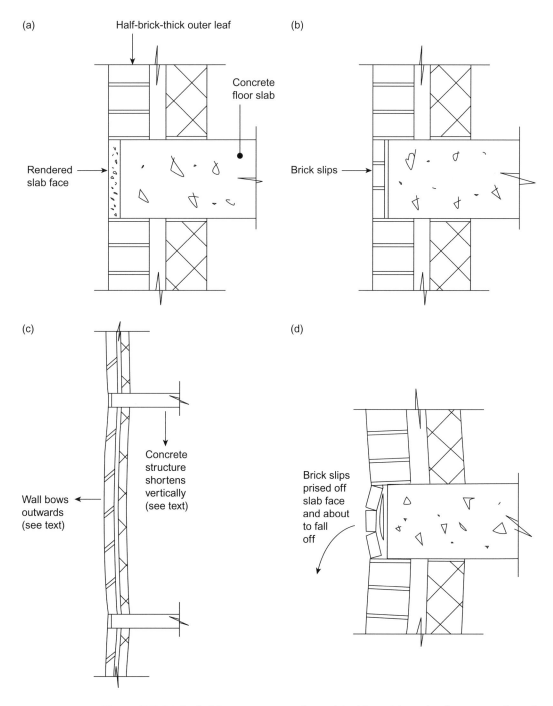

Figure 7.5 Brick cladding in concrete-framed building: (a) render facing to edge of concrete floor slab; (b) brick 'slips' used in place of render to present continuous brick face; (c) bowing of cavity wall as concrete frame shortens owing to time-dependent movements; (d) brick slips about to be pried off by pressure from bowed walls above and/or below.

sometimes other members – with mortar. Often quite a thickness of mortar was 'dubbed out' to take up variations in the concrete profile and achieve a plane surface finish. Typically, no movement joints were provided in the mosaic. As in the case of the brick cladding, the concrete would shorten over time while mosaic is dimensionally stable, so as the concrete shortened it compressed the tiling. Areas of mosaic would buckle outwards and fall off, or debonding would occur at the concrete–mortar or mortar–mosaic interface, or both. Even if this did not immediately result in the mosaic and maybe the render falling off, it would sooner or later occur (certainly on external faces) as trapped moisture froze in cold weather.

A remedial solution, similar to that for brick cladding, was to remove loose mosaic and mortar, roughen the concrete face, apply a mortar with a bonding additive to achieve the required backing line and then, using a specialist tile adhesive, replace the mosaic.

It is to be hoped that present-day construction practice will take note of current guidance in codes of practice and standards, which embodies the lessons of such problems arising from the consequences of restrained movement.

Causes and effects of movement

The common causes of movement in buildings are

- change of temperature
- change in moisture content
- applied loading
- inadequate restraint or continuity
- material decay or deterioration
- alterations or misuse
- inadequate or changed ground conditions (discussed in Chapter 6)

Change of temperature

Over the range of temperatures that buildings experience, thermal movement can be estimated from the multiplication formula learned by many in school science classes:

$$e = \alpha \times L \times \Delta t \tag{7.1}$$

where e is the linear extension (or contraction) of a component of dimension L owing to a rise (or fall) in temperature of Δt degrees, and α is the coefficient of linear thermal expansion of the material from which the component is made.

Values of α for common building materials can be found in published guidance such as Building Research Establishment Digest 228[3] and in scientific and building construction text books, although the value of α will vary depending on the elements present in the material and the material's internal structure. As an example, for various concrete types BRE Digest 228 offers a range of 5–14×10^{-6} per °C, reflecting the variability of a material containing different proportions of cement and aggregate (which itself can include crushed stone, gravel, sand or recycled waste products such as pulverised fly-ash, etc.). Timber, with its aligned fibrous structure, typically has a value for α of 4–6×10^{-6} per °C along the grain, but as high as 30–70×10^{-6} per °C across the grain.

While the dimension L is easily determined (whether it be length, width, thickness or whatever), a reasonable value for Δt is much harder to choose when considering thermal movement in an existing building. In a laboratory it is, of course, easy to heat or cool a test specimen in a sealed vessel, increasing or decreasing the temperature by a known amount and holding it constant at a known figure. (Measuring the change in length would then allow the value of α to be determined or checked.) In what is truly the 'real' world, and certainly in the UK, the sun rarely shines steadily all day, and it traverses the sky for hours before setting, so that its radiant heat falling on a building face varies throughout every day. It is rare to have an entirely still day, and even a gentle breeze will further moderate the heat gain on a building face, while wet fabric will be cooled as moisture evaporates from it. On the other hand, cold winters often include periods where the air is still and temperatures hover around freezing point for days at a time.

It is therefore not surprising that there is relatively little published guidance on temperature ranges either to be considered for the design of new buildings or for use when considering existing construction. BRE Digest 228 is one source, giving some figures for maximum and minimum temperatures that might occur outside and inside buildings in the UK. These were mainly intended for use in the design of new structures when published in 1979 (when global warming was barely recognised, so the minimum temperatures quoted may require review before too long . . .).

Minimum outside surface temperatures suggested in the Digest were in the range -20 to -25°C. Maxima ranged from 50 to 60°C for light-coloured surfaces up to an alarming 65 to 90°C for dark surfaces, recognising that dark surfaces absorb more radiant heat. (These latter figures give credence to suggestions that, on a hot, still summer's day in London, one could crack an egg against the dark granite cladding of a tall office block; the egg would then slide down the hot stone face to arrive at ground level – fried!) Internally, temperature ranges of 10 to 30°C were quoted for occupied buildings and -5 to 35°C for empty or disused buildings. Of course, different temperature ranges would be encountered in cold stores, boiler houses, laundries and the like.

As an indicative example, the 'steady-state' expansion or contraction of a brick wall 10 metres long, built of clay brickwork with $\alpha = 6 \times 10^{-6}$ per °C, and subject to a temperature change from datum of ± 20°C, is

$$\alpha \times L \times \Delta t = 6 \times 10^{-6} \times 10{,}000 \times 20 = 1.2 \, \text{mm} \qquad (7.2)$$

When considering the possible effects of temperature on existing construction, it is worth remembering that in traditional construction the external walls are relatively thick so that the building's response to temperature change is 'sluggish', whereas the modern cavity wall typically exposes a half-brick-thick outer leaf to sun and atmosphere. This leaf, often nowadays backed by thermal insulation, more rapidly responds to thermal changes.

A particular cause of temperature rise is **heat gain in freshly mixed cementitious materials**. When water and cement are mixed to make mortar, render or concrete, the chemical reaction that occurs between the two materials leads to the cement hardening as it sets, but it also generates heat, known as heat of hydration. The cement paste is sufficiently plastic to absorb the expansion due to heating, but as the hardened concrete cools it will shrink. If the concrete is free to contract then all is well, but if it is restrained by adjacent construction – for example, if concrete is placed to strengthen a nineteenth-century mill floor of cast iron beams and brick arches (see Chapter 10) – then there is a danger of the 'young' concrete cracking as it tries to contract but is prevented from doing so by being bonded to the brickwork.

The problem is potentially most severe in large or thick concrete pours, in which heat loss at the surface is slow compared with the amount being generated internally, and is of particular concern in construction intended to contain or exclude water, such as reservoirs, swimming pools, and basements. The solution is competent design, careful detailing to minimise restraint effects and to provide adequate reinforcement to control cracking, and proper control of construction.[4]

Change in moisture content

Most building materials increase in volume when wetted, and return to their original size when dry again. (Metals, glass and igneous and metamorphic rock, however, are effectively dimensionally stable.) These movements are reversible.

Timber undergoes significant initial drying shrinkage. This is hardly surprising, as a key function of the internal structure of timber is of course to conduct water throughout the tree as sap; as soon as the tree is felled, its sap begins to evaporate. Because of its unusual and distinctly non-homogeneous internal structure – memorably analogised as 'drinking straws held together by elastic bands'[5] – timber is liable to curl, warp and crack during this 'seasoning' process if not carefully sawn and stored.

Traditionally, this seasoning took time, particularly for larger sections such as beams and posts. The reconstruction of part of York Minster's roof after it was destroyed by fire in 1984 called for large oak sections in quantities that exceeded available stocks of seasoned timber, and so the design of the roof and its connections had to allow for the movements that would occur as the 'green' oak gradually seasoned in situ.[6] (Modern kiln-drying of timber needs equal skill if it is to produce material that is not over-dried, which can then result in distortion occurring after incorporation in a building as the timber regains atmospheric moisture.)

The word 'sap' has been adopted, too, in the term 'quarry sap' – the natural moisture found in quarried limestone and sandstone. Its presence often makes it easier to work the stone, which then shrinks a little as it dries to an ambient moisture content. This is a reversible movement; the stone will expand if re-wetted, although it is relatively rare for stone, once built in, to become saturated over its whole section unless weatherproofing is grossly deficient.

In addition, 'irreversible' moisture movements occur after the placing of materials containing cement or lime, as these newly hydrated materials set and lose moisture in the process. This is known as drying shrinkage. In contrast, bricks used fresh from the kiln have a minimal moisture content, but once laid they chemically absorb atmospheric moisture and expand in the process. (Salvaged bricks do not undergo this expansion when reused.)

Typical figures for reversible and irreversible movements in common building materials (Table 7.2) might appear to be of small magnitude, but they can be significant in practical construction. For example, a movement of 0.04% represents 4 mm in a wall 10 metres long.

Applied loading

Loading applied to any material results in stress, which in turn causes strain. Most building materials are relatively *stiff*, so that movement under loading is small and difficult to see. However, movement always occurs in response

Table 7.2 Typical values for thermal and moisture movement for some common building materials (based on BRE Digest 228* which gives more detailed figures for particular types of material)

Material	Typical coefficient of linear thermal expansion ($\times 10^{-6}$ per °C)	Typical reversible movement (± %)	Typical irreversible movement (+ is expansion, − is shrinkage) (%)
Stone	3–12	Limestone 0.01; sandstone 0.07; others nil	—
Cement-based materials (concrete, concrete blocks, mortar, render, etc.)	5–14	0.02–0.10 (greater for ultra-lightweight concrete)	−0.03–0.10 (greater for ultra-lightweight concrete)
Clay brickwork	5–8	0.02	+0.02–0.07
Carbon steel	12	—	—
Lead	30	—	—
Timber	4–6 with grain; 30–70 across grain	0.6–4.0 (tangential); 0.45–2.5 (radial)	—
Glass	9–11	—	—

*Building Research Establishment Digest 228: *Estimation of Thermal and Moisture Movements and Stresses: Part 2* (HMSO, London, 1979).

to loading, and this can be readily seen by using a pencil eraser as a test piece:

- Squeezing the ends of the eraser together between finger and thumb causes **compression**, which shortens it.
- Pulling on the ends causes **tension**, which extends it.
- Holding the ends firmly and pushing thumbs against fingers causes **bending**, with the concave face being in **compression** and the convex face being in **tension**.
- Holding the ends firmly and moving the hands apart while keeping them parallel causes **shearing**, in which internal compression and tension stresses act diagonally at right angles to stretch an initially rectangular shape into a lozenge.
- Holding the ends firmly and rotating them against each other causes **torsion**, in which internal compression and tension stresses act diagonally at right angles to twist the eraser along its length.

The structural elements of a building carry loads in ways that depend on what function they serve. All buildings are subject to the effects of gravity and wind, and may be subject to other loading due, for instance, to earth and water pressure (e.g. on basement retaining walls), vibrations from traffic or machinery, and earthquakes (and – sadly, often to be considered nowadays – explosions).

Gravity loading includes the building's 'dead' load – the self-weight of the structure and all other permanent elements (finishes, services, plant, etc.), as well as the 'live' or 'imposed' load arising from use (occupants, furniture, water in tanks, etc.) or from snow loading, which by its nature varies in magnitude. Gravity loading in a typical building will be carried down to the foundations, and from there into the ground, principally as follows:

- Floorboards, joists, beams, girders, etc. carry loads by **bending**, which causes **deflection** – or, crudely, sagging; they are also subject to **shear**, although this typically produces only a marginal increase in deflection.
- Trusses and lattice girders carry load by compression and tension in the various members, which also results in deflection.
- Columns and walls carry load downwards by compression, so that they shorten (but visually imperceptibly).
- Hangers and tie rods carry load by tension, so that they lengthen, again usually imperceptibly.

Wind loading is variable, as the wind constantly changes speed and direction. Slender and large structures, such as tall slim buildings, masts and suspension bridges, may need to take account of the dynamic effects of vibrations induced by wind, but more typically the wind can be considered for design and assessment purposes as a constant loading whose magnitude will depend on location, height and direction. It should be stressed that local wind load effects can be quite severe, and also that wind can apply suction as well as inward pressure to walls and roofs.

Buildings and other structures broadly resist wind loading by the presence of **walls** or **frames** (either **braced** or **unbraced**):

- Walls, often called **shear walls**, resist wind by **bending** and **shear**, acting effectively as vertical cantilevers fixed at ground level; these are stiff, so that lateral deflection or **sway** is modest.
- Braced frames – frames with columns and beams, augmented by diagonal members usually connected to the column–beam junctions – resist wind in the same way as lattice girders carry gravity loading, by compression and tension in individual members, although they deflect in a way similar to shear walls.
- Unbraced frames rely for stability on rigid joints between the columns and beams, all of which resist wind by bending (with compression in the leeward columns and tension in the windward columns); typically each member deforms into a very flat S-shape, so that each storey 'drifts' away from its neighbours above and below, and the sway is greater than that in walls or braced frames.

Most structural materials are linear-elastic in service conditions, so that if the stress doubles then the strain also doubles – Hooke's law, which is commonly expressed as

$$\text{stress} = E \times \text{strain} \tag{7.3}$$

where E is the elastic modulus, known as Young's modulus after its originator. The higher the value of Young's modulus for a material, the **stiffer** that material is.

If the stress is increased towards failure then the behaviour will vary, depending on whether the material is basically **ductile** or **brittle**. Ductile materials, such as steel or reinforced (but not unreinforced) concrete, give visible warning of overload by **yielding** or suffering irrecoverable deflection. Brittle materials such as unreinforced concrete or stone will crack and collapse if subject to excessive tension; in compression, they may give some warning of imminent failure by the development of cracking parallel to the axis of the compressive loading, as in brickwork, although dense materials such as granite and unreinforced concrete can fail explosively and without warning.

A structural material often encountered in conservation is cast iron, which is almost invariably the grey form. This contains excess carbon in the form of graphite flakes. These flakes are like slots in the material; this means that, as stress increases, the strain increases at a greater rate. The material is in fact elastic, but not linear-elastic. Because the slots have greater effect when the material is in tension, as they reduce the available cross section, cast iron subject to a given stress will strain more in tension than in compression. (The slots also give the cast iron a lower tensile strength, and cause a brittle failure.)

Most movement in response to loadings will occur immediately, but some materials undergo **time-dependent movement or 'creep'** under sustained stress, so that the initial movement is augmented by further movement later. This is due to internal relaxation in the material; movements eventually stabilise, except when the stress is close to the failure stress, when the material can 'creep to failure'.

Cementitious materials are prone to creep. Present-day codes of practice for structural concrete give attention to creep movements, which can increase initial movements two- or threefold. Brickwork also creeps, although less than concrete. Creep shortening of reinforced concrete walls or columns, combined with irreversible expansion of outer-leaf facing brickwork in buildings of the 1950s and 1960s, as described above, has often led to distress as the brickwork is gradually 'squeezed' between adjacent floors, causing bulging and occasional collapse.

Timber is also susceptible to creep under sustained loading, which can increase initial deflections by a factor of five or more. Overloaded joints in timber roof trusses can result in gradual local creep or crushing of the timber and consequent spreading of the truss feet, in turn pushing out the wall-heads on which they bear. In 'genteel' Georgian and Victorian villas, the enlarged saloon or dining-room window at ground floor level often interrupts the direct flow to ground of the load in the pier separating the windows on upper floors. The ground floor window opening is spanned by a timber 'bressumer' or large timber beam, which undergoes creep deflection over time to result in characteristic diagonal cracks in the under-sill panels on upper floors, a noticeable sag and possibly local cracking in the brickwork or render immediately above the opening, and (probably the first symptom) 'sticking' of sash or casement windows as their frames and surrounds are squeezed together.

There are many causes of **dynamic loading**, from the human footfall and fluctuating gusts of wind, through vibrating plant and machinery, to vehicle impact, explosion and earthquakes. Effects range from passing discomfort on springy floors to catastrophic failure.

In the context of building conservation, the commonest issues are 'bouncy' floors and slender finials and other rooftop features. Timber floors are often springy, especially in long-span floors, frequently above ornate plaster ceilings that cannot be disturbed. A simple way of improving stiffness is to screw an additional covering of plywood sheets through the existing floorboards into the joists, whose location can be traced from the nails fixing the boards to them. This converts the rectangular joist section into a significantly stiffer tee-section, and disperses loading onto a wider floor area.

Slender finials and similar rooftop features will flex in gusty winds. Over time there is a risk that, although no individual flexing is sufficient to overstress the material (typically iron or zinc), the repeated cyclic stressing may lead to a fatigue failure. Ideally, regular inspection would detect early symptoms such as distortion at fixing points and the beginnings of cracking, although the cost of access to such features (using, for example, a 'cherry-picker' platform) may make such inspection uneconomic unless past failures have highlighted probable future problems. Replacement features should, of course, be made sufficiently strong to withstand fatigue effects.

The effects of thermal and moisture changes, loading and ground conditions are inevitable for any particular site and building. A further cause of movement is dependent on how well or poorly the building elements are held together in place. An elementary illustration of this is the house of cards: playing cards carefully stacked to form an apparently stable 'multi-storey structure'. But the slightest disturbance will bring it down.

In buildings, particular attention needs to be given to limiting out-of-plane movements – those not in the same plane as the loading. This requires adequate lateral restraint.

It is fundamental to prevent **buckling**, the tendency of members in compression to suddenly bow outwards. Buckling is a function of **slenderness** and also of **stiffness** (as discussed above). The eighteenth-century Swiss mathematician and scientist Euler showed that the load required to cause buckling in a member is inversely proportional to the square of the length between points that provide the member with lateral restraint. Other material and member properties influence the buckling load, but for a given member cross section and material it is this length that matters.

This can be demonstrated by taking two lengths of thin stripwood – one short (say, 100–150 mm) and one long (say, 1–1.5 metres) – holding them vertically, with the base on a flat surface, and pushing down on the top. To buckle the shorter piece requires a little effort, but the longer piece will bow outwards under the least pressure.

If the shorter piece is imagined to be one storey-height of a brick wall, and the longer piece a ten-storey-high brick wall, it requires very little thought to recognise that the taller wall is barely stable; a very modest gravity load will cause it to buckle outward and collapse, to say nothing of its ability to stand up to a wind load. And yet the same thickness of wall one storey high will comfortably support a substantial gravity load, and be more capable of resisting wind load, too, by spanning vertically between floor levels.

This highlights the importance of the wall having **lateral restraint**. This is often provided by floors and roof spanning onto the wall; their weight, and the floor or roof acting as a stiff horizontal 'plate', are between them adequate to hold the wall in place at floor level. Floors butting against internal walls on either side also provide restraint, so that the wall cannot move sideways (and, being internal, it is not subject to significant wind load).

However, any room with a timber floor has two opposite walls supporting floor joists, but the other two walls have the nearest joists parallel, providing no restraint. If such a wall is external with no ties into the adjacent construction, it will rise effectively two storeys or more without lateral restraint, but it will have a lower gravity load capacity before buckling occurs and will also be vulnerable to wind loading, particularly local suction pressures.

A more severe situation occurs (not uncommonly) in end-of-terrace houses where the timber staircase is next to the brick gable wall, carried on stringers so that the stairs apply no gravity load to the wall. Here the wall may rise three or more storeys without restraint over the length of the staircase. Outward movement of the wall is often seen.

Castles, churches and great houses were typically built with thick masonry walls that were inherently able to stand higher and longer without relying on restraint from floors or roof. Walls at right angles to each other provided mutual buttressing. (Hence the survival of the walls of numerous fire-gutted or otherwise floorless ruined buildings of these types, unmolested by wind.) However, no doubt prompted by unfortunate experiences, **wall plates** – also known as pattress plates – began to appear on walls, tied back to the floor or the roof timbers by wrought iron tie rods. The plates themselves were originally of wrought iron, and later also of cast iron. A variety of shapes were used, not just circular; the aim in each case was to 'grab' a reasonably large area of masonry so that the plate was not pulled through the wall if further movement tried to occur.

Sometimes these plates appear regularly spaced at each floor level, suggesting that they were built in at the time of construction. Ad hoc occasional plates, plates at irregular spacing, or plates of more than one design all suggest later repairs.

Plates still offer one option for stabilising walls against further out-of-plane movement, and a variety of designs are available, nowadays mainly in cast iron or stainless steel. A more discreet solution, where practical, is to drill and install one or more resin anchors in the inside face of the wall at each restraint point; the anchors are attached to a steel tie that is in turn fixed to the floor construction.

Rubble-filled stone walls

Stone walls were commonly built with attention focused on the faces that would be seen. Ashlar work was dressed and coursed, but it was uncommon to course the entire thickness of the wall. The internal wall face was usually of brick or rubble with, effectively, an unbonded central cavity. Rubble stonework has a similar cross section, with some – but often not many – through-bonding stones intended to tie the two leaves together across the cavity. This was filled, more or less, with broken stone, dust and surplus mortar, which, over time and aggravated by water penetration and frost action, fragments and 'slumps' downwards, causing outward pressure on the leaves, which can then bulge outwards. Remedial treatments for this are discussed in Chapter 8.

Lack of wall bonding

It was common, particularly in the nineteenth century and in cheaper domestic construction, for party walls to be built ahead of front and rear walls. The party walls, which would then be plastered, often used lower-quality bricks which were likely to be of more irregular shape than the better quality bricks for the front elevation. As a result, it was difficult to successfully bond the walls together, and they would then be left discontinuous, with what were in effect movement joints at the corners; movements would tend to aggregate there, leading to torn wallpaper and other disruption. Structurally, the lack of wall bonding means an absence of lateral restraint similar to that described above for floors. This may lead to lateral movement, requiring remedial measures such as U-shaped stainless steel wire with turned-in ends, which can be inserted through holes drilled in the external wall bed joints and set into raked-out joints in the party wall.

Similar lack of bonding frequently occurs at the junction between the back wall and the semi-detached smaller back extensions that were very characteristic of urban terraced houses in the later nineteenth and early twentieth centuries. Leaving the back extensions down while the main houses were built allowed the builder to store construction materials in the back yards, but again resulted in unbonded wall junctions.

Twentieth-century construction

From the above it might be concluded that the nineteenth century was a time when bad practice thrived, to be swept away by the wisdom of the twentieth-century builder. Regrettably, this is not entirely true!

For example, the urge to build more decent housing economically, and to ensure that housing did not suffer the appalling dampness that caused such ill health in slums, both encouraged the wider adoption of the cavity wall in preference to the one-brick-thick solid wall which is generally now accepted as not weatherproof without additional treatment. This was typically a half-brick-thick external leaf of facing bricks or pebble-dashed common bricks, linked by galvanised wire ties to an inner leaf of half-brick-thick common bricks, later replaced by concrete blockwork which has become increasingly light in weight as thermal insulation requirements for walls have become more onerous.

The result has been relatively more 'flimsy' wall construction, which is more dependent for stability against buckling on the ties connecting the two leaves and on adequate lateral restraint from floors and roofs. Galvanising has not always proved of adequate thickness to prevent corrosion of the wall ties, and stainless steel is nowadays used for preference, while building regulations and codes of practice now highlight the need for 'engineered' lateral restraint to be provided between walls, floors and roof. The installation of 'remedial' wall ties, typically of stainless steel and drilled in from one face before being resin-fixed or secured by expanding action, has become an established part of the remedial works business.

Similarly, the introduction in recent decades of factory-produced trussed timber roof rafters demonstrated the need for conscious restraint to prevent them 'slopping' over sideways during or after construction. Before these were developed, most roofs were purpose-built after the walls were complete, with each member being cut to size and support being taken off both internal and external walls.

The trussed rafter was designed to span clear across the building between external walls, before the internal walls were necessarily built. Joints were formed with galvanised steel plates out of which spikes had been pressed at 90°, the plates then being pressed against the timber members on both sides. Rafters were intended to be placed at the same close spacings as the traditional common rafter to receive tiling battens, so with the relatively modest loadings on each it was possible to produce adequately strong rafters with quite thin timbers.

Unfortunately, these large slender assemblies could distort while being handled, and once in place were liable to rack sideways, distorting the roof unless adequately stiff diagonal bracing was fitted on the sloping roof faces to restrain the rafters. This was fairly obvious with hindsight, but the need for bracing was not always conveyed to those working with the rafters on site.[7]

This review has concentrated on deficiencies in mainly 'traditional' construction using timber and masonry, and in general twentieth-century structures of steel or reinforced concrete have inherent robustness and resistance to movement. However, the major rehousing programme of the 1950s and 1960s led to the wide adoption of precast concrete panel construction, a form previously little used in Britain, and the notorious 1968 partial collapse of Ronan Point, a block of flats in East London, triggered by a gas explosion revealed a lack of robustness in the panel system (see Chapter 11).

As time passes, what is still seen as recent construction may well be listed, and its informed conservation will require awareness of such problems.

Material decay or deterioration

In extremis, **timber decay** can lead to collapse, but local disruption is more likely. A common problem is decay of bonding timbers, which were used in brickwork mostly in the eighteenth and nineteenth centuries. They were seen as helping to tie the building together[8] and found wide use in multi-storey dock warehouses and other large buildings. In external walls the timbers, almost invariably of softwood, could rot from the outside in. If the bonding timbers were central in the wall the decay might cause no symptoms, but if – as was more common – the timbers were on the inside face, the wall could bow outwards (Figure 7.6). The remedy is to cut out the timber in short lengths and piece in bricks to replace it. (As with many building distortions, it is seldom possible to reverse the movement and 'straighten' the wall.)

Sulphate attack on brick mortar is caused by sulphates in the bricks which are leached into the mortar by rainwater. The sulphates react with the cement constituents, forming a product of greater volume. If movement can take place freely then the brickwork expands: a common example of this is the chimney stack, which leans like a banana away from the prevailing wind (usually from the south-west). If movement cannot take place freely then the mortar may fracture internally; this problem also occurs

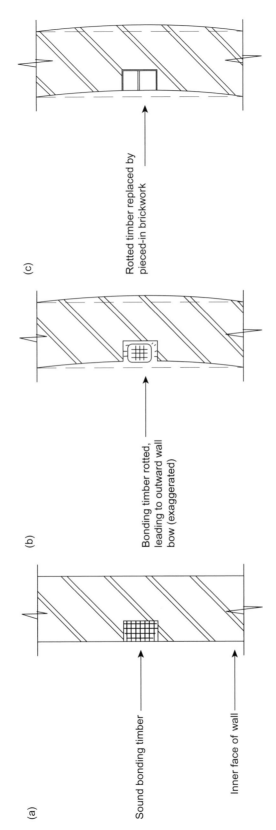

(a)

(c)

(b)

Rotted timber replaced by
pieced-in brickwork

Bonding timber rotted,
leading to outward wall
bow (exaggerated)

Sound bonding timber

Inner face of wall

Figure 7.6 (a) Sound bonding timber in external brick wall; (b) timber later rots, leading to bowing of wall; (c) rotted timber replaced by pieced-in bricks.

commonly in concrete foundations where the soil or groundwater contains sulphates and sulphate-resisting cement has not been used. The 'banana' chimney stack can usually be rebuilt using the original bricks, as the sulphate attack debonds the mortar from the bricks![9]

Alkali-aggregate reaction in concrete occurs when some silica aggregates react with cement to form an expansive gel. This results in 'popping' of surface concrete and distinctive 'map-cracking'; it develops most rapidly under conditions of alternate wetting and drying, and disfigures externally exposed concrete. It can require reconstruction or over-cladding.[10]

Corrosion (rusting) of iron and steel, of embedded steel sections or reinforcement, is triggered by water penetration onto inadequately protected metal, sometimes aggravated by chemical attack. It usually occurs in the external walls or roof, although it can also occur in damp, wet or aggressive internal environments (for example, over swimming pools or in a chemical plant). Rust is some five to ten times greater in volume than the original steel, and consequently can displace the masonry or concrete in which it is contained. The resulting movement, visible on the surface, is often the primary evidence of problems beneath.[11,12]

In riveted wrought iron and steel structures, local corrosion from water trapped at rivets or at overlaps between members can cause 'prying' apart of the metal and joint failure. This is a particularly common problem on seaside piers and other marine structures. Treatment of such corrosion can be expensive and may involve alterations to appearance, particularly in masonry-clad steel-framed buildings and on exposed architectural concrete surfaces.

It was recognised that iron and, later, steel ties in cavity walls needed to be protected against corrosion as the outer leaf was expected to be damp – a fundamental consideration to be acknowledged in cavity wall detailing. Originally, wrought iron ties were heated and plunged into linseed oil. Later, steel ties were galvanised. However, the zinc coating was often not thick enough to assure protection, especially if the brick mortar contained ash or other sulphate-bearing material so that acid attack augmented the corrosion by moisture. Nowadays, it is common practice to specify stainless steel for ties.

If corrosion reaches a point where ties become ineffective then the mutual stiffening afforded by the two leaves of the wall is lost, and they can bow or buckle as a result of the resulting slenderness.

Supplementary consequences, including decay of timber and corrosion of iron or steel tie rods, can result in **loss of restraint** to other members (see above).

Alterations or misuse

It is a rare building that has not been altered during its working life. All too often the alterations were conceived or implemented in ignorance of the consequences, or without adequate investigation. In addition, the building's occupants and users may subject it to uses – or rather abuses – that are beyond its capacity to accommodate without distress. It is therefore important when investigating the causes of movement to consider the possibility of such interventions and their consequences. Some examples indicate the range of ill-informed alteration and abuse.

Central heating pipework

Even with modern small-bore pipework (typically of 20 mm diameter) it is regrettably common – in the absence of clear instructions to be more judicious – for notches of up to 100 mm square to be cut in the joists for the pipe to cross them at right-angles. As the bending strength of a joist is proportional to the square of its depth, a 100 mm deep notch cut out of a 150 mm deep joist reduces its bending strength to $(150 - 100)^2/150^2 =$ one-ninth of the full section. If these notches were cut at or near midspan, the floor would almost certainly collapse; as heating pipes are normally run near to walls, the damage may be limited to increased deflection of the floor with possible cracking in the plaster ceiling below.

Forming new openings in trussed timber partitions

Many older houses have internal walls that are actually trussed timber partitions which support both the floor above *and* the floor below. This is very common in Georgian and Victorian terraced houses, in which the ground and first floors comprise large rooms (such as saloon and dining room) above which are smaller bedrooms. The trussed partition offered a neat solution to the structural problems of supporting floors spanning over larger spaces below. Horizontal timber beams above and below the partition are combined with diagonal studs framed into the orthodox vertical studs. Original door openings could be framed with additional diagonal studs over the opening. However, such houses are seen as all too readily adaptable for offices or professional use, and additional doors may be needed. Uninformed cutting-out of plaster and studs for a new opening may destroy the trussing action, and cause collapse.

Sometimes collapse is postponed. Removing the 'tired' lath-and-plaster either side of a partition in an attic resulted in both it and the attic floor gently disappearing into the rooms below. A later doorway had been cut into the partition, and apparently the plaster was all that held up the mutilated timberwork, thanks to its shear strength!

Overloading a floor

A Georgian town-house was taken over by a small local newspaper as its offices and printworks. Although the heavy printing press was, wisely, located at ground level, a first floor room was allocated for storing copies of the paper. Paper, although light when in sheets, is heavy in bulk. Investigation of the building, by now reconverted to a ground floor shop with a disused first floor, showed that the timber first floor had a permanent sag of some 150 mm over a span of some 3 metres. The sustained loading from stored volumes of the newspaper had caused creep deflection of the timber joists but no actual fractures. (The cheapest remedial solution, and also the most appropriate in conservation terms, would be to retain the floor as found and fix shaped timber packing over the joists to receive a new level timber board floor.)

Removal of a loadbearing wall or column

It is perhaps hard to understand how such elements as a loadbearing wall or column can be casually removed, but occupants do not always seek informed advice before opening up larger spaces! Assuming that local collapse is not triggered, a conspicuous sag in the ceiling may well result, with corresponding distortion in floors, walls and door openings above. The survival of a building after such violent alteration is reassuring proof of the adage that 'structures only fall down when they have exhausted all possible ways of standing up'.

Addition of one or more floors

It is likewise not unknown for floors to be added to a building without informed advice. Clearly, it will increase load on the structure below, including the foundations, and this is likely to produce conspicuous movement. In recent years there have been several fatal collapses of buildings in the Middle and Far East attributed to such unauthorised intervention; it has happened in the UK, too, in the past.

Excavation under or near an existing building

Excavation nearby can disturb the stability of the foundations. At worst, this can be disastrous. Some years ago a house collapsed, fortunately without casualties, when its owner had nearly completed the excavation for an intended basement extending over the plan area of the house right out to the inside face of the external walls. No application for building regulations approval had been made, and no shoring had been provided. Unsurprisingly, the external wall foundations duly slid into the hole, happily with no casualties.

Several cases have occurred where trenches for adjacent wall foundations have been dug parallel and close to an existing gable wall. The loss of lateral restraint to the soil below the gable wall foundation led to gross movement of the foundation and collapse of the wall, together with severe damage to adjacent parts of the building.

In less severe cases, excavations near existing foundations can cause visible movements. Hume (Chapter 8) rightly warns of the risk of movement arising from ill-considered excavation of trenches to assist ground drainage near damp walls.

Investigation, diagnosis and treatment of movement

These topics are covered in greater detail in other chapters, and key points are noted here by way of introduction.

It has been well said that investigation and diagnosis of structural movements and defects require three things – two open eyes and one open mind.[13] The building is the primary source of information, supplemented by available documentation; both of these must be thoroughly studied before causes can be reliably diagnosed.

Buildings can be subject to cyclical movements on a daily and seasonal basis. During the day the temperature varies, so that any point will move, if only by a small amount. This is particularly the case in taller structures, which move in response to air temperature and radiant sunlight. Precision monitoring of a target point on the building position may show relative lateral movements of several millimetres at different times of day solely as a result of temperature variations, so it is important to record the time of each reading. (The 'zig-zag' readings in Figure 7.7 represent the variations

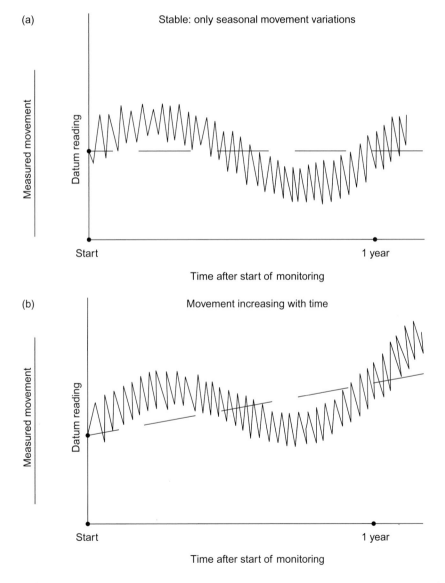

(a)   Stable: only seasonal movement variations

Measured movement

Datum reading

Start   1 year

Time after start of monitoring

(b)   Movement increasing with time

Measured movement

Datum reading

Start   1 year

Time after start of monitoring

Figure 7.7 Monitoring of movements: (a) recording seasonal variations but no trend of increased movement overall; (b) showing a trend of increasing movement overlaid on seasonal variations.

in recorded movement arising from day-to-day temperature changes as well as possible minor reading errors.)

Likewise, atmospheric temperature and humidity and ground moisture content all vary over the year. So if movement is being monitored (and provided, of course, that the building does not move so much in the interim as to demand immediate action), it is desirable to take regular readings for at least a year.

Figure 7.7 shows two plots of movement taken over a year. It can be seen that the movements follow a cyclical trend (Figure 7.7a), indicating that there is no underlying structural movement occurring. In Figure 7.7b, however, it is clear that there is ongoing movement not attributable to temperature or moisture variations.

Monitoring can include measurement of levels, out-of-plane movement, plumbness and crack width. The means used can range from simple to 'hi-tech'.[14] Regular monitoring will show not only whether movement is taking place, but whether it is continuing and at what pace. This will all help to inform the diagnosis and remedial proposals.

Diagnosis

It should be borne in mind that movement can result from more than one cause, with damage such as cracking forming more than one pattern. There must be confidence that the right diagnosis has been made, based on adequate information. It would, for example, be embarrassing, and worse, to spend money underpinning one part of a building believed to be suffering from subsidence, only to find that the other part carries on rising as a consequence of heave due to removal of nearby trees!

Repair of movement damage

The need for repair must be established first. Typically, there are three principal reasons for carrying out remedial treatment:

- To restore structural adequacy – this ensures safety and is not negotiable.
- To restore serviceability such as weathertightness – this is usually necessary.
- To restore appearance – the need for this is debatable.

Repair or other remedial treatment, if required, should follow conservation principles and be sympathetic to the existing construction. Treatment to restore appearance should be considered, bearing in mind that, unless very carefully executed, it may well be more unsightly than the damage. A classic example of this is the clumsy 'filling' of cracks with mortar, which highlights rather than conceals their presence. Filling of cracks with hard mortar may also transfer problems elsewhere; once a crack has formed it can act as an (unintended) movement joint, possibly relieving other areas from damage.

Another unwelcome intervention is the cutting of vertical movement joints in existing masonry, usually accompanied by their sealing with mastic; however, this may offer a way of controlling the 'bookend' effect (see above) in a terrace of masonry buildings that is less disruptive than providing bracing to stabilise the terrace ends.

Further reading

This is a short personal selection only, from an extensive literature.

Alexander, S.J. and Lawson, R.M., *Design for Movement in Buildings*, Technical Note 107 (CIRIA, London, 1981).
Building Research Establishment, *Estimation of Thermal and Moisture Movements and Stresses: Parts 1–3*, Digests 227–9 (HMSO, London, 1979).
Building Research Establishment Information Papers (various and numerous).
Concrete Society, *Non-structural Cracks in Concrete*, 3rd edn, Technical Report No. 22 (Concrete Society, Slough, 1992).
Construction Industry Research & Information Association, *Movement and Cracking in Long Masonry Walls*, Special Publication 044 (CIRIA, London, 1986).
Richardson, C., *AJ Guide to Structural Surveys* (Architectural Press, London, 1986).

Endnotes

1   C. Richardson, and A.G. Messenger, 'The "bookend" effect', *Structural Engineer*, **78**, 13 (2000), 19–27 and discussion **79**, 13 (2001) 30–32.
2   British Standards Institution, BS 5628-3: 2005 *Code of Practice for the Use of Masonry: Materials and Components, Design and Workmanship* (BSI, London, 2005).
3   Building Research Establishment Digest 228, *Estimation of Thermal and Moisture Movements and Stresses: Part 2* (HMSO, London, 1979).
4   Concrete Society, Technical Report No. 22, *Non-structural Cracks in Concrete*, 3rd edn (Concrete Society, Slough, 1992).
5   P. Ross, *Appraisal and Repair of Timber Structures* (Thomas Telford, London, 2002), p. 39.
6   *Ibid.*, pp. 198–210.
7   British Standards Institution, BS 5628-3: 1998 *Structural Use of Timber: Code of Practice for Trussed Rafter Roofs* (BSI, London, 1998).
8   S. Johnston, 'Bonding timbers in old brickwork', *Structural Survey*, **10**, 4 (1992), 355–62.
9   Building Research Establishment Good Repair Guide 15, *Repairing Chimneys and Parapets* (Construction Research Communications, London, 1998).
10 Institution of Structural Engineers, *Structural Effects of Alkali-Silica Reaction: Technical Guidance on the Appraisal of Existing Structures* (ISE, London, 1992).
11 P. Gibbs, *Corrosion in Masonry clad Early 20th century Steel framed Buildings* (Historic Scotland, Edinburgh, 2000).
12 P. Pullar-Strecker, (ed.), *Concrete Reinforcement Corrosion: From Assessment to Repair Decisions* (Thomas Telford, London, 2002).
13 P. Beckmann, and R. Bowles, *Structural Aspects of Building Conservation*, 2nd edn (Butterworth-Heinemann, London, 2004), p. 44.
14 Building Research Establishment Digests 343–4: *Simple Measuring and Monitoring of Movement in Low-rise Buildings: Part 1 – Cracks; Part 2 – Settlement, Heave and Out-of-plumb* (BRE, Watford, 1989).

8 Repairs to historic structures

Ian Hume

Traditional versus modern repair methods

Ideally repairs should be carried out using traditional methods and the same materials that were used in the original structure. However, sometimes this results in an unacceptably high degree of loss of fabric and other methods have to be sought. Modern materials, where they have a proven life span and well-known behavioural patterns, may prove to be equally, sometimes more, valuable. For example, the selective use of resins can be effective in making hidden or unobtrusive fixings and for the repair of decayed timbers with valuable mouldings. This chapter looks at the pros and cons of traditional and more modern repair methods.

Repairs and strengthening work should be executed honestly, with no attempt at disguise or artificial ageing, but should equally not be obtrusive. All solutions should, if possible, be reversible; that is to say, they should be capable of being taken out if there is no more need for their continued existence or if a better solution can be derived in the future. It is often felt necessary to ensure that repairs are easily dateable by an interested party, but it is good if they fit generally with the character of the structure so as not to stand out. Repairs, particularly in structural voids and in agricultural or utilitarian situations, need not be invisible but should always be in sympathy with the original fabric of the structure.

Timber repairs

Problems with timber fall into two basic categories:

- local decay due to fungal or beetle attack
- lack of strength due to decay, original use of undersized members or change of use demanding greater strength than is available

Additionally, earlier and inadvisable changes (either deliberate or accidental) sometimes create weaknesses that have to be addressed.

Ideally, of course, one should seek ways of avoiding repair altogether by looking closely at the stress and deflection limits used. The type and quality of the timber are other matters for careful consideration. It is clear that many old timbers are stronger than their modern counterparts, that higher permissible stresses may be used and that a higher value for the modulus of elasticity would reduce calculated deflections. Old, softer and more flexible finishes might allow the deflections permitted by the codes of practice to be exceeded with safety, and where there are no ceilings below, these deflections may be exceeded even further without distress.

The structure must be examined for signs of distress or lack thereof as this will give important clues as to the need or otherwise for repair. The usual questions must be asked. Has the structure moved? Has it moved recently? Is it currently 'live'? What is the rate of movement? How much more movement can it accommodate before repairs are needed? Consideration should be given to load testing to prove the structural adequacy of something that cannot be justified by calculation. However, in spite of such preliminary work, repairs to many structures are necessary for the survival of the structure as a whole.

There are several levels of repair and the first step is to consider additions to the structure that do not involve removing anything or damaging it in any way. Items such as steel brackets and additional joists fall into this category, but these often need to be hidden or at least to be visually unobtrusive.

The next level of repair to be considered is work which causes minimal damage but which does not destroy significant amounts of historic fabric, such as inserted flitch plates and bolts to repair splits. It is quite feasible to strengthen and stiffen timber beams to a marked degree by flitching (that is, cutting a vertical slot in the centre of the beam and dropping a steel plate or a number of steel reinforcing bars into this slot). When bolted together or resin-bonded in position, the beam becomes composite steel and timber and will be significantly stronger than the plain unassisted timber. If the beam supports a ceiling, it is possible to cut a slot that does not penetrate the full depth of the timber beam but stops perhaps 30 mm short. Slots can be cut by drilling a series of pilot holes, then cutting out the slot with a chainsaw using a guide to ensure a straight cut.

Further down the road of undesirability is the addition of steels to the sides of beams to strengthen them, which would involve cutting off all the tenons of the floor joists; again, this is sometimes necessary to save more important parts of the structure. Yet another alternative may be to glue timber or fix steel plates on the top and bottom of the timber beam, but if there is an important ceiling below this method is not practicable. Sheets of plywood screwed to floor joists stiffen up a springy floor without doing any damage to the historical integrity of the building.

Clearly there are times when the internal structure of a building is totally beyond redemption owing to massive dry rot attack, fire or whatever, and significant rebuilding may be called for.

There are no hard-and-fast rules for the repair of structures, and the idea that this or that type of repair is always suitable for some specific task is not sensible. The use of resins is acceptable but must be considered very carefully. The evidence to date is that resins have a long life, but in historic building terms, measured in hundreds of years, the life of a resin repair may not be adequate.

Walls

Walls can suffer from a multitude of problems. They are constructed from different types of materials and the problems can vary from material to material, although there are a number of common problems such as

- ground and/or foundation problems, settlement, heave, undermining, trees
- thermal effects
- lack of tying of walls to other elements such as floors
- lack of tying between internal and external skins
- structural movement due to matters such as roof spread, vibration or impact

The **pointing** of a wall is its first line of defence. If this is weak, the integrity of the wall is threatened: the mortar between the stones or bricks will be softened and eroded, the stone or brick will be vulnerable to attack by water, and frost damage will occur. The mix to be used for the repointing is all-important, a very hard pointing often doing more harm than good. The style of the pointing is vital, as the wrong style can change the character of the building beyond recognition. The repointing must begin with the removal of the existing pointing to an adequate depth. Pointing should be removed only where it is decayed, and left intact where it is sound; the resulting recess must be clean and the new pointing inserted correctly. It is a skilled and time-consuming task, like so much of the work related to ancient monuments. An extension of pointing is the resetting of loose masonry. Loose masonry can be dangerous, and it encourages the ingress of water and plant growth.

Small improvements on a reasonably satisfactory structure push its factor of safety up. For example, pattress plates and tie rods can ensure that a wall which is distorted moves no further by fixing it to the diaphragm action of the floors.

Where facades are parting company from party walls reinforced concrete stitches were often inserted to tie them together, but these stitches are of a very different material from the walls and can sometimes lead to problems. A better solution might be to install drilled-in anchors. Resin-fixed ties in a herringbone pattern can be also be used to tie a facade wall to a floor, thus fixing the wall securely to the diaphragm action of the floors. The traditional way of dealing with bulging walls is to insert ties drilled through the wall to terminate in pattress plates on the facade. On aesthetic grounds this is not always to be recommended, but it can often be quite acceptable.

Victorian brick walls are often constructed in two skins. The outer skin might be built with large numbers of snap headers to give the appearance of a thicker bonded wall but is in fact more or less unbonded. There are simple means of anchoring this external skin to the internal skin in the manner of remedial wall ties.

Medieval (and other) walls are generally constructed of two skins of masonry to form the external and internal faces of the wall, with the gap between filled, more or less solidly, with rubble and mortar. This rubble core can settle over the years, causing one or both of the faces of the wall to bulge. Settling of the core can be due to water ingress, foundation movement or vibration. Where this has happened the two skins begin to separate. The installation of drilled-in, resin-fixed **anchors** can offer a solution. These anchors can either be a simple stainless steel ribbed or threaded bar or a helically twisted flat bar, cementitiously or resin-grouted in position. A patented system of a stainless steel bar or tube encased in a sock to prevent loss of grout into voids in the wall can also be used. Expanding anchors should not be used as the expansion will almost certainly split the material into which they are being fixed. All anchors must be made from stainless steel.

Where the rubble core has settled, a masonry wall or column may contain a considerable percentage of voids. Sometimes this is acceptable, but frequently it is decided that these voids are risking the structural integrity of the structure by weakening the masonry or by allowing water to seep in. The strength of the wall can be greatly increased by **grouting** – that is, feeding into the wall quantities of liquid mortar. The mix for the grout must be appropriate to the conditions, and the amount fed in at any one time must be carefully controlled to avoid the risk of the pressure of the liquid grout bursting the wall. The grout used is almost always cementitious, using only a very small amount of cement, if any. On very rare occasions a resin grout may be used in small quantities. A gravity feed system is usually used, and pressure grouting should generally be avoided as there will be a risk of blowing off the face unless the pressure is very low and very carefully controlled.

Grouting fails one of the principles of conservation: it is not reversible – once in, it is there forever. This makes choosing the right grout mix critical. Like any material used in the consolidation of a monument, its strength should not vary greatly from that of the original material. A masonry wall is essentially of a flexible construction: grouting with a strong material is not necessary and can be detrimental.

Fabric consolidation of ancient monuments

In addition to the considerations of pointing, grouting and underpinning discussed above, ancient monuments have some particular considerations. By their very nature as buildings which have been deliberately destroyed – for example, at the Dissolution of the Monasteries, during the Civil War, or simply by being quarried for their useful building materials – some ancient monuments may have dangerous overhangs or precariously leaning walls. In such cases, **additional support** is sometimes needed to ensure the long life of the remains. This is always problematical, and a variety of techniques are available. Sometimes it is possible to build up a support in corework (rough racking). Sometimes a sympathetic, but out-of-character support in, say, stainless steel is acceptable. If reconstruction is a possibility, is there sufficient evidence of what previously existed? Extra support, if it begins at ground level, will need a new foundation. This means an excavation either by, or under the supervision of, an archaeologist.

Either as a result of their deliberate destruction or as a result of more recent natural events, ancient monuments can suffer **cracking**. Sometimes their piecemeal building programme has resulted in **straight joints** between adjacent sections. It must be said that if these planes of weakness have been in existence for a long period then the need for repairs should be closely questioned. If there is doubt, it will be helpful to install simple but accurate structural monitoring. However, sometimes a need is established and it is decided to improve the connection across the discontinuity. This can result in the use of steel (always stainless) or reinforced concrete, again preferably with stainless steel reinforcement. Such ties should be buried in the wall and refaced using the original material. It is important to record all repairs, particularly hidden ones. Opening up an unsafe area of a structure to carry out a repair only to discover that the repair has already been done is not a unique experience!

Modern drilling techniques have made possible the installation of **long tie bars** through the length of a wall. It is possible to drill in excess of 10 metres through relatively thin walls (500 mm or less) in order to install stainless steel tie bars. The bars are typically 25 mm square or in diameter. A recently developed technique involves a hollow tie bar covered in a fabric sock being inserted into the hole. Grout is pumped into the tube, emerging eventually into the sock, which prevents the bonding grout from being lost into voids in the wall. The ends of the tie bar can be anchored to a pattress plate or to some hidden fixing, thus tying the structure together most effectively while still maintaining its flexibility.

The use of steelwork in historic building repairs

It is often necessary to incorporate structural steelwork as strengthening and/or as a repair method in historic buildings, for example where beam ends have rotted, earlier alterations have been done unwisely, floors have to be strengthened owing to either weakness or the need to carry an increased load, or where decay or movement has caused a weakness.

It is not proposed to suggest here any particular details, as repairs to historic structures usually have to be designed for each individual case. However, there are some general guidelines.

Mild steel or stainless steel?

As repairs to historic structures are almost always intended to be long-term solutions to particular problems, using a material with a limited life is not ideal. Mild steel will corrode whereas stainless steel will not. The requirement for long life demands the use of stainless steel, though limited financial resources sometimes preclude this.

It is suggested that where steel is to be totally buried in a wall, or where ends of steel members are to be supported in an external wall that may allow the passage of damp or where the steelwork is to be exposed to the weather, stainless steel should always be used. However, if the steelwork is in a dry environment, particularly where it is easily accessible, such as in a roof space, or accessible but only with difficulty, as in a floor structure, then mild steel is an acceptable alternative. Mild steel can be galvanised (at some cost) but at least should always be painted with a good protective system.

It might seem that putting a stainless steel end on a mild steel beam could be a solution to some of these problems. However, corrosion problems sometimes arise (owing to electrolytic action) where mild steel and stainless steel are in contact, and this has to be avoided.

Installing structural steelwork

It must be remembered that very often steelwork will be required in large sections and/or long lengths and therefore will be very heavy. This is not a problem in new works where cranes are often available. When dealing with historic building repairs, the difficulties are compounded by limited access and the fact that materials have to be manhandled. Also, installing a new beam presents problems as the beam, which may have to sit in pockets in the walls, is of necessity longer than the gap between the walls. These problems often demand the use of splices and joints, which have to be carefully designed.

Active versus passive repairs

It is usually advisable to design strengthening systems and repair methods to historic buildings as being active rather than passive. It is often helpful if the newly installed repair/strengthening system takes up load immediately (active repair) rather than waiting (passively) either for further movement to take place or for the repair/strengthening system to move a little before it takes up load. This may demand that the repair/strengthening system be jacked or pre-loaded in some way. It will also demand that care be taken to ensure that the repair does not need to move itself to a significant degree before carrying load. This may mean that slightly larger sections need to be used so as to reduce deflection on long spans. It is important that slip at splices and joints be avoided wherever possible.

Slip at splices and joints

One way of ensuring that splices and joints do not slip would be to site-weld the connections. However, there are very few historic structures

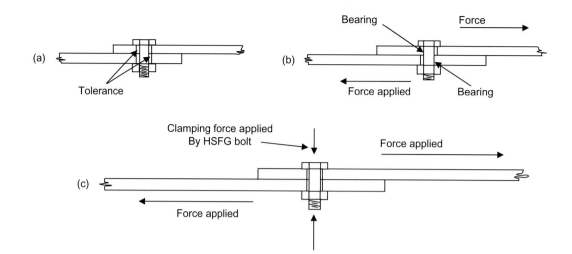

Figure 8.1 (a) The bolted connection before loading; (b) the bolted connection after loading; (c) how a high-strength friction grip bolt works.

where site-welding could be permitted even under the most stringent of controls. The fire risk is just too great. As welding is not a practical proposition in most cases, bolts have to be used.

Unless the load is along the length of a bolt, bolts usually work in shear. Holes are drilled through the metal to be connected and the bolt or bolts inserted and tightened. The holes have to be slightly oversize so that the bolts can be fitted without difficulty (Figure 8.1a). When the joint takes up load, it slips so that the sides of the holes bear on the bolts (Figure 8.1b). This slip allows the joint to move, and the repair deflects or moves slightly in some way. In some cases, such as long-span beams, this movement can be significant, thus demanding that the part of the structure has also to move before it can be carried by the repair/strengthening.

High-strength friction grip (HSFG) bolts work in a different way. They are used to clamp the metal together very much in the fashion that a carpenter's 'G' cramp is used to clamp pieces of wood together (Figure 8.1c). HSFG bolts are just as easy to install as normal bolts but the meeting faces of the metal to be joined must not be painted; neither must the ring around the bolt holes where the washers will bear. HSFG bolts also have to be tightened to a specified torque using a torque wrench. Some HSFG bolts have load-indicating washers that show, by various means, when the specified torque has been applied with a normal spanner.

Underpinning

Underpinning a building is expensive, but it may be vital to its long-term future. Without underpinning, the building may continue to settle and eventually collapse. There are times when there is no alternative. However, underpinning is often unjustified and a waste of time and money, and it can result in a great deal of disturbance to the historic fabric and destruction of the archaeology on which the building sits.

There are several **methods** of underpinning. It can be carried out in traditional fashion by excavating beneath the foundations and filling the cavity with concrete or with piles – sometimes large diameter, sometimes so-called 'mini-piles'. In some cases, post-tensioning a reinforced concrete ring around the base of the walls can result in less intervention into the historic fabric of a structure.

It is essential to examine the structure carefully, to study its problems in depth, and to investigate its structural history and surroundings. It is equally important to establish a good, accurate monitoring system and to keep good records, to ensure that drainage is working efficiently and that water is being drained away from the structure adequately. Finally, it is necessary to carry out a thorough ground investigation. If all this is done and if the monitoring shows significant movements, it may be necessary to underpin the building. In most cases this will not be necessary.

French drains

A French drain is a trench that has a land drain installed at the bottom and has been backfilled with shingle or similar coarse stone. Modern techniques include lining the sides of the drain with a geotextile filter membrane that will stop the transmission of fines into the French drain (Figure 8.2). The

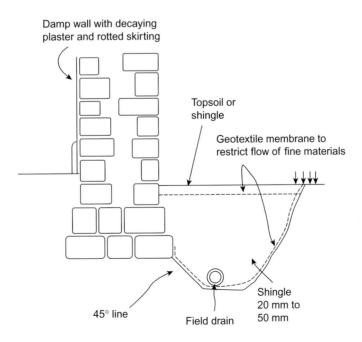

Figure 8.2 French drain. Excavation must not go beneath the wall or encroach within a 45° line from the base of the wall.

147

purpose of such a drain is to change the pattern of drainage in a certain area. French drains may be used in fields and other open spaces, but this discussion relates to their use close to buildings.

Similar to French drains are 'dry areas'. These may be open trenches around a building with or without drainage, or may be similar in construction to French drains but without a land drain installed at the bottom. Unless built with a drainage system, they will not disperse water but will allow moisture to evaporate from the base of a wall. Dry areas may serve to collect water, particularly if the ground is not free-draining, and may well cause more problems than they solve.

Problems are often caused by bad drainage. Blocked drains and broken gutters or downpipes can all cause excessive wetting of the ground with associated risks of subsidence. Efficient rainwater disposal methods and good below-ground drainage, regularly inspected and running to a soakaway or main drains, are important.

Why might a French drain be needed?

The usual reason for installing a French drain is to ease the situation where damp problems exist within the body of an external wall. This usually shows itself as rising damp which can result in damp and decaying plaster within a building and damp and decaying stonework or brickwork externally. Panelling may become damp and rotted. Quite clearly, damp problems should not be allowed to persist. Other means of controlling the damp problem, such as the insertion of a damp-proof course (preferably not involving chemicals), might be considered in preference to the installation of a French drain, but often these have their own problems. These problems have been written about elsewhere.

Before any other remedial measures are attempted, it should always be ascertained that both the roof drainage and existing below-ground drainage are working properly. Advice in assessing the cause of the damp problem and the suitability of any proposed solutions should always be sought from an experienced professional.

Dangers

There are inherent dangers in the use of French drains and dry areas in that they may change the flow of water, not always to the best advantage. The ground may dry out excessively, and while this may perhaps relieve any rising damp problems it can create problems of settlement of the building.

Most importantly, it must be ensured that the excavation for the French drain or dry area does not undermine the foundations of the wall that it is intended to help. As noted above, foundations of historic buildings do not always go very deep. Often, particularly in the case of mediaeval buildings, the walls are founded only about 150 mm below the existing ground level. In this case the French drain/dry area will have to be constructed at some distance (say, one metre) from the wall so as to avoid undermining the foundation. Its effect on any rising damp may therefore be limited.

Excavation for the French drain will take away the horizontal resistance to outward wall movement. This may be critical if the wall is fragile and has a tendency to bulge sideways. The backfilling to the trench will have to be well compacted so as to avoid settling of the fill with consequent movement of the ground and structures adjacent to it. It is best to compact each 150 mm of fill before the next layer is put in.

Precautions

It is always wise to carry out some trial excavations before deciding on the installation of French drains/dry areas in order to ascertain the bottom of the foundations, the existence of anything buried, such as graves or archaeology, and the type of ground. It may well be necessary to seek listed building or scheduled monument consent before carrying out excavations of any sort.

If the ground is already of a free-draining type, little may be gained by inserting French drains or dry areas; however, if the ground is of a clay type then benefit may be expected.

The top of the French drain can be backfilled with topsoil (over a further layer of geotextile membrane), left with the coarse material exposed, or covered with an open channel that will collect and disperse surface water. Such channels are prone to leaking and thereby concentrating the water in one spot if they are not properly and constantly maintained.

The installation

As with all drains, French drains need to be maintained regularly. Therefore the land drains must be laid to good falls, and must ensure that any water they collect is taken well away from the building and fed either to a main drainage system, to a specially constructed soakaway or to a nearby watercourse. Again, as with all drains there must be a generous supply of rodding eyes to facilitate access should the system become blocked, and there should be access points at all changes of direction.

The alternative of digging a trench and leaving it unfilled (a dry area) may result in its filling with water and debris, and the situation will be exacerbated rather than relieved. Such a system should be drained.

The use of drainage composites might also be considered. These are prefabricated sheet materials and use a three-dimensional core made from modern, long-lasting, plastics with a geotextile filter membrane fixed to the surface. These are fixed to the wall surface below ground level. Any water moving towards the building passes through the filter membrane, runs down the three-dimensional core into a drain and is piped away from the building. Specialist advice on the use and installation of these materials should be sought.

Conclusion

It may be considered that having no drainage system at all is better than having a badly neglected one, as blocked drains can often concentrate water into one localised spot rather than allowing the water to distribute itself more evenly around the building. It is usually concentrations of water that cause problems. However, if there are no other options to the solution of a damp problem and it is felt that any new drainage installation can be properly maintained, French drains may well be at least a partial solution.

Further reading

The Building Research Establishment (BRE) publish a great deal of useful information on building problems and building repair.

Ashurst, John and Nicola, *Practical Building Conservation*, vols 1–5 (Gower, Aldershot, c.1988).

Beckmann, Poul, *Structural Aspects of Building Conservation* (Butterworth-Heinemann Ltd, London, 2004).

Bray, R.N. and Tatham, P.F.B. *Old Waterfront Walls, Management, Maintenance and Rehabilitation* (CIRIA, London, 1992).

Brereton, Christopher, *The Repair of Historic Buildings* (English Heritage, London, 1995).

Construction Industry Research and Information Association, *CIRIA Report 111: Structural Renovation of Traditional Buildings* (CIRIA, London, 1986).

Davey, Ken, *Building Conservation Contracts and Grant Aid*, (Spon Press, London, 1992).

Highfield, David, *Rehabilitation and Re-use of Old Buildings* (E & FN Spon, London, 1987).

Institution of Civil Engineers, *Conservation of Engineering Structures* (ICE, London, 1989).

Mills, Edward D. (ed.), *Building Maintenance and Preservation* (Butterworth, London, 1980).

Mitchell, Eleanor, *Emergency Repairs for Historic Buildings* (English Heritage, London, 1988).

Powys, A.R. *Repair of Ancient Buildings* (London, 1929).

Robson, Patrick, *Structural Repair of Traditional Buildings* (Donhead, Shaftesbury, 1999).

Weaver, Martin E., *Conserving Buildings: Guide to Techniques and Materials* (Wiley, New York, 1993).

Wright, Adela, *Craft Techniques for Traditional Buildings* (B.T. Batsford Ltd, London, 1991).

9 Numerical modelling of masonry structures

Dina F. D'Ayala

Masonry as a material

Masonry is a composite material made of units of various types arranged regularly in space and separated by a cement paste called mortar in which the units are embedded (the mortar can be omitted to form dry stone walls). The units are traditionally either

- **manmade:** clay-fired bricks, earth bricks, concrete blocks or other industrially produced blocks obtained by pouring a paste into a mould and then letting it set and harden
- **natural:** stone, either as rubble or dressed

or more recently

- **reconstituted stone**

The units are laid down following a regular pattern, in a succession of horizontal layers alternating with beds of mortar and vertically staggered so as to avoid continuous vertical joints. As a result, the horizontal and lateral faces of the units are embedded in mortar and there should not be direct contact between units.

However, for dry stone masonry no mortar is used and the stone units are simply stacked directly on top of each other with some lateral staggering. The order and regularity with which the units are arranged strongly influences the mechanical properties of the masonry. In this respect, random rubble stone masonry represents the lower end of the spectrum while brickwork represents the upper end, the units being standardised and resulting in the most regular arrangement. Depending on the unit used, we can identify the masonry as brickwork, ashlar, rubble stone and so on.

Mortar is made of **fine aggregate, sand, water** and some type of **cementitious binder** – lime historically and Portland cement more recently. Gypsum, hydrated lime and mixed cement and lime are also used, and some sands like pozzolana act as binding agents. Also, additives are used to improve the properties of the mortar.

The strength and durability of the mortar depends on the mix proportion, the cement:water:aggregate ratio. This also influences its stiffness and hence its propensity to crack.

The layout of units and type of mortar critically influence the final mechanical characteristic of the masonry, and while today this has been reduced to few options, the Romans were well aware of the implications, as shown by different types of 'opus' used for different purposes. This was to a certain extent also well known to medieval masons, who very often used a mixture of stone and brick and variable courses and types of mortar.

As a form of construction masonry is relatively simple and cheap, and although in certain circumstances brick- or stone-laying may require highly skilled labour, it is a form of construction that lends itself to use by very small building contractors and, ultimately, to self-build. Also, construction in brickwork is adaptable from an architectural point of view, allowing substantial freedom in the layout of internal spaces and the distribution of openings, and hence allowing good adaptability to different climatic conditions. From an environmental and structural point of view, masonry performance depends on the performance of mortar and units and on their interaction. Present-day codes of practice provide guidelines for the best coupling of mortar mixes and brick types so as to optimise both strength and environmental performance in the resulting wall.

The structural performance of brick masonry buildings depends on four levels of connections. First, within the fabric of the wall the integrity and shear resistance are influenced by the level of bond between mortar and bricks; hence it is essential that the brickwork is properly constructed, allowing for the best possible bonding, and subsequently it is important that bed and head joint are regularly repointed so as to ensure the maximum possible surface of contact.

The second level of connection concerns the leaves of brick walls. Current standards require, for instance, that there should be regularly spaced ties between the leaves of a cavity wall, so as to ensure monolithic behaviour and redistribution between the two parts of the wall. In vernacular historic construction, walls would typically be made either of solid brickwork one or two bricks thick or of two outer leaves with a cavity filled with rubble material to improve the thermal capacity of the wall. Connection between the two leaves was ensured through thickness or by using headers placed at regular intervals in the body of each leaf.

The third level of connection concerns corner junctions where the wall returns. This ensures three-dimensional behaviour of the masonry box and the redistribution among walls of lateral forces.

The fourth level of connection is between walls and horizontal structures. This particularly influences the seismic performance of the building.

Given the distribution of the two components – units and mortar – and their physical characteristics, masonry is very difficult to model and analyse mechanically, yet historically, in various configurations, it is the most used material for the built environment with around 80% of the present-day building stock being either built of masonry or having non-structural masonry components.

In order to describe masonry as a structural material, its strength and stiffness need to be defined. We need a constitutive law (the relationship between stress and strain for the whole range of the material) and a failure criterion (to define the strength of the material under general three-dimensional stress conditions).

In principle, in should be possible to define a constitutive law for masonry by defining the constitutive law for each component and then deriving the constitutive law of the composite material by some technique of homogenisation. In other words, masonry can be considered as a homogeneous material by means of distributing the characteristics of the two components in their occurring ratio over the entire volume of material to be considered. Several experimental studies have been conducted to relate the strength of the resulting masonry to the strength of the units and the mortar – and the results can be usefully applied to the general analysis of masonry structures. It is evident that such a model would overlook the distribution of crack patterns and other localised aspects of masonry behaviour that in reality occur. This approach may be satisfactory for new masonry structures, but it can only partially apply to existing structures.

From a qualitative point of view, the units can be considered as the stronger, stiffer element and the mortar as the weaker, more flexible element of the composite material. Therefore the strength of the masonry will be dependent on the strength of the mortar while its stiffness should be more related to that of the unit. Investigation of historic masonry requires a high level of skill, expertise and technical knowledge. This ranges from the sampling, analysis and chemical techniques involved in testing stone of all ages and origins, to special test methods for assessing the in situ structural properties of a historic building. This chapter is only concerned with the mechanical characteristics of the component materials and how they combine to produce the characteristics of the resultant masonry.

From a structural point of view we are interested in knowing

- compressive, tensile and shear strength and how these are related to each other, and which of these governs failure
- Young's modulus and Poisson's ratio for the elastic range, secant modulus at failure
- ductility, or the ratio between strain at failure and strain at elastic limit

As masonry is a composite material, we need to know these parameters for each of the component materials as well as their geometric lay-out and ratio. The parameters listed above refer to uniaxial loading and deformation conditions for a given material. However, given the particular way in which masonry is composed, it can always be considered in a two-dimensional state of stress. Moreover, the material is not isotropic; it behaves differently when loaded uniaxially along different axes. In particular, the compressive strength of a masonry panel is maximum along an axis perpendicular to the bed joints and minimum along an axis parallel to the bed joints, while the tensile stresses are minimum in an axis perpendicular to the bed joint and maximum along an axis parallel to the bed joint. This is mainly due to the fact that both tensile and compressive failure are dependent on the maximum tensile strength, which is maximum along an axis parallel to the bed joints. However, it is also essential to define the characteristic shear strength – the strength associated with a condition of pure shear load – in terms of the material's structural behaviour as defined by the bonding strength between units and mortar.

From the above it is evident that, together with uniaxial stress–strain relationships, it is essential to define two- and three-dimensional failure criteria, both with respect to the principal stresses space (analogy with Von Mises or Tresca criteria) and in the sigma-tau plane (analogous with the Mohr-Coulomb criterion for soils). In drawing those failure domains, it should be considered that the strengths in tension and in compression are different and that, owing to the anisotropy, these are different depending on the relative orientation of the acting forces and the bed joints.

Structural assessment of historic masonry building

When conducting an assessment of the structural behaviour of historic masonry buildings by the use of analytical tools, one of the main problems encountered is the collection of data concerning the mechanical features.[1] The preservation of the integrity of the building, and the lack of homogeneity resulting from additions and alteration occurring over a long period, often work against each other in the provision of reliable in situ test results. While it is reasonably simple to extract single bricks and perform tests on a number of samples to obtain significant mean values, to extract undisturbed mortar samples is a much more difficult task. Moreover, tests on extracted masonry wallets might be limited by the historic importance, artistic value and structural soundness of the building being considered.

One major problem for the analysis of masonry structures using numerical tools is the need for homogenisation owing to the high computational costs associated with a direct simulation of the components when the analysis concerns real three-dimensional structures. Different homogenising techniques have been proposed by Pande,[2] Urbanski[3] and others, all relying on the correct identification of, sometimes, several constituents' parameters.

The following section defines a numerical procedure directly linked to a database developed by the author, which, given the topological and historic data of the masonry, enables a reliable estimate of the mechanical parameters to be introduced in a standard finite element (f.e.), non-linear programme, without performing extensive destructive tests. The upgradable database collects the mechanical data from published tests that have been carried out on historic masonry of various periods and in different locations. The data is analysed statistically and a number of interpolating regression curves are drawn, which relate the geometric and mechanical parameters of the units, mortar and resulting masonry, or some of their non-dimensional ratios. The values of the masonry parameters obtained from the regression curves are used as input in the non-linear structural analysis procedure.

The database is built in Microsoft Access for WindowsXP©, compiled from papers providing complete information about masonry, units and mortar in terms of geometric and physical characteristics, modality of tests, number of samples, and mechanical features. Papers dealing with either historic or new masonry are considered, the distinction between the two classes being related to the aim of the study. Thus for some sets of data the mortar or masonry samples may not be old but reproduced historic masonry in laboratory conditions. Actual historic masonry structures are considered to be those of fifty or more years of age built with non-engineered techniques. The age and location of the samples are entered on the database to allow for comparisons of test results carried out in the same geographical area (thus using similar component materials and craft techniques) or in different areas but of similar date.

The sources reviewed include international brick, block and masonry conferences and earthquake engineering conferences, specialist international journals, international conferences on conservation and a number of regional conferences and specific reports. Of some 700 papers reviewed to date, only about one-tenth had complete sets of data suitable for the database. Two separate databases are considered for brick and stone units. It is interesting to note that papers relating to specific buildings only rarely provide complete data on the constituent materials.

The tests considered were uniaxial or triaxial compression tests, rupture tests, shear-bond tests and direct tension tests, carried out on the units, the mortar and the masonry as a whole, and performed according to the relevant recommendation of the International Standards Organisation (ISO) or European Committee for Standardisation (CEN). The majority of the data is used to establish correlation between parameters of the same material – mortar or unit – while the compression test presents correlated data sufficient to allow a statistical analysis of the influence of the components' parameters on the masonry. The level of occurrence in the data of the compressive strength is 80% for the mortar, 97% for the brick or stone and 71% for the resulting masonry. The occurrence for the values of the elastic modulus is 29%, 59% and 42% respectively.

A first group of regressions relates the compressive strength of the masonry to the compressive strength of the units and the mortar, and to the heights of the units, the bed joints and the masonry sample, and their ratios. A second group relates the elastic modulus E of the masonry to its compressive strength, to the elastic modulus of the units or the mortar, and to the heights of the units or the bed joints, or their ratios.

The first set of regressions shows that the compressive strength of the mortar bed joint has a greater influence on the compressive strength of the masonry than does the strength of the unit. The similar distribution of the data and shape of the resulting curves suggests combining the influence of the two parameters in a formula as follows (Figure 9.1):

$$f_{cw} = 0.538f_{cm} + 0.241f_{cb} \qquad (9.1)$$

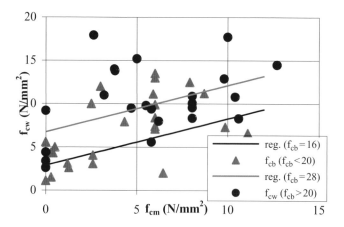

Figure 9.1 Equation (9.1) for discrete values of f_{cb}.

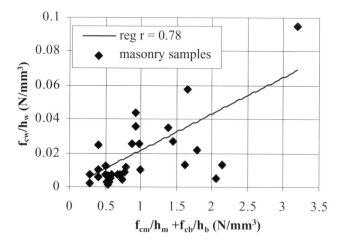

Figure 9.2 Equation (9.2) regression coefficient r = 0.78.

The high sensibility of the masonry strength to the height of the mortar bed joint was also highlighted and a very good correlation (r = 0.78) was obtained relating the masonry strength normalised with respect to the height of the sample, and to the sum of the strengths of the two component materials, each normalised to its height (Figure 9.2):

$$\frac{f_{cw}}{h_w} = 0.0216 \cdot \left(\frac{f_{cb}}{h_b} + \frac{f_{cm}}{h_m} \right) \qquad (9.2)$$

The regressions define the direct proportionality between the elastic modulus of the unit, mortar, masonry and their related compressive strength (Figure 9.3). The distribution of points over a wide range and the high values of the correlation coefficient in the three cases (0.935, 0.655, 0.937, for mortar, brick, masonry) make these curves highly reliable. Such a good

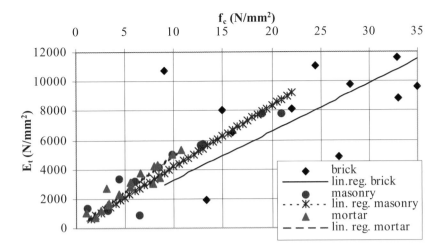

Figure 9.3 Regression of E_t (f_c).

correlation enables us to propose, in the absence of direct experimental tests, the use of those curves to define the elastic modulus when the strength of the material is known. It is worth noting that the slope coefficient for the masonry curve is $c = 417$, more than half the value suggested by the Eurocode 6 for the short-term secant modulus in new construction ($c = 1000$).[4] However, considering the maximum effect associated with creep, the long-term value of the slope coefficient would reduce to $c = 660$, which is still 1.5 times greater than the one obtained with the regression.

Finite element procedure

To date, finite element analysis of masonry structures within the typical design office environment has been hampered by the lack of simple yet reliable constitutive models to define appropriate mechanical properties for the material. This is particularly true of existing masonry buildings, because the requirement to assess their material properties entails extensive destructive testing. The commonly used method of circumventing this problem has been to extrapolate the constitutive laws of concrete to masonry. This, however, completely overlooks the orderly composed nature of masonry and the fact that the weakness of the material is concentrated at specific locations – in the bed joints.

The strength of this approach lies in the parallel use of the database and a preliminary finite element analysis to generate equivalent homogeneous material properties for the masonry based on those of the constituent bricks and mortar.[5] The preliminary finite element analysis simulates numerically the standard compression and bond test by modelling in two or three dimensions the individual bricks and mortar layers separately with their own failure criteria and constitutive law. These are derived from the database when the location and age of the masonry structure and composition of the mortar are known, together with the geometry of the units, thickness of the mortar and their compressive strength. The numerical simulation allows a wide variety of stress conditions to be considered, enabling the definition of a proper constitutive law and failure domain for the composite material. The values of the relevant parameters obtained in this way are verified by comparison with the database regression curves.

Once the masonry properties are in such a way defined, a coarser mesh can be used to model larger portions of the structure up to the entire building. Each plate-shell element thus simulates the masonry as a homogeneous orthotropic material, using a smeared crack model and a modified Mohr-Coulomb failure criterion for the post-elastic behaviour. The constitutive law is approximated by a tri-linear curve. The algorithm is made up as follows:

- A pre-processor prepares the f.e. model, stores the material data, and defines the elastic limit of the analysis under the given load condition. It also defines the number of increments and an initial incremental step for the load. On the basis of the material properties given, constitutive law and failure domains for each material are also defined.
- The main processor which solves the f.e. problem for a given incremental step is provided by the Algor V17© commercial package.
- The post processor checks the state of stress at the centre of each element with reference to the failure domain, accordingly modifying the values of the stiffness parameters and operating the redistribution of the internal state of stress to the adjacent elements by equivalent nodal forces, when an element fails.

A three- or four-node plate-shell element with five degrees of freedom (d.o.f.) per node is used, allowing for the simulation of complex three-dimensional problems. Two failure criteria are used to allow for the non-associative nature of the materials. The first failure criterion, of the Rankine type, is defined in the principal stress plane and is used to define the state of stress internal to the single element of mortar or brick (Figure 9.4). A tension cut-off is included to take into account the reduced strength under biaxial tension. The bond between mortar and unit and the shear behaviour of the units are defined by the Mohr-Coulomb-type criterion shown in Figure 9.5 with respect to the stress σ normal to the plane of the joint. The state of stress on the edges of the elements is verified with respect to this failure domain to define shear failure of the joint and direction of slip. The same failure criteria are used after homogenisation for the macromodelling, using the parameters for the masonry obtained by the simulation of the compression and shear bond test. A linear elastic tensile behaviour is assumed until the cracking surface is reached. The material becomes then orthotropic, with characteristics defined for the direction parallel and normal to the crack. No variation of direction of the crack has been considered within the single element of mortar or brick. The reinforcement is simulated by bar elements connected at each node of the plate shell elements forming the mortar bed joints. During the elastic phase the bond with the mortar

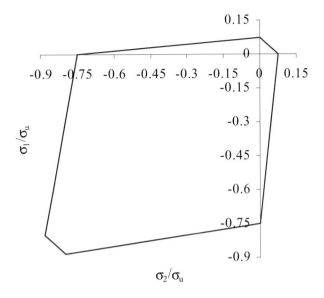

Figure 9.4 Rankine-type failure domain.

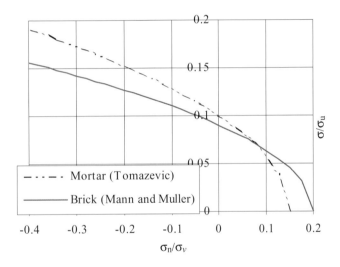

Figure 9.5 Mohr-Coulomb-type failure domain.

is considered full. The behaviour after cracking is simulated by a uniaxial elasto-plastic model applied in the bar axial direction only, the stress released at the crack being applied at the common node on the bar.

Application to experimental work

The finite element procedure described above has been applied to simulate the tests conducted by Cook at the University of Bath,[6] in collaboration with Karlsruhe University, on fourteen specimens of full-scale spandrel walls, which modelled the process of 'crack damage–repair–continued movement up to further damage'. The criterion of success was the degree to which the damaged element, after a repair consisting of reinforcement of two bed joints, could tolerate further bending movement without re-aggravation of the original damage.

These tests were confined to spandrel walls of single-leaf brickwork, while the connection to piers was simulated by equivalent pre-stressing. Two types of masonry were tested, with different geometries of unit and different mortar mixtures. The overall geometry of the spandrel walls, and in particular the h/l ratio, was, however, kept constant. According to the regression analysis performed on the database, the height of the bed joint has substantial influence on the strength of the masonry, and it was kept constant while the height of the unit was varied.

The information on the material parameters was reduced to the compressive strength of mortar measured on cubes and brick for both cases, with one partial compression test per set, performed directly on the spandrel wall and aimed at defining the masonry initial tangential modulus. This value was kept for reference but not introduced initially as a datum in the f.e. analysis. Also, a number of five-brick stack tests had been performed, to provide a value of strength for the masonry. There was no indication of bond or tensile strength for any of the materials.

The finite element model simulated half of the spandrel tested in practice owing to the two halves being theoretically symmetrical. An assymetrical crack pattern indicated that this was not the case in reality, however, but without information on the causes and quantification of the asymmetry it was not possible to include this aspect in the numerical model.

On the basis of the data available, the initial tangent elastic modulus for mortar and bricks was derived from the database, together with their tensile and shear strengths. The finite element simulation of five-brick stacks and masonry wallets based on this data showed a good agreement with the available experimental data. Therefore the chosen values were also used to simulate the shear bond test on triplets. Although there was no relevant experimental data, these were equally carried out to compare the two resultant failure domains for the two types of masonry; the Karlsruhe one is smaller than that at Bath, in agreement with the lower strength of the components.

A different way to obtain the initial tangent modulus of the two components is to use the results of the spandrel test, applying some rather simple theoretical models and the standard homogenisation procedure in reverse order. Using the equation for a deep beam with fixed ends and concentrated load (Timoshenko), the modulus at cracking could be obtained when a given value for the ratio E/G is established (chosen as 2.5 according to Hendry[7]). This yields the values collected in Table 9.1 for the two sets of tests.

From these values, using the homogenisation equation as follows

$$E_w = \frac{E_j(h_b + h_j)(l_j E_j + l_b E_b)}{h_j(l_j E_j + l_b E_b) + E_j h_b(l_j + l_b)} \qquad (9.3)$$

Table 9.1 Tangent modulus test results

Test set	Mortar			Brick			Masonry		
	$E_{//}$	$E_{reg.}$	$E_{eq.\ 4}$	$E_{//}$	$E_{half\ brick}$	$E_{reg.}$	E_{test}	$E_{reg.}$	$E_{Timoshenko}$
Bath	6290	5000	4950	15697		10000	8300	6000	7079
Karlsruhe		2000	2754		5950	6500	5283	5000	5176

the value of tangent modulus of mortar could be calculated for a given estimate of the brick tangent modulus (Table 9.1).

The experimental tests, for which the only variable parameter was the number of brick layers and the geometric ratio h/l, showed quite scattered results, not only in terms of first crack load but also in term of stiffness. The parameter that seemed to be fairly constant in most of the tests was the cracking bending strain. Moreover, the two sets of tests did not show considerably different crack loads or initial stiffness for similar ratios of h/l, notwithstanding the consistent difference in the materials used.

The author believes that a main reason for this is the relevant part that could have been played by friction between the upper plate and the specimen, an effect which will initially show as an increase in stiffness and in cracking load. Although it has not been measured, given the rather high precompression applied at the spandrel's ends this effect might have been of the same order of magnitude in terms of stiffness as the one produced by the materials' properties. This would also explain the rather sudden drop in load capacity following the initial cracking.

Two different strategies were followed to simulate the test numerically. One used the value of Et for mortar and bricks obtained as mentioned above. This would yield lower values of first cracking load than that obtained by the experimental test. The difference in stiffness would be converted in an equivalent spring system applied horizontally at the level of the plate with a limiting force equal to the one provided by friction at the plate, having assumed a friction angle of 30°. In this way the values obtained compared very well with the test results. However, in the absence of more detailed experimental evidence it would be wrong to assume that this was the only cause for a discrepancy in the results.

The introduction of reinforcement was analysed by simulating one of the spandrel specimens in which the reinforcement was introduced at an initial state, before any loading was applied. As expected, this model showed the same initial elastic behaviour as the unreinforced one until first cracking occurred. At this point the reinforcement appeared to be quite effective in increasing the load capacity for an increasing deformation of up to 30% more than the initial elastic limit.

Application to a real case

Finally, a homogenised mesh was analysed on the basis of the parameters derived from the smaller test for the Bath case. The reduction in computational effort is considerable, having reduced the d.o.f. to one-third and the bandwidth even further. The results, in terms of both load capacity/ deformation and crack pattern, reproduce well the experimental results. However, it is not possible to localise the single failure to the bed joint or the unit.

A review of the scientific literature on reinforced masonry and strengthening techniques of damaged masonry from the last twenty years shows that while the research has focused extensively on the damage and repair of masonry due to loading in the lateral and horizontal plane and to the design specification of new reinforced masonry to such loading,[8] only marginal attention has been paid to the effects of subsidence on ordinary buildings.[9] In fact the conventional wisdom is that this problem can only be solved by intervening directly with the foundations. However, papers by Pfeffermann and Haseltine[10] and by Valsangkar et al.[11] demonstrated that the use of properly distributed bed joint reinforcement in new masonry structures above foundation level can significantly improve the stress distribution in the wall and prevent cracking due to uneven settlement.

Such a view has been substantiated by the results of research completed under funding from the EPSRC, the German DFG and the Italian CNR-GNDT, which shows that bed joint reinforcement can be very effective in repairing existing buildings damaged by settlement and earthquake. This work, in part conducted at Bath by Cook,[12] on testing of isolated spandrel walls was successfully simulated by using non-linear analysis techniques which can model mortar and brick/block as individual materials.[13] It would be desirable to extend such findings to the entire fabric of a building, though the difficulty of conducting extensive tests on full-sized structures is evident.

Based on the experimental results discussed above, and using a simple homogenisation technique derived from worldwide testing data, we will now present an extension of the study by numerical analysis to simulate the crack pattern within a building facade and describe how this can be altered and reduced by insertion of bed joint reinforcement at appropriate locations.

A case study building in Great Pulteney Street, Bath, is examined, the choice of which follows the availability of a settlement profile and a thorough photographic survey. Also, the scale of the settlement – 260 mm differential settlement – and its sinusoidal shape, representing an extreme case, are particularly suitable to highlight the effectiveness of the procedure. A brief history of the building follows, together with a summary of significant alterations. A non-linear finite element analysis of the building is then presented in detail and its results discussed.

Nos. 42–51 Great Pulteney Street: archival research

Great Pulteney Street is the centrepiece of the Bathwick estate, a major late eighteenth-century urban development by the architect Thomas Baldwin, east of Bath's city centre. Great Pulteney Street is 1000 feet

(c. 300 metres) long and 100 feet (c. 30 metres) wide, enclosed by three ranges of terraced houses on the south side and two on the north. The street was built on an artificial causeway to bring the ground floor of the houses above the river flood level. The basement walls and arches would have been built over an initial level of fill and the causeway then completed up to the level of the street.

The soil below the causeway is alluvium of varying height and extent, overlying silt and clays. The Geological Survey of Great Britain shows the passage from alluvium to a second terrace of gravel half way along the axis of Great Pulteney street at the western end of the central south terrace.[14] The depths of the two formations are not given, and they should be considered more as an indication of a change in the course of the riverbed than as differing strata.

The present case study is of a terrace of twelve houses at the south-east end of the street, nos. 41 to 52 (Figure 9.6). The settlement profile as surveyed by D. Cook[15] (Figure 9.7) is juxtaposed against the elevation so that the two horizontal scales are roughly the same. The settlement along the entire length of Great Pulteney Street mainly occurred underneath the region of the two extreme blocks on the south side of the road. The settlement under the case study block presents several reversals of curvature along the longitudinal axis of the block with an increase in magnitude from the eastern end toward the western end. Interestingly enough, the adjacent terrace, built a few years earlier, does not show comparable settlement. It should be noted that the settlement profile has been obtained by survey

Figure 9.6 Elevation of nos. 42–51 Great Pulteney Street, Bath, by Thomas Baldwin, from a lease of 1791.

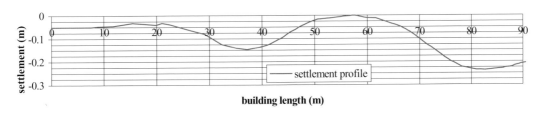

Figure 9.7 Settlement profile as surveyed at cornice level in 1992 by Cook.

at cornice level. The crack pattern, surveyed by close inspection of the facade above and below ground, confirms the settlement shape.

Archival research, mainly aimed at identifying possible causes for the uneven settlement along the longitudinal axis of Great Pulteney Street, failed to reveal specific reference to the state of the construction and preservation of the individual houses, or to structural faults or defects. Deeds indicate that nos. 42 to 51 were the last to be built in the street, the initial lease being dated 1791. The individual houses were built by different contractors at different times, as was the practice in Bath. Deeds and mortage documents indicate that the houses were built over a period of at least five years and probably in a random sequence, perhaps resulting in disturbance to foundations when work to adjacent houses started and hence some level of tilting or distortion of party walls and facade. One such case might have occurred between nos. 50 and 51.

Given the vicinity of the river bed and the original levels of the ground, a relevant line of inquiry concerns the record of major floods in the area. Floods are recorded in 1703, 1725, 1774[16] and 1797,[17] but it is doubtful that than any of these could have influenced the Great Pulteney Street causeway. A major flood is then recorded in 1809, probably the most damaging flood that Bath has ever experienced, with great areas of the city under water.[18] The maximum water level recorded for this flood is 3.81 metres above the Pulteney Weir, which would have been just sufficient to flood the basements in the street and possibly erode the base of the causeway,[19] though the flooding, however dangerous, could not possibly on its own account for the double reversal of curvature in the settlement profile.

A further hypothesis that might help explain the settlement profile is the presence of a buried channel or localised alluvial formation as a result of a change in the course of the river. This would comply with the approximate distance of 40 metres between the two relative maxima of settlement (Figure 9.7). The hypothesis could be verified by a fine grid of bore hole investigations in the area, which at the time of writing were not available.

To summarise, the evidence from a number of different lines of inquiry would suggest the following. The settlement could have been caused by an initial uneven compaction of the fill creating the causeway and the soil's superficial strata by the action of the fill. This could have been caused by the combined effects of lack of accuracy during erection, time lag of construction of adjacent units and, possibly, the presence of a buried channel. The initial uneven settlement could have been amplified in time by the erosion of the fill and soil beneath caused by flooding. The influence of the change of profile of the water table owing to the construction of the nearby Kennet and Avon Canal has not been studied so far.

Numerical model

The numerical simulation of the terrace was undertaken, not to prove or disprove the different hypotheses concerning onset of the settlement but to identify a relatively non-obtrusive way of reducing the effects of such settlement.

The analysis was restricted to the western half of the block, between nos. 46 and 52. The analytical method followed is presented in detail elsewhere,[20] and here the specific application to this case will be discussed. The first obstacle in conducting such an exercise is the lack of detailed data on the mechanical parameters of the masonry and the impossibility of conducting any in situ test or removal of material for laboratory testing. For this reason a number of simulations of small portions of the masonry were analysed in detail, to reproduce monoaxial compression and shear strength tests.

The compression test was carried out on models of overall dimensions 1.40×1.30 metres, reproducing the exact layout, bed joint dimensions and ashlar arrangement as in the piers of the actual building. The strength and mechanics parameters of the stone were derived from literature, while the strength and elastic modulus of the lime mortar was obtained by tests of cubic samples prepared with a $1:3$ mixture and aged for ninety days. While the values obtained would not correspond to the present values of the in situ mortar, it can be assumed that they are representative of the original state of the mortar in the wall soon after construction. Great care was taken in representing the random distribution of head joints in the masonry by analysing ten different models. The analysis shows that as long as the number and frequency of head joints are respected, rather than their precise location, the results in terms of strength only vary by 5%. However, an increase of 20% in the number of joints results in increased deflections with a range of the equivalent tangent modulus E_m between $4250 \, N/mm^2$ and $7500 \, N/mm^2$.

A detailed survey of the piers and spandrels shows that while the number of bed joints is constant throughout the facade, the number of head joints varies quite considerably, owing partly to the original fabric and partly to subsequent alterations. Hence it was decided to use a single value of the initial tangent modulus for the masonry $E_m = 4500 \, N/mm^2$, which represents the lower 5% of the distribution of ten compression tests.

In Figure 9.8 the results for two different arrangements of head joints are compared, and the crack pattern for one of the two cases at two different stages is shown by the model insets. In Figure 9.9 the points representative of the state of stress are indicated for each mortar element, and the corresponding failure curve in terms of $\sigma\perp - \sigma//$ (stress perpendicular and stress parallel to the bed joint, respectively). The points have been classified in relation to the type of failure. The limitation of this choice of failure criterion is apparent with respect to the points located in the compression–tension zone (blue diamond points). In this area the state of stress, and hence the orientation of principal stresses, is highly influenced by the presence of shear. This is taken into account in the numerical procedure by the definition of a Mohr-Coulomb criterion, in which for each point a complete Mohr circle is compared with a Coulomb-like σ-τ criterion and the condition of intersection of the two curves is imposed for failure.

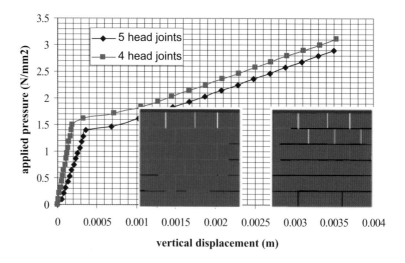

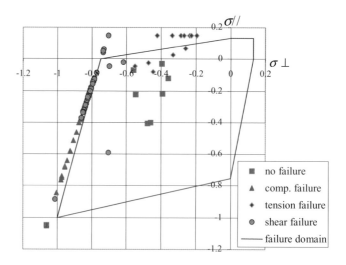

Figure 9.8 p-δ curves for compression test of wallets: white joints indicate tensile failure, black compression.

Figure 9.9 Distribution of state of stress for mortar joints.

The same procedure is used for the analysis of the whole facade. However, in this case, given the overall dimension, it would have been impossible to simulate mortar and stone in separate elements. Therefore the size of the finite element was chosen so as to include a horizontal joint and at least one head joint, and its parameters are those of the resultant masonry, rather than of either of the constituent materials. It was discussed above how the initial tangential modulus was chosen on the basis of the compression test. This was also used to define the compressive strength $\sigma_c = 6.5\,\text{N/mm}^2$. The characteristic shear strength τ_k was calculated by simulation of a number of tests on triplets with different sizes of stone. The mean value obtained is 0.49 N/mm^2. The tensile strength was taken as 60% of the τ_k. The triplets were also used to define the Mohr-Coulomb criterion – that is, the relation between shear strength of the joint and the applied normal compressive stress.

The facade is constituted of shell elements, with beam elements simulating the reinforcement and connected to the same mesh as the shell elements. The choice of the two elements is made so that there is compatibility of displacement at the nodes. Relative slip between the stone and the reinforcement, which will occur once the mortar cracks, is not considered in this analysis. While this introduces a fictitious reduction of the opening of the cracks, there is at the moment not enough experimental evidence in literature to substantiate any reliable model. It should also be noted that the model has been purposely kept as homogeneous as possible along the facade, disregarding architectonic peculiarities of the original design. This, if it might partially impair the perfect correspondence of results, on the other hand generalises the crack patterns and the behaviour associated with the introduction of reinforcement to similarly proportioned long terrace facades generally. Hence the model should be regarded as a prototype rather than as a replica of the case study.

The three storeys above ground are simulated in the model. The settlement is induced by boundary elements connected to the lower row of nodes to which finite displacement is applied in successive increments. The overall shape of the settlement is maintained from the start, although there is no evidence, as stated earlier, that the surveyed final shape corresponds to a single event or that the settlement evolved linearly with time. The model is constituted of 3263 nodes for approximately 9000 d.o.f. and 2547 plate elements. It should be noted that the areas above the windows have the same properties that are found elsewhere, as there were no lintels in the original design. The model is analysed in the original conditions and then with some bed joint reinforcement introduced. In both cases the self-weight of the facade and dead and live loads associated with the roofing are applied in two initial increments so as to obtain the state of stress associated with this condition. The intermediate floors are assumed to span between the party walls, as was common at the time. The settlement is simulated by fifty increments, of which ten are until onset of the first failure and forty to completion of the analysis. The total run time on a Pentium machine is approximately two hours, including data post-processing and graphic output for each increment.

Discussion of results

Original configuration

The horizontal tensile strain at which the masonry would fail is 75 microstrain, and this is reached for 45% of the total settlement. In the hogging region above no. 48, ten elements, representative of as many joints, reach cracking, while in the sagging region, which has a smaller radius of curva-

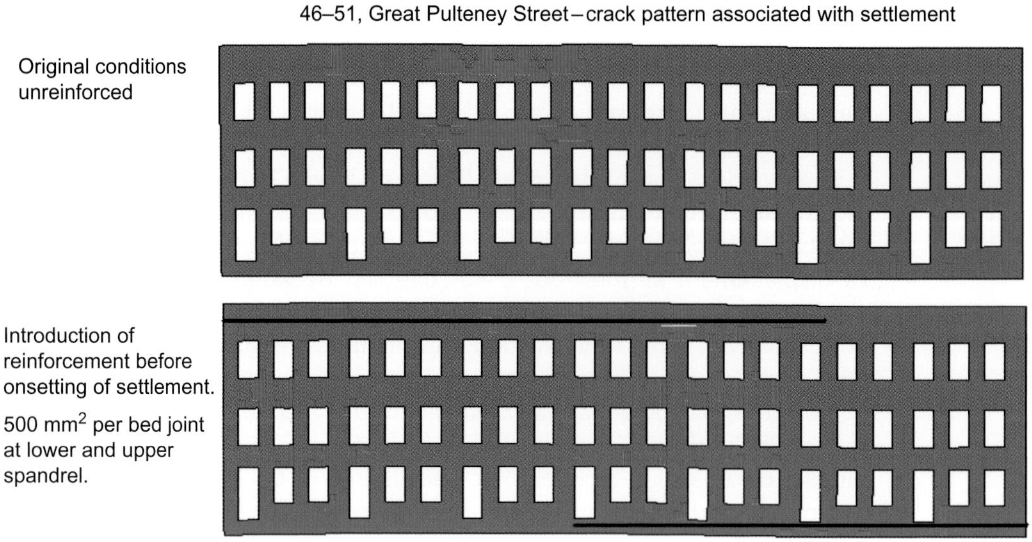

46–51, Great Pulteney Street – crack pattern associated with settlement

Original conditions
unreinforced

Introduction of
reinforcement before
onsetting of settlement.

500 mm^2 per bed joint
at lower and upper
spandrel.

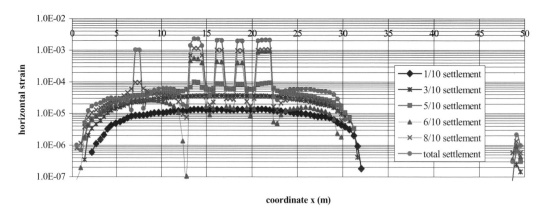

Figure 9.10 Computed crack pattern associated with surveyed settlement.

Figure 9.11 Distribution of horizontal strains at top spandrel in original configuration (+ve only).

ture, only two elements are broken underneath no. 51. This was confirmed by a visual inspection carried out on site. Figure 9.10 shows the pattern of failed elements (darker colour) for both cases, while Figures 9.11 and 9.12 show the distribution of horizontal strain associated with a given location along the facade at the second row of elements from the top for the two cases respectively. Elements reach failure here initially for 50% of the total settlement in the spandrel above the windows. As the settlement increases the cracking deepens in the fabric, reaching the second and then the first floor spandrels, whose crack pattern is completely developed when 65% of the total settlement is applied.

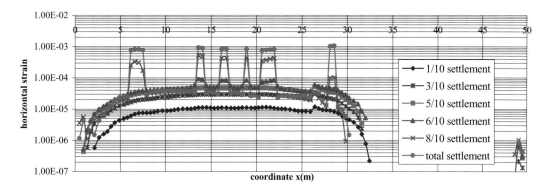

Figure 9.12 Distribution of horizontal strains at top spandrel in reinforced configuration (+ve only).

Of course, not all of this cracking is due to pure bending, especially at the second floor spandrel where the shear stresses will be high and comparable with the bending stresses. However, in the region of contraflexure, where the associated bending moment is relatively low compared with the corresponding shear, it may be noted that only a minority of elements are cracked. This cracking, particularly evident over no. 50 both in the model and in reality, only occurs for 80% of the settlement, or for a value of settlement twice the one that causes bending crack. This is in agreement with the experimental evidence collected by Cook.

Strengthened configuration

The strengthened configuration only differs from the original one by the insertion of reinforcement in two bed joints at the ground floor level and at the roof level. The reinforcement in each bed joint is made of four thin plates of 5 mm thickness and 25 mm width, which can be inserted in the masonry by use of an angle grinder. The plates have a corrugated surface for bond enhancement and characteristics similar to concrete reinforcement. In the present case the reinforcement is passive as no prestressing has been induced.

The results show that the bending strain limit is reached for 60% of the settlement, an increase of 10% compared with the previous case, and that corresponding total horizontal strains are about 20% smaller (Figures 9.11 and 9.12). But most importantly the analysis shows that a great portion of the facade is spared any damage as the cracking is confined to the upper spandrel. The reinforcement results are quite effective and its stress is maintained in the elastic region, at a maximum of 200 N/mm^2.

However, this greater stiffness in the regions of maximum bending entails greater shear distortion in order to accommodate the same amount and shape of settlement. This occurs mostly in the regions of contraflexure. The shear cracks start appearing for 65% of the total settlement and fully develop only for the complete settlement. This cracking could have been partly avoided by using a smaller amount of reinforcement or, better, an alloy of lower stiffness. Figure 9.13 best illustrates this concept by compar-

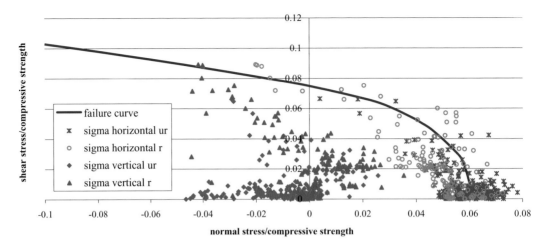

Figure 9.13 Mohr-Coulomb-type failure curve and state of stress of failed element in two perpendicular planes for the unreinforced and reinforced case.

ing the state of stresses in two perpendicular directions for the two cases for the failed elements. Failure always occurs for relatively low values of associated normal compression. However, in the unreinforced case the tensile failure is reached for a very low value of the associated shear stresses. The presence of reinforcement in the second case allows shear stresses to develop and hence a greater degree of distortion to take place before failure is reached.

Conclusions

The present study shows that, from a range of experimental results obtained from different authors, it is possible to derive a number of regression curves and evaluate the strength and elastic modulus of masonry from those of its components. Although several parameters of the experimental work simulated and relevant to the f.e. analysis were not explicitly measured, the use of the regression curves and homogenisation techniques enabled satisfactory results to be obtained using numerical simulation. This identified some aspects of the experimental work that can be improved. The technique will be used to extended the analysis to real structures that are subject to settlement.

The present study is concerned with the behaviour of long terraces built of masonry and subject to differential settlement and with methods of reducing the associated damage. The f.e. non-linear numerical procedure proved to be a valid instrument of analysis, reproducing the original crack pattern and predicting the behaviour associated with the introduction of the bed joint reinforcement.

As the results show, the introduction of reinforcement at appropriate locations along the bed joint considerably reduces the cracking associated with bending failures. However, a sensitivity analysis should be conducted in order to tailor the amount and type of bed joint reinforcement for minimum disturbance to the original fabric. It is evident that the technique is most effective if the reinforcement is introduced before the onset of settlement or as soon as it is detected. But, as with this particular case study, where the movement is historic and apparently stabilised, the best practice is always not to interfere, apart from carrying out repointing and partial substitution of the most damaged stones.

Acknowledgements

Thanks go to David Cook and Paul McCombie of the Department of Architecture and Civil Engineering, University of Bath, for enlightening discussion about the local geology, to the National Rivers Authority, South Western Region, and to Colin Johnson, archivist, Bath Record Office.

Endnotes

1 A.W. Page, 'Influence of material properties on the behaviour of brick masonry shear wall', *Proceedings of the VIII IBMAC* (Dublin, 1988).
2 J.S.Lee, G.N. Pande, J. Middleton and B. Kralj, 'Numerical modelling of brick masonry panels subjected to lateral loading', *Computers and Structures*, **61**, 4 (1996), 735–45.
3 A. Urbanski, J. Szarlinski and Z. Kordecki, 'Finite element modelling of masonry walls and columns by the homogenisation approach', *Computer Methods in Structural Masonry*, **3** (1995).
4 European Committee for Standardisation, ENV 1996-1-1, *Eurocode 6: Design of Masonry Structures: Part 1-1*, Brussels 1995.
5 D. D'Ayala and A. Carriero, 'A numerical tool to simulate the non-linear behaviour of Masonry Structures', *Proceedings CMEM 1995*, Capri, Italy.
6 D.A. Cook, S. Ring and W. Fichtner, 'The effective use of masonry reinforcement for crack repair', *Proceedings of the Fourth International Masonry Conference*, vol. 2 (1995), pp. 442–50.
7 A.W. Hendry (ed.), *Reinforced and Prestressed Masonry* (Longman, London, 1991).
8 R.G. Drysdale, A.A. Hamid and L.R. Baker, *Masonry Structures: Behaviour and Design* (Prentice Hall, New Jersey, 1994).
9 C.J. Anumba and D. Scott, 'Development of an expert system for the diagnosis and repair of subsidence damage to masonry', *Computational Method in Structural Masonry 3* (Lisbon, 1995), pp. 339–49.
10 O. Pfeffermann and B.A. Haseltine, 'The development of bed joint reinforcement over two decades', *Proceedings of the Third International Masonry Conference* (1994), pp. 91–3.
11 A.J. Valsangkar, J.L. Dawe and C.K. Seah, 'An evaluation of masonry wall–foundation interaction using finite element method', *Proceedings of the Third International Masonry Conference* (1994).
12 D.A. Cook, S. Ring and W. Fichtner, 'The effective use of masonry reinforcement for crack repair', *Proceedings of the Fourth International Masonry Conference*, vol. 2 (1995), pp. 442–50.
13 D. D'Ayala and A. Carriero, 'A numerical tool to simulate the non-linear behaviour of masonry structures', *CMEM 1995*, Capri, Italy.

14 Geological Survey, Sheet 265, scale 1 : 63360, Chessington, Surrey, 1965.

15 D.A. Cook, S. Ring and W. Fichtner, 'The effective use of masonry reinforcement for crack repair', *Proceedings of the Fourth International Masonry Conference*, vol. 2 (1995), pp. 442–50.

16 Bristol and Avon Local Land Drainage District, Land Drainage Survey Report (March 1978), par. 1.6: Flooding history.

17 Palmer's index to *The Times*, Wednesday, 20 September 1797, page 2 col. c.

18 Ibid. footnote 5.

19 From OS plan ST7565SW (June 1964). The surface level above the Newlyn datum is 69.78 feet (21.27 metres), while the peak water levels between Grove Street and Pulteney Weir would read 70.10 to 69.26 feet (21.34 to 21.11 metres), according to the 1960 recorded levels of flood, whose profile can be considered similar to those of 1809.

20 D. D'Ayala, 'Numerical modelling of masonry structures reinforced or repaired', *Computer Methods in Structural Masonry 4* (Swansea, 1997).

10 Use of iron and steel in buildings

Michael Bussell

Introduction

The three ferrous metals used in building are cast iron, wrought iron and steel, this order also defining the sequence in which they were introduced for significant structural use. The heyday of cast iron was the period from the late eighteenth century to the late nineteenth century, while wrought iron flourished from about 1840 until the beginning of the twentieth century. Both materials were then overtaken by the ready availability of structural steel at competitive prices.

Of the three, cast and wrought iron are both structurally 'extinct', in that cast iron is no longer used in new structures while wrought iron is no longer made. However, cast iron is still widely used non-structurally, for example in rainwater goods and railings, and there are many surviving buildings that incorporate structural cast and/or wrought iron (as, too, do many bridges and other structures). An awareness and understanding of these materials and their use in buildings is therefore essential, so that they can be conserved appropriately. The same consideration, of course, applies also to steel structures.

This chapter begins with an outline historical review of the use of iron and steel, primarily in building structures. The materials, their characteristics, and their conservation in material terms are described in the next volume in this series: *Materials & skills for historic building conservation*. The present chapter closes by considering ways in which iron and steel structures can be adapted for continued use while following conservation principles.

Cast iron

Early use of structural cast iron

In the 1770s, slender circular cast iron columns were tentatively used in several churches, but the first significant structural use of cast iron in Britain was the 1779 Iron Bridge across the River Severn (Figure 10.1). Indeed, it was the world's first major cast iron arch bridge, with a span of 100 feet (c. 30 metres). Interestingly, joints between members were based on car-

Figure 10.1 Iron Bridge, Shropshire across the River Severn, cast at the nearby Coalbrookdale Works in 1779.

pentry methods, with wedges, dovetails, and mortices and tenons serving as connections.

A driving force for the introduction of structural cast iron was the industrial growth taking place at the end of the eighteenth century. Multi-storey buildings such as textile mills, factories and storehouses were being built in large numbers, and traditional floors of timber were very vulnerable to fire. The fire risk was very high in mills and factories, where there was a potentially incendiary combination of machine lubricating oil, rags and other combustible waste, and candles used for lighting. Storehouse floors of timber were equally vulnerable, with valuable and often highly combustible contents (such as kegs of rum in naval dockyards).

So a material such as cast iron was seized upon as offering 'fireproof' construction, although its development was prolonged. (Today such construction would not be called fireproof, but rather 'incombustible', as the exposed and unprotected cast iron columns and beams could be weakened by exposure to fire.) A cotton mill of 1792 in Derby had cast iron columns in place of timber posts, but still employed timber beams, encased in sheet iron and plaster for fire protection, with timber fillets as springings for brick vaults. This building has been lost, but the world's first multi-storey building with both its columns and beams of cast iron still stands in Ditherington on the outskirts of Shrewsbury, Shropshire (Figure 10.2). It was built as a flax mill (for making linen) in 1797; rectangular openings in the central row of columns accommodated the line-shaft which powered belt-driven textile machinery. It saw various subsequent uses including that of

Figure 10.2 Ditherington Mill, Shrewsbury, Shropshire of 1797, the world's first iron-framed multi-storey building, using cast iron for both beams and its cruciform-section columns.

a maltings. Grade I listed for its importance in technological history but disused for some years, it has now been purchased by English Heritage and a brighter future is in prospect.

Cast iron columns

Being strong in compression, cast iron was ideal for use in columns. As cast iron is formed by being poured molten into a mould, sectional and elevational variations of profile were readily achieved. The earliest column sections were cruciform (+), soon followed by hollow circular sections. These cooled more rapidly and with less risk of shrinkage cracking than a solid square or circular section. A modest entasis was often incorporated into the shaft, following classical influence that could also be seen in the fluting of circular columns and most obviously in column heads of Doric, Ionic and Corinthian profile.

Column bases, in contrast, were usually relatively simple, with an enlarged plate (or simply a lip on some larger columns) to spread the load, stabilise the column, and sometimes engage a corresponding flange on the column below, to which it might be bolted.

Column joints usually occurred at floor level. The column below would often have an enlarged head or 'table' to receive floor beams, while the column above would engage on a spigot or a continuation of the column below. Occasionally a 'saddle' would be formed to allow beams to pass through the column head. In general, gravity loads from above were transmitted directly to the column below rather than through timber beams (weak in cross-grain compression) or metal beams (with the risk of web crushing or buckling unless stiffened).

Circular hollow columns were often used as down pipes, particularly in large single-storey sheds and factories where saw-tooth toplit roofs made any other means of rainwater disposal difficult. In rare cases such columns were used instead as vertical risers for a steam heating system – and in one case, reportedly, as gas pipes!

H-section cast iron columns found some use in naval dockyards and factories with overhead gantry cranes. They should be distinguishable from later wrought iron or steel H-columns by their thicker flanges and their integral end-plates. Dating of the construction can be helpful, too – even small rolled wrought iron H-columns were not introduced before c.1850, while steel columns were not rolled until the late 1880s.

Cast iron beams

The relative weakness of cast iron in tension was a disadvantage where beams were concerned. The famous civil engineer Thomas Tredgold erroneously believed that the bottom (tension) flange of a beam should be of the same size as the top (compression) flange, but work in the 1820s by Eaton Hodgkinson, a scientist and mathematician, led to the adoption of I-section cast iron beams, with the top flange being about one-quarter the area of the bottom flange. (This was an early example of what is nowadays called research and development.)

The bending stresses in a beam increase towards midspan. This was understood by Victorian engineers and ironfounders, who responded by varying the beam profile. 'Fish-belly' or 'hump-backed' elevations and similar convex bowing of the flanges on plan are common; the moulding and casting process made such variations very easy to achieve.

Longer beams could be cast in sections, and joined by bolts. Beams were sometimes strengthened by 'trussing' with wrought iron tie rods. The failure in 1847 of three-piece trussed cast iron beams with poorly conceived wrought iron tie rods on Robert Stephenson's Dee Rail Bridge near Chester led to a Royal Commission of Inquiry into the use of cast iron in railway structures. (This contributed in part at least to the subsequent wider use of wrought iron in place of cast iron, particularly for beams and girders.)

The end face of a beam supported on circular columns was often formed as half a circle with projecting lugs on either side. It could then sit on a narrow ledge at the column head, being held in place with wrought iron bolts through the lugs connecting it to the adjacent similar beam. Alternatively, adjacent beams could be connected by wrought iron rings heated and then shrunk onto D-shaped studs projecting either side of the beam ends, or simply bolted to the top of the column.

Cast iron frames

The cast iron frame was widely used, particularly for larger industrial and commercial buildings, throughout much of the nineteenth century. Although wrought iron beams and girders were available from c.1850, frames entirely of cast iron continued to be built. Many notable all-cast-iron-framed textile mills were built in the 1860s, particularly in the textile centres of West Yorkshire and Lancashire. In this context it should be made clear that 'framed' refers specifically to the internal structure of columns and beams; mills, factories, storehouses and the like were almost invariably enclosed by thick masonry external walls, not least to exclude burglars. These walls stabilised the building against wind forces, so that the internal columns and beams had to support only the gravity loads of the building itself, its users, and their machinery and goods.

A major structural development was the **rigid frame**, in which the joints between the columns and beams are made stiff enough to stabilise the frame without the need for heavy masonry walls. Possibly the earliest surviving rigid-framed cast iron structure is the two-storey former fire station in Portsmouth Dockyard of c.1844, whose upper floor had to support the very substantial weight of a large water tank that fed the dockyard's fire main. The columns are braced by haunched beams that provide the necessary rigidity; the external wall cladding of corrugated sheeting makes no contribution to stability. Later rigid-framed structures usually had some wrought iron members, and so are considered below.

Large numbers of smaller all-cast-iron-framed structures were built and many survive, often with delightful decorative features. Conservatories and greenhouses are usually relatively austere, but bandstands and pier shelters, for example, can amply show the ability of cast iron to form pleasing architecture.

Other uses of cast iron in buildings

- **Arches**: cast iron arches are seldom found in buildings, but were widely used in bridge engineering, from the Iron Bridge of 1779 until the late nineteenth century. The arch form made effective use of the good compressive strength of cast iron to carry heavy loads (as from canals, roads and railways), and its generous headroom gave clearance over other transport routes including navigable waterways.
- **Trusses**: in view of its weakness in tension, it might be surprising that some complete trusses were made in cast iron. (The shorter-span trusses of the Crystal Palace – see below – are excellent examples.) More generally, it was widely used for compression members in trusses assembled from individual components.
- **Minor structural elements**: cast iron was much used in the nineteenth century for secondary lattice elements such as cantilever brackets supporting railway station platform roofs. Often the 'mouldability' of cast

iron is used to its full, with such brackets comprising a riot of geometri-cal patterns, leaves, flowers, fruits, etc. In austere contrast are the simple concave-triangular cantilevers, braces and beam sections to be found in industrial and commercial buildings. Cast iron was also much used for lintels over openings, as decorative mullions dividing windows, and in wall plates anchoring wrought iron tie rods. Flat or profiled solid plates were often used as flooring in larger buildings. Open-tread plates were also made, particularly for staircases and access ways.

- **Handrails, railings, balustrading to staircases, etc.**: cast iron was a common material for these barriers, despite its known poor resistance to tension and impact loading.
- **Screw piles**: the screw pile was an ideal foundation solution in poor ground and in marine works such as jetties and piers. Formed as a shaft with, typically, a single large-diameter helical thread, screw piles were an alternative to timber piles as a simple means of carrying loads without having to excavate in waterlogged and difficult ground conditions.
- **Notable non-structural uses**: these include lamp posts, pipes of all sorts, gates, bollards, grilles, household fittings such as boot-scrapers and – not least – the 'slates' roofing the Houses of Parliament.

Connections in structural cast iron

As noted above, gravity loads were generally transmitted by direct bearing from beams onto column heads and from one column to the column below. Wrought iron bolts were used to ensure that elements were placed in their intended locations, and to retain them there, secure against disturbance such as machinery vibration that could lead to a beam gradually 'walking' off its bearing if it were not held in place.

Rivets were not used to connect cast iron elements, at least not by those who understood the material, as the clamping forces exerted as the rivets cooled and contracted could fracture the brittle cast iron sections.

Wrought iron

Pre-industrial use of wrought iron

Wrought iron masonry cramps were occasionally used in Greek and, later, Roman construction, and subsequently. Iron nails were widely used but were costly, being hand-made, while major structural joints in timber frames were usually made by shaping and rebating the intersecting timbers, using (usually hardwood) dowels to provide a simple pinning connection and relying on transfer of forces in compression wherever practicable.

Non-structural 'ironmongery' was used for moving parts subject to wear – hinges, latches, locks, window frames and the like – while non-ferrous metals were widely used in later periods, with lead and copper for sheet roofing and lead for water supply being common. Like cast iron, wrought iron was commonly used for railings.

Ambitious masonry structures such as Wren's St Paul's Cathedral in London were often provided with wrought iron ties to restrain circumferential tension forces, while the development of timber trussed roofs for larger spans led to the use of wrought iron to reinforce joints subject to tension; the larger spans were not easily achieved with timber alone. Wrought iron was also incorporated, in strip or bar form, as reinforcement to masonry. The Louvre in Paris has such ironwork dating from the 1660s.

Early suspension footbridges using wrought iron rods as the chains are known to have been built in China from the seventh century AD.

Early use of structural wrought iron

In the early 1820s, wrought iron angles and tie rods came into limited use as the internal elements in composite roof trusses, combined with timber principal rafters. Iron-to-iron connections were typically made by riveting, iron-to-timber connections by bolts or straps. But the real spur to the wider use of wrought iron in structures was industrial growth, just as it spurred the development of cast iron as outlined above.

The need for improved road communications to carry freight (before the coming of the railway) called for longer-span bridges. Thomas Telford, for example, was charged with improving the London–Holyhead road, a key link between Britain and Ireland. Spanning the wide fast-flowing Menai Strait was a challenge, to which Telford responded by designing a suspension bridge (Figure 10.3) – the longest span of this type yet attempted (579 feet/177 metres). Wrought iron was the only material then available that could carry the large tension forces that such a large span induced in the suspension chains. The bridge opened in 1826. Much of the original wrought ironwork has been replaced by steel, but the span still impresses.

The railways in their turn created new structural demands. Stations such as the large termini needed large and imposing roofs. One of the earliest was at Euston in London, where arguably the first all-wrought-iron roof trusses were erected in 1837.

The first wrought iron I-beams, of modest size, were rolled in Britain and France in the late 1840s. However, the demand for long-span railway bridges capable of carrying heavy locomotives was beyond the capacity of these small sections. Once again, it was the crossing of the Menai Strait that called for a very substantial bridge, this time conceived by Robert Stephenson. The notion of trains running *inside* twin large wrought iron tubes made up from riveted plate was simple, but the engineering had to be proved, particularly for the two central spans, each of 460 feet (140 metres). Model testing showed that the slender plates would buckle unless stiffeners were provided, while the top and bottom flanges were made up of rectangular cells, again to prevent buckling. The bridge was opened in

Figure 10.3 Thomas Telford's 1826 Menai Bridge over the fast-flowing strait between Anglesey and the North Wales mainland, a key element in his improvement to the London–Holyhead road (and thence to Ireland).

1850 and served well until, sadly, its ironwork was irreparably damaged by fire in 1970. Its spans were replaced by steel arches carrying both road and railway, although a small section of one tube has been preserved on the mainland side of the bridge.

Wrought iron beams and girders

The commonest wrought iron beams were small rolled I-beams, often compounded with riveted flange plates. Plate girders were made up largely from plate, with angles (sometimes tees) joining plate sections and providing stiffness to resist buckling, all joined by rivets. Such girders – to be found in buildings as well as bridges – may have flange plates added towards midspan to increase bending strength, and web stiffeners (angles or tees) to enhance shear resistance and/or to resist concentrated web loads. Because of this, they may not be easily distinguishable from steel; knowing the construction date may be helpful, but both materials were in use during the 'overlap' period of the 1880s and 1890s.

Angles and tees were often used as secondary beams supporting wrought iron floor plates and as purlins, or even battens, in pitched roofs.

Beams and plate girders were sometimes used in pairs, for example in crane gantry girders. The extreme example of this combination of elements was the pair of huge tubes in the Menai Strait Railway Bridge mentioned above. Brunel developed the use of closed tubes, most notably for the top boom (really a strut rather than a beam) in the spectacular 'suspension arch' Royal Albert Railway Bridge near Plymouth.

Wrought iron columns

Wrought iron was not so widely used for columns as cast iron. The latter was stronger than wrought iron in compression, and remained readily and cheaply available throughout its lifespan as a structural material, so it was widely used for columns until supplanted by steel around the end of the nineteenth century. Wrought iron columns, when used, would generally be either I-beams or built-up plate sections, with or without additional flange plates.

Wrought iron frames

Wrought iron building frames became common in the second half of the nineteenth century, particularly for single-storey industrial and commercial use as in railway stations, arcades, factories and sheds. Because of the continued use of cast iron for columns, single- and multi-storey structures combining both materials are common. These make the best use of their respective merits – the compressive strength of cast iron, and the tensile strength and ductility of wrought iron. Stability to such frames was provided by the rigidity of the unbraced frame (particularly in single-storey sheds), by diagonal bracing or by loadbearing masonry walls. Two landmark structures are noted below.

Lost now, but well documented, Joseph Paxton's iconic Crystal Palace, erected in London's Hyde Park for the 1851 Great Exhibition, clearly showed the potential of iron and glass to create memorable architecture. The ironwork included cast iron columns and the shorter-span floor trusses, while wrought iron was used for longer-span trusses and the diagonal bracing that tied the structure together and provided overall stability. Sadly, the Crystal Palace was destroyed by fire in 1936, having been re-erected in south London after the original exhibition closed.

Arguably of greater historical importance, if less well known than the Crystal Palace, is the four-storey Boat Store of 1858–60 in the former Royal Naval Dockyard at Sheerness, Kent. This can fairly claim to be the first multi-storey rigid-framed building in the world, with cast iron I-section columns and secondary beams, and riveted wrought iron primary plate girders and roof trusses. As with the Portsmouth Dockyard fire station, the external walls are of corrugated sheeting and there are no internal walls, so stability is entirely reliant on the rigidity of the column–beam joints. This building is a precursor of the modern high-rise steel frame, although being within a military establishment its existence was not widely publicised, and its historical importance was realised only quite recently.

Wrought iron arches

These, both lattices and plate girders, were often used for the roofs of larger buildings including railway stations. They could be cheaper than might be expected, as they would be fabricated in much the same way as a straight plate girder, with only tapered web plates and kinked flange plates distinguishing them. The most notable example is the roof over the train shed of St Pancras Station in London. Its lattice arches span 240 feet (73 metres), the largest roof span ever built when the station opened in 1868. (Listed Grade I, the train shed is being carefully restored and adapted for its new role at St Pancras International, the London terminal for the Channel Tunnel Rail Link.)

Wrought iron trusses

Wrought iron came into its own for trusses, beginning as strapping for timber roof trusses and then replacing some or all of the timber elements. From the first all-wrought-iron trusses of 1837 at Euston Station until steel became readily available at the end of the nineteenth century, most roofs of any span beyond the domestic scale were carried on trusses, either entirely of wrought iron or using wrought iron for the tension elements. The wrought iron elements were typically angles and tees for compression members, and flats or rods for carrying tension. Sections of the trusses would be riveted together in the workshop or on site before being lifted into place on temporary falsework, and bolted or site-riveted together. The knowledgeable use of wrought iron by Victorian engineers and iron companies produced roofs of considerable lightness and elegance (Figure 10.4).

Figure 10.4 Roof over platforms at Huddersfield Station, West Yorkshire, completed in 1850.

Wrought iron ties

Wrought iron was the natural nineteenth-century structural material for carrying tensile loads, and as such was exploited as straightforward rod, chain, cable and linked bars.

Rod could be rolled directly from flat bar. The rolling process produced a rod with excellent longitudinal strength, and it could be easily worked to form a flattened end which could then be drilled to receive a pin. Alternatively, it could be threaded for a nut (as in wall tie rods secured by cast iron wall plates). Such rods were widely used as components in 'composite' structures, such as trusses, trussed beams, timber partitions and so on as well as in direct applications such as hangers, wall tie rods, and – notably in the Crystal Palace – diagonal bracing.

Chain, cable and linked bars were widely used in suspension bridges but seldom in buildings.

Other uses of wrought iron in buildings

- **Minor structural elements**: as wrought iron became more cheaply and readily available in the early nineteenth century, its use in various strapping and tying roles increased. Joints in timber roof trusses were increasingly reinforced by wrought iron straps, reducing the need for complex and costly timber joints. Wrought iron floor plates were occasionally used flat, but the ductility of the material meant that they could easily be pressed into a domed shape that increased their load and spanning capacity. The plates would typically be covered by concrete or loose fill to produce a level floor surface. Later in the nineteenth century, some stronger floors were built with **trough decking** – wrought iron plate, profiled like modern steel sheet piling sections, laid horizontally and filled with concrete. This was used in some mills and similar industrial buildings, but was much more widely used in bridge decks.
- **Handrails, railings, balustrading to staircases, etc.**: wrought iron was widely used for these elements. The malleability of the iron allowed very decorative designs to be produced.
- **Notable non-structural uses**: these included gates, brackets, decorative door hinges and many other household items.

Connections in structural wrought iron

Riveting was the normal method for connecting compound wrought iron sections as they were being fabricated, and also for site connections in many instances. Wrought iron bolts were also used, particularly for site connections. Slack in tie rods could be taken up using turnbuckles, or by driving pairs of tapered cotters or wedges into a slot within the overlapping enlarged end pieces of the tie rods. Columns were secured to foundations, where judged necessary, by long through-bolts or by ragged Lewis bolts.

Steel

Early use of structural steel

Although Bessemer had patented his 'converter' for the bulk production of steel in 1856, technical difficulties with the common iron ores and demand from other industries meant that structural steel was slow to be introduced. (See *Materials & skills for historic building conservation*.)

It was 1877 before the Board of Trade approved the use of steel in bridges, and 1887 before the first British structural steel section tables were issued by the iron and steel maker Dorman, Long. By now the first 'sky-scrapers' were being erected in Chicago and New York, some mixing iron and steel in their structures. In Britain the first major steel bridge – the Forth Railway Bridge – was opened in 1890. It is less clear when and where the first British steel-framed building appeared. The often-claimed 'first' is a warehouse in West Hartlepool of 1896, but there are other contenders, and construction historians still have work to do on this subject.

It might seem paradoxical that the chronology of early steel-framed construction in Britain is much less clear than that of cast and wrought iron, despite its being more recent. But the transition from wrought iron to steel between the early 1880s and about 1900 was to a large extent a 'seamless' transition, as the two materials have similar properties and both could be connected by riveting and bolting.

Steel beams

One notable difference between the two materials was that the manufacturing process for steel produced large ingots, from which larger structural sections could be rolled. A large rolled steel section could be used in place of a compound wrought iron section riveted up from components such as plates and angles, and overall was cheaper when the fabrication costs of the latter were taken into account.

Early steel sections, like wrought iron sections, were rolled in a wide variety of weights and thicknesses for a given nominal size. This was wasteful and led to difficulties and arguments over deliveries from the numerous steel makers. An early standardisation initiative in the early twentieth century was for steel sections, undertaken by the Engineering Standards Committee, forerunner of the British Standards Institution. This began in 1901 with BS 1, followed soon after in 1903 by the first edition of BS 4 *Structural Steel Sections*. This listed I-beams up to 24 inches (610 mm) deep, known as British Standard Beams (BSB). Later developments were the introduction of New British Standard Beams and New British Standard Heavy Beams (1921) and a replacement range of BSBs (1932). An entirely new range of Universal section profiles appeared in 1959, covering both beams and columns. Imperial units were superseded by SI (metric) units in the early 1970s, and further section profile changes followed. Similar developments affected channels, angles, tees and other sections.

Steel columns

The available size and strength of rolled steel, and its competitive price, led to its rapid adoption for columns in preference to cast or wrought iron. Individual I-beams were immediately useful as stanchions; compound stanchions were also commonly used to support heavier loads, with I-beam elements tied together by riveted lacing or battening.

An early alternative was the solid forged circular steel section, available in diameters up to 12 inches (305 mm). Ideal for commercial properties where floor space was at a premium, these compact sections had substantial compressive load capacity. Their low perimeter/area ratio also assured a relatively good fire resistance compared with I-sections. Fixings could not be made in the usual ways to such massive sections; instead, the head of the column might be turned on a huge lathe, forming a rebate to receive thick bearing plates that provided support for beams, and also served as baseplates. Less commonly, plates were drilled to the diameter of the shaft, heated and then shrunk onto it. Butt joints between adjacent shaft sections could be secured by inset steel pins, and relied on direct bearing for load transmission.

Hollow steel tubes were produced from the start of the twentieth century in round, square, hexagonal, octagonal and other shapes. These were initially rolled from plate sections which were then riveted together. They are relatively uncommon as structural columns before World War II, but have been much used in recent decades, commonly in the form of hot-rolled circular and rectangular hollow sections.

Steel frames

The Ritz Hotel in London's Piccadilly (1906) is a notable early steel-framed structure. From the outset of steel usage, the frames of multi-storey buildings included perimeter columns and beams that were subsequently encased by masonry walls. This is in contrast to the typical cast-iron-framed building, where – as noted above – the external walls were loadbearing with no columns. The advantage of using steel perimeter columns and beams was that the complete skeletal steel structure could be erected quickly, allowing floors and roof to be progressed while the masonry facades, which were slower to build, could follow behind. The Ritz was built at a time when the London building regulations still required the external walls to be sized for thickness as if they were loadbearing, despite the presence of the steel frame. Changes to the regulations in 1909 allowed such walls to be treated as non-loadbearing infill panels, when they could be thinner. These changes also introduced the first regulatory figures for loadings and permissible stresses on beams and columns of cast and wrought iron and steel. (See also the next volume in this series: *Materials & skills for historic building conservation*.)

A potential problem with perimeter steelwork encased in masonry is that of corrosion, which can occur as water penetrates poorly made or poorly maintained masonry joints and at other vulnerable points such as decayed or damaged flashings. Rusting may be unnoticed, or – if the steel is in contact with the enclosing skin of masonry – it will swell as corrosion proceeds and either crack or displace the masonry. Investigation and repair can be expensive, disruptive and potentially unsightly.

Welded structural steelwork was introduced before World War II. A notable early example is Simpson's (now Waterstone's) in London's Piccadilly. Built in 1935–36, its facade was innovatively conceived as a series of deep plate girders welded to stout columns at either end with long column-free bands of glazing, but wrangles with the London County Council – the building control authority – led to a more orthodox design being adopted, with columns at intervals along the facade.

It is hardly necessary to point out that the steel frame developed over the twentieth century to become, with its reinforced concrete counterpart, the natural choice for the structure of offices, factories, multi-storey dwellings, public buildings and many other building types. This period witnessed a transition from riveted construction in mild steel to welded construction, often in high-yield steel, nowadays often working compositely with concrete. A further notable change was from the heavy uninsulated masonry facades built in the earlier part of the twentieth century to the lighter but well-insulated cladding systems, often of metal and glass, which are attached to frames but afford no contributory stiffening as did the earlier masonry envelopes.

Other uses of steel in buildings

- **Arches**: steel arches are rare in buildings, but this structural form has been and remains favoured for longer-span bridges.
- **Trusses**: these can be found in almost every twentieth-century building type, ranging from the single-storey shed to the football stadium and the concert hall. Originally riveted, they are nowadays welded.
- **Foundation grillages**: these comprised one or more layers of steel beams under columns and walls, each acting as a spreader to distribute heavy loads over a larger ground area. For durability they were invariably concrete-encased.
- **Floor and tread plates**: pressed and rolled steel floor plates have been used in solid, perforated, 'domed' and 'buckled' forms. The 'Durbar' type of solid steel plate with raised non-slip 'bumps' is a common variety, its name redolent of Imperial India, and is often found on external fire escape stairs.
- **Other structural and non-structural uses**: steel generally replaced wrought iron in uses as described above.

Connections in structural steel

Riveting was the primary means until the middle years of the twentieth century, although bolts were also widely used. The first attempts at welding using an oxyacetylene flame were made c.1900, while electric arc welding (as is now generally used) was developed from the 1920s and used on a number of building structures before World War II. High-strength friction grip bolts were introduced in the late 1950s; these clamp the joined parts together and transmit loads by friction, not unlike rivets.

Composite elements

Cast and wrought iron, and later steel, were often used compositely, with one another or with other materials (masonry, timber and later concrete), to produce elements that employed each material efficiently, and sometimes achieved other benefits such as 'fireproof' construction.

Some commonly found examples are as follows:

- Cast iron beams were sometimes reinforced with an integral wrought iron rod or bar in the tension zone, to improve bending capacity. The wrought iron would be placed in the mould where, with its higher melting point, it would not liquefy when the molten cast iron was poured in. Ornamental cast brackets and cantilevers are found with similar wrought iron reinforcement.
- Trussed beams combined the tensile strength of wrought iron tie rods or tie bars with the compressive strength, initially of timber and later of cast iron. Such forms allowed longer spans to be tackled using multiple castings, relying on bearing between cast iron sections in compression, rather than on bolts which would have to provide continuity in the vulnerable tension zone, were the beam not trussed.
- Composite trusses, particularly roof trusses, were common. Tension members would be wrought iron flats or rods, while the compression members could be in timber or cast iron, and of squat section to resist buckling forces.
- An early combination of iron and masonry was the so-called 'jack-arch' floor, in which brick (or occasionally stone, and later concrete) barrel vaulting was supported by, and sprang from, beams. These were initially of timber, supplanted by cast iron beams from the 1790s. The shaping of the bottom flange to provide a secure springing for the masonry units also conveniently added metal to enhance the weaker tension zone. The vaulted construction supporting a level floor meant that the greatest floor depth occurred on the beam lines. It was thus practical to use structurally efficient hump-backed cast iron (and occasionally fabricated wrought iron) beams with a level soffit, embedding the beams in the fill – usually loose or lime-cemented masonry rubble. Wrought iron tie rods were commonly provided to resist spreading of the arches under load – sometimes embedded wholly or partly in the vaulting for fire protection, sometimes exposed.
- Another iron–masonry combination, albeit not structurally composite, was again intended to be fireproof. In this, stone slabs were carried directly on small secondary cast iron beams such as upright or inverted tees, which often sat into 'shoes' cast onto the side of the main cast iron beams.

- Various patented 'fireproof' floor systems were developed in the later nineteenth century. These relied on the insulating effect of (usually) fired-clay infill blocks to protect the iron beams or secondary joists in case of fire. Many systems are still to be found.
- Wrought iron, and later steel, plates were often used with timber beams, either with two plates enclosing the timber, or with a single plate sandwiched between two timbers, all bolted together. The result was a 'flitched' beam (flitched means 'sliced').
- A very common construction from the later nineteenth century for floors and flat roofs employed iron (later steel) joists wholly or largely embedded in concrete. This was known as 'filler joist' or 'joist-concrete' construction. Early concrete was lime-bound; Portland cement came later. The aggregate might be broken brick, clinker from domestic or commercial coal-burning, and sometimes even stones and sand. The joists were typically spaced at 2–4 foot (0.6–1.2 metre) centres and the concrete was then placed. It spanned between joists as a series of shallow arches. The concrete soffit was level with or below the joist soffits, while the top was level with or above or below the tops of the joists. Projecting top flanges were common where timber or other flooring was to be laid, as in residential accommodation. Filler joists were widely used in institutional and commercial buildings, and later in blocks of flats. They offered good acoustic and fire separation between floors. This form of joist construction continued well into the twentieth century, with steel joists replacing wrought iron, although it was eventually ousted by reinforced concrete.

Conservation and reuse of iron-framed and steel-framed buildings

The treatment and repair of iron and steel as materials is covered in the next volume in this series: *Materials & skills for historic building conservation*. Here, some more general advice is offered on sympathetic approaches to the conservation and reuse of particular iron-framed and steel-framed building types.

Understanding the structure

An informed approach to any conservation project involves a study of the structure to establish its construction and condition. Framed structures can broadly be divided into those whose construction is 'naked and unashamed' – that is, those whose elements and connections are largely exposed – and those in which the frame is largely buried in masonry or finishes:

- Typical building types with generally unclad frames include mills, factories, storehouses, single-storey sheds, conservatories, covered markets, canopies and other structures, mostly dating from the nineteenth century.

- Clad frames are more common in commercial buildings such as offices and banks, and in twentieth-century public and multi-storey buildings generally (as fire regulations increasingly called for protection to exposed steelwork).

Whether the frame is unclad or clad will influence not only the scope and cost of investigations but also the approach to the work necessary to conserve the structure and adapt it as necessary for future use. It is clearly easier to examine and record an exposed structure than one that is buried. Before beginning investigations it is important to make documentary searches – especially of surviving drawings, but checked against the as-built structure. Physical opening up of a listed building for investigation purposes may well require consent, and should therefore first be discussed and agreed with the local authority, or with the national heritage body through the local authority.

Compatible reuse and sympathetic intervention

With knowledge of the structure, thought can be given to the future use of the building. The conservation principles of 'minimal intervention' and 'conserve as found' argue for changes or new uses that have the least adverse effect on the structure. A new use with a floor loading requirement less than or no more than that of the original usage is preferable.

Studies, particularly at the University of Manchester, have contributed greatly to present-day awareness of structural cast iron, its properties and its performance. This has reduced the possibility of 'heavy-handed' intervention, as assessment may be based on higher allowable stresses.

At the same time, it may be found on careful assessment that parts of the structure are under-strength by modern assessment criteria – even for the original use! This is particularly likely in the case of cast iron beams when tension stresses due to bending are considered. (Cast iron columns will more often be shown to have adequate strength.) Solutions are available that allow the retention of the under-strength elements; for example:

- Introducing new beams alongside the existing beams to share the floor loading, relieving stresses on the cast iron. This has the additional advantage that it is largely reversible, although some removal of existing fabric along the line of the new beams will be needed. This approach was successfully used for the floor over the King's Library in the British Museum, spanned by some of the largest cast iron beams ever made.
- Removing 'useless' deadweight from the floor, such as the loose rubble fill often placed over brick barrel vaulting carried on cast iron beams, as often found in mills and other structures. Thick flagstones were often laid over the fill, and these too could be carefully removed for reuse elsewhere. If the removed weight is equal to or greater than the new user loads then the beams can be argued to have proved themselves 'by performance' – i.e. they have carried the equivalent of the future

loading without failure for a long time, possibly a century or more. (However, the stresses in the beams should still not be significantly higher than current assessment limits, as beams loaded to a level closer to their failure load may well sustain the load for a long time before suddenly failing.) Even if the removed deadweight is less than the new user loads, it still narrows the margin between available and required strength.

- Removal of the rubble fill exposes the cast iron beams, whose strength could then be augmented by casting lightweight concrete in place of the fill. The concrete bonds to the rough surface of the cast iron, forming 'composite' beams of greater strength than the cast iron alone.

Each of these solutions is 'discreet', and may offer the difference between a structure being judged (however reluctantly) to be inadequate for future use, and being justifiable for retention (not least to the local building control authority).

Fire protection

Reuse may demand upgrading the building's fire resistance, which can be a particular challenge where the iron or steel structure is exposed, as for example when a redundant dockside warehouse or a textile mill is being converted to apartments or office use. Exposed beams and columns – especially cast iron columns with elegant mouldings – may require physical protection to prevent strength loss in fire, with the risk of collapse. Routine solutions adopted for commercial new steelwork include sprayed coatings, board enclosures and encasement in concrete, and these could be applied also to existing structures. However, a more sympathetic solution is the use of an intumescent coating, in which a relatively thin formulation is applied to the metal faces without unduly impairing their appearance. In the event of a fire, the coating foams up to form an insulating casing, controlling the temperature rise in the metal. Still thinner intumescent coatings are in prospect.

An alternative approach for beams encased by brick-vaulted or concrete floors, but with exposed bottom flanges, is to consider fire-engineering principles and assess the 'heat sink' effect of the massive floor structures. Here again, the temperature rise of the metal is tempered by the slow heat absorption of the adjacent floor fabric, so that the loss of strength in the beams is more gradual. Calculations may show that no fire protection is needed, allowing the flanges to remain exposed to view.

Further reading

The following is a personal selection only, from an extensive literature.

Bannister, T., 'The first iron-framed buildings', *Architectural Review*, **107** (1950), 231–46.

Bates, W., *Historical Structural Steelwork Handbook* (British Constructional Steelwork Association, Ascot, 1984).

Bussell, M., *Appraisal of Existing Iron and Steel Structures* (Steel Construction Institute, Ascot, 1997).

Cossons, N. and Trinder, B., *The Iron Bridge: Symbol of the Industrial Revolution* (Moonraker Press, Bradford on Avon, 1979).

Gale, W.K.V., *The British Iron and Steel Industry: A Technical History* (David & Charles, Newton Abbot, 1967).

Gale, W.K.V., *Iron and Steel* (Longman, London, 1969).

Gibbs, P., *Corrosion in Masonry clad Early 20th century Steel framed Buildings*, Technical Advice Note 20 (Historic Scotland, Edinburgh, 2000).

Giles, C. and Goodall, I.H., *Yorkshire Textile Mills: The Buildings of the Yorkshire Textile Industry 1770–1930* (HMSO, London, 1992).

Jackson, A.A., 'The development of steel framed buildings in Britain 1880–1905', *Construction History*, **14** (1998), 21–40.

Mainstone, R.J., *Developments in Structural Form*, 2nd edn (Architectural Press, Oxford, 1998).

Paxton, R.A., 'Menai bridge and its influence on suspension bridge design', *Transactions of the Newcomen Society*, **49** (1978), 87–110.

Porter, A., Wood, C., Fidler, J. and McCaig, I., 'The behaviour of structural cast iron in fire: a review of previous studies and new guidance on achieving a balance between improvements in fire resistance and the conservation of historic structures', *English Heritage Research Transactions: Vol. 1 – Metals* (1998), 11–20.

Sutherland, R.J.M. (ed.), *Structural Iron, 1750–1850: Studies in the History of Civil Engineering, Volume 9* (Ashgate Variorum, Aldershot, 1997).

Swailes, T. and Marsh, J., *Structural Appraisal of Iron-framed Textile Mills: ICE Design and Practice Guide* (Thomas Telford, London, 1998).

Thorne, R. (ed.), *Structural Iron and Steel, 1850–1900: Studies in the History of Civil Engineering, Volume 10* (Ashgate Variorum, Aldershot, 2000).

Tilly, G., *Conservation of Bridges* (Spon Press, London, 2002).

Trinder, B. 'Ditherington flax mill, Shrewsbury: a re-evaluation', *Textile History*, **23**, 2 (1992), 189–223.

Warland, E.G., *Modern Practical Masonry* (Donhead, Shaftesbury, 2006) (illustrates embedded steel framing used in masonry walls).

Williams, M. with Farnie, D.A., *Cotton Mills in Greater Manchester* (Carnegie Publishing, Preston, 1992).

11 Conservation of concrete and reinforced concrete

Michael Bussell

This chapter sets out to illustrate the use of concrete in buildings over the last century and a half, and gives guidance on the conservation of concrete and reinforced concrete. The development of concrete and its constituents as *materials* is described in Chapter 5 of the next volume in this series: *Materials & skills for historic building conservation*.

Early use of unreinforced concrete

A notable early user of concrete was the architect Robert Smirke, who employed it in the foundations of many of his major works in the late 1810s and 1820s. The concrete was lime-based, with stone aggregate rammed into place. The benefits of such construction were not lost on others, and the unreinforced concrete foundation was widely used as a cheaper and simpler alternative to the brick or stone footings, which involved more labour. A major if little-known example of such work is the foundation raft of the Houses of Parliament in London.

For superstructure use, the concrete block – precast in a form, and then bedded in place with mortar – was an early component. William Ranger, an enthusiastic advocate of concrete, took out a patent for making blocks as early as 1832. Some examples of these early block-built houses must survive, their unusual structure perhaps masked by stucco and plaster.

An early form of floor using concrete was Fox and Barrett's patent of 1844, in use for half a century. Between cast iron and later wrought iron joists, at spacings of typically 18 inches (45 mm), closely spaced timber laths were placed. Over these laths and in the gaps between them mortar was laid, and a plaster ceiling applied to the underside of the strips, bonding to the underside of the mortar. On top of the mortar was placed a thicker layer of weak concrete which spanned between the iron joists and, together with the plaster ceiling, provided them with fire protection.

From the 1850s a number of patents were taken out for proprietary floors using concrete, particularly exploiting its 'fireproof' properties. Two of the commonest are noted here. The Dennett floor comprised concrete arches spanning between cast or wrought iron beams; temporary formwork supported the wet concrete and was removed after the concrete had hardened. Richard Moreland, a structural ironwork stockist and fabricator, patented several variants on the concrete floor. The best known was used for the floors of George Gilbert Scott's Midland Grand Hotel at St Pancras Station in London. Slender wrought iron bowstring lattices were placed to span between wrought iron floor girders, and corrugated iron was laid onto the lattices, the corrugations running parallel to the floor girders so that the iron sheet as laid could readily flex to follow the curved profile of the lattices. Lime concrete was then laid on top of the corrugated iron, which was left in place as permanent formwork.

A later variant of the arched concrete floor was the filler joist floor, in which secondary iron or steel joists at quite close spacing (typically 0.6–1.2 metres) were placed to span between the main beams. Flat timber formwork was then fixed to the underside of the joists or just below, and concrete was poured to come level with or just above or below the top flanges of the joists. This form of construction was quite widely used in many building types from the late nineteenth century until it was finally superseded by reinforced concrete between the two World Wars. A fuller account of filler joist construction appears in Chapter 10.

A number of houses and other buildings were constructed in unreinforced concrete – also known as 'mass' concrete. A notable survivor is the 1883 Swedenborgian New Church in Waldegrave Road, Anerley, south London (Figure 11.1). This neo-Gothic structure, now converted to flats, was built by the Concrete Building Company and probably designed by its

Figure 11.1 The neo-Gothic, unreinforced mass concrete Swedenborg Church, Waldegrave Road, south London, 1883, by W.J.E. Henley.

manager W.J.E. Henley. The thick walls superficially appear to be of weathered red sandstone, although closer inspection reveals the horizontal joint lines between successive pours of concrete, and the rounded aggregate, while the pillars, arch jambs and oriel surrounds are of a lighter-colour denser concrete, probably precast and then placed before the adjacent walling concrete was poured. The unreinforced structure appears to have required no significant repair in its working life, in contrast to many buildings with unclad reinforced concrete structures, in which corrosion of the reinforcement has cracked or spalled the concrete and required remedial work.

Early use of reinforced concrete

W.B. Wilkinson, who had taken out a patent for reinforced concrete in 1854 that seems to have been ahead of its time in view of the lack of attention it attracted, built a small reinforced concrete house in Newcastle upon Tyne in 1865. This survived until it was demolished in 1954; fortunately, it was at least recorded by a structural engineer. Apart from this, there were only isolated instances of reinforced concrete being proposed or used structurally before the 1890s, certainly in Britain. In France, Lambot built concrete boats reinforced with wrought iron rods, and Monier made large plant pots similarly reinforced.

More relevant to building construction was the cladding system patented by W.H. Lascelles in 1875. Thin precast concrete panels, in one of several colours, were lightly reinforced with wrought iron rods (probably only to avoid damage during handling), and fixed – perhaps improbably – to *timber* studding. The system also embraced decorative concrete mouldings that could easily be mistaken for terra cotta, but were undoubtedly both cheaper and quicker to make. Examples survive on the Central Buffet and Dock Manager's Office buildings on the north quayside of the Royal Albert Dock in east London.

The 'serious' beginnings of reinforced concrete construction in Britain date to the 1890s (interestingly, the same period in which structural steel was ousting cast and wrought iron). In 1892 François Hennebique, an entrepreneurial French contractor, secured his first British patent for his concrete construction system, which rapidly developed to become the most widely used system in the country before World War I. In 1897 he built Weaver's Mill in Swansea Docks, a very functional flour mill and granary whose utilitarian appearance and superficially poor condition were undoubtedly factors leading to its demolition in 1984. Hennebique was intensely careful about using sound materials and workmanship for his projects, sourcing all the materials (except possibly the water!) from his own supplies in France, and likewise the labour. The work on site was supervised by his British agent, L.G. Mouchel, who founded the eponymous consulting engineering practice that designed many of Hennebique's structures; it still – as Mouchel Parkman – holds the original records of many of them. As was common with such structures, it was load tested on completion to prove its adequacy. Floors were generally designed for the substantial loading of 3 cwt/sq. ft (16.1 kN/m^2); packing areas with sacks of grain up to the ceiling – literally the upper limit to the loading to be carried – produced minimal slab deflections of about 1/20th of an inch (just over 1 mm), an entirely successful result.

What is possibly now the oldest surviving reinforced concrete structure in Britain was built as a Co-operative Wholesale Society warehouse on the Quayside at Newcastle upon Tyne, mostly between 1897 and 1900 (Figure 11.2). This was designed for even higher loadings than Weaver's Mill, in view of the varied nature of goods to be stored in it – 6 cwt/sq. ft (32.3 kN/m^2) – and again a load test was successfully carried out. After standing empty for a number of years and escaping the demolition that removed many of its neighbours, the building was transformed into the Malmaison Hotel by Terry Farrell & Partners. A contributory factor to this possibly unlikely reuse is the building's location at the northern end of Wilkinson & Eyre's 'blinking eye' Millennium Footbridge, facing the Baltic Art Centre and Sage Music Centre across the Tyne.

Reinforced concrete in this early period offered an economical and fire-resistant form of commercial and industrial construction. Typically, a grid

Figure 11.2 The Malmaison Hotel, Newcastle upon Tyne, built in 1901 as a warehouse for the Co-operative Wholesale Society, converted by Terry Farrell & Partners.

of downstanding beams in two directions at right angles supported fairly thin slabs and was carried on columns, often at relatively close spacings except where there was an operational need for larger spans. Columns and beams were carried through onto external elevations, with either brickwork or thinner concrete walls infilling the spaces between them. The only concession to decorative treatment was external render, which, when neglected, hardly makes them prime candidates for retention, especially when sited in run-down areas zoned for regeneration.

Perhaps the most notable structure built in Britain before World War I was the 1909 Royal Liver Building at Pier Head, Liverpool, another Hennebique structure (architect: W. Aubrey Thomas). At 51 metres high to the general roof level, and with an overall height of 94 metres to the beaks of its Liver birds, it was the world's tallest concrete building when opened. Unlike the more utilitarian concrete structures of the period, this building was clad in granite; it was Liverpool's nearest counterpart to the Manhattan skyscrapers that rose above the ocean liners docked at the other end of the British–American transatlantic route.

Although Hennebique was probably the most successful concrete specialist from the beginning of the twentieth century onwards, many rival concrete systems were introduced with greater or less success in this period. These offered anything from the supply of reinforcement, or the supply plus design of the structure, to the complete 'package' including its construction – what today is called design and build. British architects were swifter than civil engineers to see the potential of concrete, not least its *apparent* need for only minimal maintenance compared to iron or steel structures.

Many different reinforcing bar profiles were adopted, partly to avoid infringing existing patents but also to ensure that the enclosing concrete gripped and bonded to the bars – an essential requirement if the two materials were to work together. Many if not most of the systems used in Britain were actually 'imported' from abroad, such as the Kahn and Indented Bar systems from the USA, and the Monier, Coignet and Considère systems from France.

Notable developments in reinforced concrete construction

Gradually, patents expired and some systems fell out of use, so that **reinforcement** profiles become more standardised, based on round mild steel bars or 'deformed' bars – mild steel cold-worked to increase its strength and also to provide an irregular surface to improve the bond to the concrete.

Early reinforced concrete construction, as already noted, typically involved concrete floor slabs supported on downstanding beams spanning onto columns and/or walls. This was an arrangement derived from iron and steel construction, in which beams were invariably necessary. The mouldable nature of concrete, however, meant that an alternative form of construction was possible, in which the slabs spanned directly onto columns without using beams. This idea germinated first in the USA, with several engineers and contractors patenting, testing and building such **flat slabs** in the 1900s, followed by Robert Maillart in Switzerland in the 1910s.

The advantage of the flat slab in purely commercial terms was that it reduced the floor-to-floor height of the building (with a resultant saving in the cost of the building envelope for this reduced height). Britain was slower to exploit the flat slab, with possibly its first substantial example being a Liverpool match factory of 1919; the structural designer was Sven Bylander – incidentally also responsible for the steel framing of the 1906 Ritz Hotel, London (see Chapter 10).

A key design issue for a flat slab was to ensure that the slab did not shear through at the column faces and slide downwards. (This can be mimicked by pressing a sheet of paper or thin cardboard downwards onto a pencil point.) So either the slab had to be thicker overall, which added unnecessary concrete, or the junction had to be made stronger. The latter was the obvious choice.

There were two options for strengthening the junction: a 'head' and a 'drop'. The former was smaller and deeper than the latter, which was typically a square or rectangular shallow downstand. The form of the head tended to be dictated by the cross section of the column it served: a circular column typically generated an inverted conical head, whereas a rectangular column had an inverted pyramidal head. (Nowadays, economy tends to favour another alternative – providing shear reinforcement within the slab depth.)

The clean line of the soffit of a flat slab floor, free of beams, appealed to architects. It also allowed columns to be located freely without the 'tyranny' of a regular grid of beams. As such it appealed to Modern Movement architects in the 1920s and 1930s, who also were enthused by the free-form potential of concrete generally. Owen Williams, the notable architect-engineer, was a keen advocate of flat slabs, particularly for large industrial buildings such as the factories he designed in the 1930s for the Boots pharmaceutical company in Beeston, Nottingham.

Reinforced concrete when poured in situ is inherently 'monolithic', with rigid connections between columns and beams, providing stiffness and strength to resist wind loading and providing overall stability. On taller buildings, though, it is usually simpler and more economical to take advantage of **walls** around staircases and lift shafts, and make these of reinforced concrete rather than masonry. These walls, of course, are capable of carrying gravity loads and can take the place of columns, an obvious advantage especially for dwellings, where heavy walls between adjacent flats provide sound insulation and fire separation, while the absence of columns make the interior spaces more flexible.

The engineer Ove Arup was actively involved in the Modern Movement in the 1930s, while working for the contractor J.L. Kier, rather than as an independent consulting engineer (which he was to become later). The 1935 Highpoint I flats in Highgate, north London, designed with the architectural team of Tecton and built by Kier, are a good example of the imaginative use of concrete from this period. Structural concrete walls are used for the upper seven storeys of flats and the penthouses, while at the ground floor the perimeter walls become columns or 'pilotis', providing the maximum amount of free space here in accordance with principles expounded by Le Corbusier. The balcony balustrades are distinctive features, formed of concrete in place of the more conventional metal railings. The walls were built using 'climbing formwork', which also supported the working plat-forms and eliminated the need for scaffolding down to ground level. This technique well illustrated the contractor's approach to simplifying construc-tion, saving time and money.

Slabs spanning onto walls were widely used after World War II in the post-war housing reconstruction programme, in what was variously called **box-frame** and **crosswall** construction. The former term reflected the fact that the 'frame' here comprised slabs and walls rather than beams and columns, while the latter clearly described the typical floor plan of a block of flats, with the structural walls *across* the block, from front to back, acting as party walls between the flats. These walls provided wind resistance and stability on the long elevation, while the more modest stability needs of the shorter elevation were usually met by stair and lift shaft walls.

For other construction in the years immediately after World War II, rein-forcement in particular was in short supply, being in effect rationed. This encouraged some interesting roof designs that exploited the strength of unreinforced concrete which, like brick and stone, makes efficient **arches, domes, vaults** and **shells**. A notable example was the Brynmawr rubber factory in South Wales, designed by the structural consultants Ove Arup & Partners working with Architects' Co-Partnership, opened in 1951 and built to bring regional employment. The main production floor was roofed by nine equal domes, rectangular on plan. Each spanned some 82 feet by 63 feet (25 metres by 19 metres), so that in a plan area of nearly 4500 m^2 there were only four columns. The minimum concrete thickness in the domes was a mere 3 inches (76 mm), thickening towards the corner springing points. Derelict for many years, it was regrettably demolished despite being listed Grade II*, showing all too clearly that – without concerted local support and viable reuse – even such a notable building can be lost.

Many other shell roofs of this period – over bus garages, markets, fac-tories and the like – were architecturally more modest but their large clear spans can still impress.

Another construction technique whose use was stimulated by the short-age of materials for post-war reconstruction was, paradoxically, **prestressed concrete**. The high strength of the steel used meant that less was required than for conventional reinforced concrete. Although patented by Eugène Freyssinet in France in 1928, post-war government buildings, such as a Stationery Office store and a telephone exchange of 1953 in Kilburn, north-west London, were among its earliest applications in Britain.

Later applications of prestressed concrete exploited its spanning capabilities, for example at St Catherine's College, Oxford (1964, Arne Jacobsen and Arup), with its slender prestressed roof beams over the main dining hall, and the 1964 Royal College of Physicians in Regent's Park, London (Denys Lasdun and Arup), with prestressed wall beams supporting the library over the entrance, delivering its weight onto three slender columns.

Prestressed concrete has also been widely used in precast slabs, joists and beams, both in mass-produced proprietary form and purpose-designed, for flooring, roofs and bridges.

In situ concrete is poured in its final position – typically piles, foundations, floor and roof slabs, walls and frames. There is only the one chance of getting in situ concrete right, unless by demolishing it and rebuilding. **Precasting**, typically in factory conditions, offers better quality control and the opportunity of accepting the precast elements before they are installed. 'Off-the-shelf' standard structural units, such as concrete floor joists and bridge beams, are precast in large quantities. Concrete cladding panels lend themselves well to precasting, with better conditions to achieve consistent quality. Richard Seifert's thirty-six-storey Centrepoint office tower at St Giles Circus, London (1962–67, and listed 1993), is among the most notable buildings to use precast structural cladding – which allowed this tall structure to be erected without scaffolding – here, with a polished finish (Figure 11.3).

Figure 11.3 One of the more conspicuous additions to the skyline in the twentieth century was Centrepoint, London, 1962–67, by Richard Seifert.

Durability

Plain or mass (unreinforced) concrete is not usually subject to significant durability problems, although earlier structures with low cement contents are prone to weathering-out of the surface cement paste, leaving an unintentional (but often quite pleasing) exposed aggregate finish.

Durability concerns focus on reinforced or prestressed concrete, in which atmospheric oxygen and moisture can under certain circumstances reach and act on the embedded steel, which then starts to corrode. The rust, being larger in volume than the original steel, then starts to force or 'spall' off the concrete cover, allowing further corrosion to proceed. Other factors can act to aggravate the process. The repair and remedying of corrosion damage can be a challenging and expensive process, and raises particular difficulties when the problem occurs in 'architectural' exposed concrete, whose appearance will almost inevitably be altered by such work.

Factors affecting the durability of reinforced concrete

Cement content

Freshly hardened concrete provides a highly alkaline environment, giving passive protection against corrosion to the reinforcement. A well-compacted mix with a generous cement content, a low water–cement ratio (see below), and suitably graded aggregates results in dense concrete with minimal voiding and pores, which is more resistant to the ingress of oxygen and moisture. Until recent decades cement content was generally regarded as significant principally in terms of strength, but it is now appreciated that it influences durability, so that minimum cement content is now typically chosen based on durability and exposure first, and strength second.

Water–cement ratio

Early reinforced concrete needed a 'sloppy' mix to flow into and fill the shutters, as only hand punning tools were then available to compact the concrete. This inevitably meant a high water–cement ratio. The significance of the water–cement ratio as a determinant of concrete strength was not understood until Duff Abrams' 'law' in 1919, which in essence stated that strength was inversely proportional to water–cement ratio – the less water, the stronger the concrete. Upper limits on the water–cement ratio are now prescribed in codes for reinforced and prestressed concrete, essentially providing only sufficient water to ensure hydration of the cement content.

Compaction

The importance of mechanical compaction to expel air and produce dense concrete was established by Eugène Freyssinet in 1917.

Cover

The pioneers of reinforced concrete realised that concrete cover was needed to protect reinforcement from corrosion, and also from fire, which could heat the steel and cause it to lose strength. It also ensured bond between the concrete and the full perimeter of the embedded reinforcement. Modest cover, in combination with 'lean', poorly compacted mixes low in cement (but with a generous water–cement ratio), was often – and still can be – inadequate in service exposure conditions, leading to early corrosion problems.

Congested or misplaced reinforcement

Congested or misplaced reinforcement often contributed to inadequate cover. Sometimes the specified cover could not be achieved on all faces with the reinforcement bent as dimensioned by the designer or detailer when tolerances were taken into account. And sometimes the problem was just poor workmanship, either in fixing steel with adequate cover initially or in not tying it adequately to avoid displacement of the steel during concreting.

Carbonation

As noted above, fresh concrete is a highly alkaline environment. Over time, however, atmospheric carbon dioxide can permeate from the surface into the concrete, reducing its alkalinity. If the carbonation face reaches the reinforcement then it no longer has the benefit of this passive protection and can begin to corrode in the presence of oxygen and moisture. Carbonation occurs more slowly in dense, well-compacted concrete, and obviously the greater the cover, the longer it will take for carbonation to reach the steel. Its depth of penetration into the concrete is roughly proportional to the square root of elapsed time.

Chlorides

Chlorides aggravate corrosion of steel in concrete. They originate from several sources, some in the concrete mix itself and some from outside:

- calcium chloride that was added to the concrete mix in cold weather to accelerate the setting process – its harmful effects were recognised and it is now no longer permitted as an additive
- poorly washed marine aggregate rich in salt
- sea water and marine spray (seafront structures as well as those in the sea)
- de-icing salts applied to highways and carried, mainly in solution, into the fabric of bridges, car parks, etc.

Cracking

It should not be forgotten that reinforced concrete, and some prestressed concrete, has to crack under service loads causing flexure or direct tension, as a consequence of strain compatibility. Present-day codes offer detailing guidance on provision of quite closely spaced reinforcement to ensure adequate limitation of crack width, but older structures may not be so well provided. Cracks, of course, offer an easy path for atmospheric oxygen and moisture, as well as attracting accelerated local carbonation.

Exposure conditions

Clearly a structure in a dry internal environment is at lower risk of corrosion damage than those that are in external or aggressive environments.

Durability of 'architectural' exposed concrete

Many concrete structures, particularly of the 1960s and 1970s, were conceived as architecturally 'brutalist' constructions in which the concrete was exposed, usually with some form of patterning or treatment such as board-marking or bush-hammering of the surface concrete, and expressed joints. Additional care in design and construction was necessary when the concrete was 'architectural' and would be exposed. Particular areas where corrosion problems might begin are noted below.

There is of course also the matter of appearance. Detailing of exposed concrete in urban and roadside Britain, still a fairly dirty environment, presents challenges to architects and their collaborators. It should take account of the visual effects of differential cleaning and staining where rainwater does or does not run over the concrete. But this is not really a structural matter!

Concrete finishes

Deeper cover should have been specified and provided when the cast concrete faces were to be worked after the formwork had been stripped, for example where aggregate was to be exposed by acid-etching or following use of a retarder, or where the concrete was to be bush- or pick-hammered. Hammering in particular may remove up to 50 mm or more of concrete, to leave a coarsely pitted surface; so it was important both that the specified initial cover should be adequate for the intended depth of concrete removal, and that the hammering did not exceed this depth.

Expressed joints

It was common in such work for the architect and contractor to agree a regular pattern of vertical and horizontal construction joints. To mask any colour differences and the 'junction' lines between adjacent pours, the joints often had a shallow formed rebate, usually trapezoidal, to allow easy removal of the formwork. This locally reduced the cover to the steel, and so should have been allowed for in detailing and on site.

Material issues

Unsound aggregates

There have been problems with unsound aggregates that react adversely with the cement or contain material that impairs performance of the concrete and/or the reinforcement. Such aggregates have often been waste materials, chosen for use without awareness of their deleterious properties. Common examples include

- clinker and 'breeze' (wholly or partially burned coal or coke), which may
  - expand when used in concrete
  - contain unburnt material that reduces the concrete's fire resistance (and indeed may support combustion)
  - contain compounds of sulphur and other elements that reduce the alkalinity of the concrete and contribute to reinforcement corrosion
- mundic, taken from mining spoil heaps (in Devon and Cornwall mainly), and expanding shales (Lowland Scotland), which react with the alkaline cement to produce an expansive product, causing cracks in concrete and concrete blockwork
- reactive silica aggregates, which react with the cement to form an expansive gel, leading to 'popping' of surface concrete and distinctive 'map-cracking' – a process known as alkali-silica or alkali-aggregate reaction; it needs moisture and develops most rapidly under conditions of alternate wetting and drying, so (unfortunately) disfigures externally exposed concrete

High alumina cement (HAC)

Unsound aggregates raise issues of durability, performance and/or appearance, but have not led to failures. However, there were three partial roof collapses in 1973–74 where precast HAC beams were involved. HAC developed strength very rapidly, with 80% of final strength after twenty-four hours being typical. Hence it allowed more efficient use of expensive equipment, notably steel moulds used for long-line mass-produced proprietary precast prestressed units such as floor and roof beams, of which reportedly some $17\,000\,000\,m^2$ were built, nearly all between 1945 and the mid-1970s. Over time the HAC 'converted' as a result of internal chemical changes, resulting in a more porous concrete and a consequent loss of strength. Originally it was believed that this conversion would occur only at higher temperatures, and be accelerated by higher humidity. However, investigation of the three failures (happily, with no casualties) led to major investigations of HAC and HAC structures. These showed that, even in temperate and relatively dry conditions, the HAC was converting, and could also be subject to alkaline attack, particularly in warm humid environments.

The government set up Sub-committee P of the Building Regulations Advisory Committee to review the technical evidence and make recommendations. It was found that a long-term lower-bound strength of fully converted HAC could be adopted, and hence the long-term strength of units could be predicted. From this it was possible to 'clear' all domestic floor and roof construction of the beam-and-block type with beams up to 10 inches (254 mm) deep, provided loads and spans were within the manufacture's tabulated range. Guidance was also provided on the assessment of non-domestic HAC construction and 'non-standard' HAC elements. HAC is banned in new structural work; there have been no further HAC failures since 1974.

Some specific design and construction issues

The following defects generally arose from a combination of inadequate understanding of material behaviour, and inadequate construction practice. It is to be hoped we all know better now!

Woodwool formers

Woodwool formers were quite widely used in the 1950s and 1960s to provide permanent formwork to ribbed concrete floors, usually above suspended ceilings. Proprietary formers were available, where the designer had to adopt the spacing and depths on offer, or the woodwool could be made up to profiles as required by the design, particularly for longer-span floors. The concrete design code at the time, CP 114, did not explicitly call for links to be used in ribs, and so – for economy – often only bottom bars were detailed in the ribs. Woodwool can soften when wet, and might well have been standing out in rainy conditions before concreting started. So when placing began (a) the bars could sink on their spacers towards (or even into) the woodwool; (b) compaction could disturb the bars and push them off their spacers or move them sideways or together, reducing the scope for concrete to fully envelop them. If the design was 'tight', with large-diameter bars in a narrow rib, the steel might even act as a barrier to stop any concrete reaching the bottom of the form. The result was inadequate or even no cover to the steel, with the following potential problems for the reinforcement:

- inadequate corrosion protection
- inadequate bond with the concrete
- inadequate fire protection

The woodwool, being permanent, masked any such defects, which often come to light only when, for example, a building is being refurbished with new services and ceilings. It is difficult to fix a drop-rod anchor bolt into woodwool or steel where there is no concrete!

Hollow-tile floors

The problems in hollow-tile floors are similar to those with woodwool formers and are found in structures of the same period. Hollow clay blocks (not really tiles), typically 12 inches (305 mm) square and available in depths from 3 to 10 inches (76–254 mm), were laid in rows between 'slip' tiles 3–5 inches (76–127 mm) wide, which formed a permanent soffit for the concrete ribs. The blocks, of course, saved weight compared with the concrete in the lower part of the slab, while both these and the slip tiles had a castellated profile on the soffit to act as a key for ceiling plaster applied directly. Although the tiles would not, unlike woodwool, soften when wet, the same problems of displaced bars and inadequate concrete encasement could occur, again only to be found when there was cause to remove slip tiles.

Mosaic-clad concrete

Mosaic tiles were a common form of cladding from the 1950s to the early 1970s, applied directly to concrete faces. Typically, cement render was applied to off-the-shutter concrete, 'dubbing-out' to a constant plane surface and providing an adhesive for the mosaic. Sheets of tiles on paper backing were pressed into the render and lined up, with the paper backing being soaked off when the render had hardened. The tiles were then grouted. Movement joints were not often provided in the mosaic. Also, the concrete face was often not roughened to provide a key for the render. Typical results of this were

- poor initial bond between the render and the concrete and/or tiles
- further loss of bond arising from (a) thermal movements of the tiles, (b) shrinkage and creep of the concrete, both producing shear forces in the interfaces
- mosaic near ground level, in particular, being loosened by frost when wet from splashed-up rain, and by folk kicking it
- patches of mosaic falling off

Nowadays, the render typically would incorporate a bonding agent and be secured to the concrete surface, suitably roughened, while the mosaic tiles would be secured to the render using a modern purpose-formulated adhesive. Movement joints would be provided in the mosaic and render to reduce the potential effects of concrete shrinkage and creep.

Some general site issues

Inadequate support or tying of reinforcement

Customarily the contractor was responsible for providing spacers both for cover and to support top steel. If too few or too flimsy spacers were provided (to save money), traffic before concrete was placed could push the top reinforcement down. If not detected and remedied, this reduced the bending capacity against hogging moments – a problem, particularly, in cantilevers! Insufficient tying of reinforcement could result in the steel moving around during concreting, leading to misplacement, inadequate cover or blockage of concrete flow, as noted above for woodwool formers.

Grouting of post-tensioned sheaths in prestressed work

Subsequent investigations have shown that grouting was often not fully effective in filling the sheaths, which was usually specified for durability. This could lead to air and water entering the sheaths, causing corrosion and potential failure of the tendon(s).

The above two examples highlight the following issue.

Inadequate supervision

Construction work was often not adequately supervised. For example, on a building which had lost a brick panel in high winds, a subsequent wall tie survey revealed many areas of backing concrete wall with the specified brickwork restraint ties all in place, but others with no ties at all. This could perhaps be correlated to the presence or absence of the Clerk of Works on particular days . . .

Structural failures: Ronan Point

Four people died in the partial collapse in 1968 of Ronan Point, a twenty-two-storey block of flats in east London, following a gas explosion. This was a high-rise structure using precast concrete panels for both wall and floor units, based on an existing system. The explosion blew out a load-bearing wall panel at the eighteenth floor, removing support from the floors above, which in turn fell and removed the entire corner of the block. The inquiry into the collapse highlighted a number of issues, not least that the potential for 'progressive collapse' of the structure was not considered either by its designers or in the then current codes of practice and building regulations. Codes now explicitly address 'robustness', and building regulations require consideration of disproportionate collapse – both as a direct consequence of this failure. Robust connections and alternative load paths were identified as essential. More recent events have justified this view. (See Griffiths *et al.*, 1968.)

Conservation of concrete

Introduction

Events such as the Ronan Point collapse (1968) and the high alumina cement 'scare' (1973–74) have combined with the often poor weathering performance of exposed concrete to give the material's reputation a dent, although equally a number of notable concrete structures are now listed in recognition of their architectural and historic interest.

In recent decades much has been learned – sometimes the hard way – about what is needed to produce sound, durable concrete structures, and with the knowledge gained there is no reason why sound concrete structures cannot today be designed and built. The conservation of existing concrete – particularly where it is exposed and subject to damage from reinforcement corrosion – is a more challenging task!

Investigation and assessment

Investigation and assessment of defects can generally follow the procedure described in Chapter 5. Concrete structures are 'opaque', and so as much relevant information as possible should be sought from original drawings, specifications and other records on construction details and condition, as well as the original design information. Even with the latest non-destructive testing equipment, it is not easy to determine such information without expensive and disruptive opening up.

Appraisal of Existing Structures, published by the Institution of Structural Engineers, contains useful guidance on structural investigation and assessment, both generally and also as specifically applicable to concrete. Topics include possible information sources, recognition of symptoms and diagnosis of possible causes of defects, and methods of testing. A selection of other published aids to investigation and assessment of concrete is included in the further reading list at the end of this chapter.

If strength assessment is required, it should be noted that most concrete beam and slab design until after World War II employed the elastic, modular ratio, permissible stress approach. Present-day load factor or ultimate strength limit state assessment can be applied in assessing the capacity of older concrete. This will generally give an increased resistance moment based on the concrete in compression, but the limiting factor will usually be the tensile capacity of the reinforcement. Guidance on shear capacity is, however, currently more cautious than in the past, especially for ribs, lintels and the like, for which nominal shear reinforcement used not to be called for, and it will be prudent to follow this guidance.

Repair and remediation

Concrete repair has in recent years become – regrettably, many would say – a major field of activity within the building industry. The Concrete Repair Association (www.concreterepair.org.uk) and the Corrosion Prevention Association (www.corrosionprevention.org.uk) both offer guidance on repair methods. So too do the Building Research Establishment (www.brebookshop.com) and the Concrete Society (www.concrete.org. uk), also with a wide range of published guidance on the investigation and assessment of existing concrete construction (some of which is listed below).

Corrosion damage

Severely cracked or spalled concrete and/or corroding reinforcement will generally point to the need for treatment to restore durability, even if the loss of section is not yet structurally significant. Clearly a view has to be taken, particularly if the damage is widespread and the structure is 'mundane', as to whether partial or total replacement would not be a more cost-effective and neater solution. There are a variety of repair methods, among which are the following:

- 'Traditional' repairs, cutting out the damaged concrete and reinforcement, cleaning corroded steel, splicing new steel into place, and replacing the removed concrete with a mix often containing a bonding additive to ensure that it adheres to the original concrete and provides the required cover.
- Applying an impermeable coating to the concrete (after repair) to enhance its future protection (often used on external concrete to mask weathering, repel dirt and improve appearance).
- Electrochemical 'realkalisation' of the concrete, aiming to re-passivate the steel.
- Electrochemical extraction of chlorides.
- Cathodic protection using an impressed current.

A combination of two or more methods may well be needed on any particular job.

Treatment of other common defects

Typical solutions for other defects described above (which, if widespread, again might justify replacement) are as follows:

- Unsound aggregates: 'overcoat' the elements to enhance fire protection and/or resistance to water ingress.
- High alumina cement: this does not currently appear to be causing concern, although clients might well ask for an appraisal when HAC is identified in a particular structure.
- Woodwool former and hollow-tile floors: remove formers and slip tiles and apply 'traditional' corrosion damage repair as above.
- Mosaic-clad concrete: difficult to repair in situ; more practical to remove loose mosaic and apply new matching tiles using modern adhesive formulations.
- Brick cladding and concrete nibs: if there are stability and safety concerns, replace with stainless steel angles supporting brickwork, properly tied back and with horizontal movement joints; if less severe, check for presence and adequacy of wall ties and install new ties if necessary; rake out horizontal joint below brick slips, check adequacy of slip bonding and form sealed movement joint.
- Grouting post-tensioned tendons: test with air pressure for 'through' voids; assess tendon condition by *careful* local opening up; consider whether careful de-stressing and replacement is needed; re-grout sheaths.

Regrettably, it is practically impossible to achieve an 'invisible mend' where the concrete has been damaged, so careful thought needs to be given to treatment of the repaired surfaces. A coating applied over the entire concrete surface would achieve a visual unity, rather than having patches of new concrete within the original (probably now weathered) surface. Such issues become more challenging when the structure has been listed as of architectural or historic interest, for which such a repair will usually require listed building consent and consultation with the heritage authorities.

Further reading

The following is a personal selection only, from an extensive literature.

American Concrete Institute, Building Research Establishment, Concrete Society and International Concrete Repair Institute, *Concrete Repair Manual*, 2nd edn (2003).

Bate, S.C.C., *High Alumina Cement Concrete in Existing Building Superstructures*, BRE Report 235 (HMSO, London, 1992).

British Standards Institution, BS 8221-1 *Code of Practice for Cleaning and Surface Repair of Buildings: Part 1 – Cleaning of Natural Stones, Brick, Terracotta, and Concrete* (BSI, London, 2000).

British Standards Institution – a growing number of BS EN Standards for Products and systems for the protection and repair of concrete structures – test methods with a range of Standard numbers – see the BSI website www.bsionline.bsi-global.com.

Building Research Establishment Digests:

389: *Concrete Cracking and Corrosion of Reinforcement* (1993).

402: *Static Load Testing: Concrete Floor and Roof Structures within Buildings* (1995).

405: *Carbonation of Concrete and its Effect on Durability* (1995).

444: *Corrosion of Steel in Concrete: Part 1 – Durability of Reinforced Concrete Structures; Part 2 – Investigation and Assessment; Part 3 – Protection and Remediation* (2000).

455: *Corrosion of Steel in Concrete: Service life Design and Prediction* (2001).

Concrete Society Technical Reports:

No. 30: *Alkali–Silica Reaction: Minimising the Risk of Damage to Concrete* (1999).

No. 36: *Cathodic Protection of Reinforced Concrete* (1989).

No. 44: *The Relevance of Cracking in Concrete to Corrosion of Reinforcement* (1995).

No. 50: *Guide to Surface Treatments for Protection and Enhancement of Concrete* (1997).

No. 51: *Guidance on the Use of Stainless Steel Reinforcement* (1998).

No. 54: *Diagnosis of Deterioration in Concrete Structures: Identification of Defects, Evaluation and Development of Remedial Action* (2000).

Currie, R.J. and Robery, P.C., *Repair and Maintenance of Reinforced Concrete*, BRE Report 254 (HMSO, London, 1994).

Dinardo, C. and Ballingall, J.R., 'Major concrete repairs and restoration of factory structures: Uniroyal Ltd, Dumfries, Scotland', *Structural Engineer*, **66**, 10 (1988), 151–60; and discussion, *Structural Engineer*, **67**, 3 (1989), 55–6.

Griffiths, H. *et al.*, *Report of the Inquiry into the Collapse of Flats at Ronan Point, Canning Town* (HMSO, London, 1968).

Institution of Structural Engineers, *Appraisal of Existing Structures*, 2nd edn (SETO, London, 1996).

Macdonald, S. (ed.), *Concrete: Building Pathology* (Blackwell, Oxford, 2003).

Macdonald, S. (ed.), *Modern Matters: Principles and Practice in Conserving Recent Architecture* (Donhead, Shaftesbury, 1996).

Macdonald, S. (ed.), *Preserving Post-war Heritage: The Care and Conservation of Mid-twentieth-century Architecture* (Donhead, Shaftesbury, 2001).

Pullar-Strecker, P., *ICE Design and Practice Guide: Concrete Reinforcement Corrosion: from Assessment to Repair Decisions* (Thomas Telford, London, 2002).

Sutherland, R.J.M., *et al.* (eds), *Historic Concrete: Background to Appraisal* (Thomas Telford, London, 2001).

Reference sources:

- The libraries of the Institution of Civil Engineers and the Institution of Structural Engineers (the latter originally founded as the Concrete Institute) both hold excellent collections.
- The Concrete Archive held at the Institution of Civil Engineers in London is a large repository of documentary information on systems and reinforcement, together with samples of concrete and reinforcement.
- The Concrete Society (www.concrete.org.uk) and its Advisory Service cover a wide range of topics relating to the use and care of concrete.

12 Fire safety and historic buildings

Steve Emery

British Standard 7913:1988 *The Principles of the Conservation of Historic Buildings* recognises in paragraph 7.2.2 ('Protection against fire') that 'fire is the greatest single threat to the fabric and contents of any building and, in the case of an historic building, the loss of authentic fabric in a fire is irretrievable'. This chapter is arranged to reflect the specific measures that the British Standard recommends, but expanding and updating these.

Establishment of a written fire safety policy

For a private dwelling, a 'fire safety policy' may be no more than a plan of action in case of fire, but for larger residential properties, commercial premises, museums, art galleries and other places of work, a policy statement should be prepared along the following lines:

[This organisation] is committed to providing a high standard of fire safety in its property or properties. The aim is to minimise the risk of fires occurring in order to ensure the safety of employees, contractors and visitors.

All reasonable and practicable measures will be taken to reduce the risk of fire and minimise its effect by providing effective fire safety management.

[This organisation] will comply with its statutory responsibilities under all current fire safety legislation and will conduct fire risk assessment/s as required.

Fire safety arrangements will be regularly audited to ensure that standards are maintained.

All fire safety and firefighting equipment will be tested and maintained in accordance with the relevant British Standard or manufacturer's specification.

All employees will receive fire safety instruction when starting with the organisation and continuation training at regular intervals, to include fire drills.

The Fire Safety Manager will be responsible for all fire safety matters and will receive the appropriate support from the organisation. The Fire Safety Manager will report to the Chief Executive/Managing Director/etc.

Fire Wardens will be appointed to help the Fire Safety Manager to undertake his duties, to undertake first response firefighting and ensure effective evacuation in case of fire.

Special precautions will be adopted for any extraordinary events such as building works, public events, firework displays, etc.

Appointment of a named person to be responsible for all fire matters

A fire safety manager should be appointed. This person should be in a position of authority, preferably at senior management level, so that he can take control of all fire safety matters and be in a position to implement the fire safety policy and any fire safety improvements. He should nominate employees as fire wardens to help him carry out his duties.

Preparation of a fire safety manual

This manual should detail

- an explanation of the fire safety strategy
- procedures to be followed in case of fire
- the fire safety provisions provided for the building, ideally annotated on a plan, which should include
  - fire-resisting walls and partitions
  - fire-resisting doors and shutters
  - position of fire barriers
  - position of fire detectors, break glass call points, sounders and indicator panel
  - position of emergency lights, firefighting equipment, exit signs, fire procedure notices and other signs
- the design documentation of each fire safety system to show the standard to which it has been installed, any deviations from that standard and its use
- detailed maintenance and testing procedures
- staff roles in the event of fire and their responsibilities, authority and accountability
- salvage and damage controls
- staff training programmes
- fire brigade access and firefighting facilities
- building services

The fire safety manual should be kept on the premises and maintained by a competent person. It should be available for inspection by the relevant enforcing authority.

Installation of a fire detection and alarm system

A fire alarm and/or detection system should be provided for each historic property as appropriate for the risk. British Standard 5839 Part 6 is the appropriate guidance for residential premises and British Standard 5839 Part 1: 2002 provides guidance for all other uses of premises. Fire alarm systems can be installed to provide property protection or for life safety, both of which should comply with BS 5839. It is important that a system exists to transmit the fire alarm signal to the fire brigade when the premises are unoccupied. The normal method of providing this facility is to route any fire alarm actuation to a central monitoring station, which can call out the fire brigade, or if required verify that it is a genuine call.

The positioning and choice of detectors is significant in historic buildings. The siting of **point smoke detectors**, particularly where there are ornate ceilings, often leads to conflict. The ideal position for detectors is, as detailed in the British Standard, as central as possible. For visual reasons they are often placed close to the wall above the door, so that they cannot be seen upon entering the room.

Recent smoke testing in a variety of premises has shown that natural air currents influence the movement of smoke in the early stages of a fire as much as the convection currents set up by the fire. Doorways and windows often provide these natural air currents, which very effectively keep the smoke away from the detectors, rendering them useless. Detectors that are recessed or placed above holes in the ceilings or hidden behind beams and lights are also ineffective.

In large rooms with ornate ceilings the use of **beam detectors** could be considered. These have a transmitter and receiver, and work when the beam is interrupted by smoke. The beam is not very wide, so there is no guarantee that smoke will interrupt it on the way up. The beam detector should therefore be located as near to the ceiling as possible, so that when the smoke spreads out it will interrupt the beam, causing it to actuate. The lower the beam is located, the longer it will take for the smoke layer to fill down to it.

Aspirating systems, also known as air sampling systems, only require a small sampling tube to be inserted through the ceiling, so visually they are ideal. They either have a central sampling point, so that air from all the rooms covered is drawn along tubes to it, or there are a number of local sampling points connected to fewer tubes. There are some points to bear in mind:

- The size of the tubes between the small bore tube, which penetrates the ceiling, and the sampling chamber may make it difficult to install sympathetically. Lifting of floorboards above will be required.
- There needs to be a large enough space for the sampling chamber, which should be conveniently located to avoid long pipe runs.
- The noise of the fan, which is running continuously, may be obtrusive in certain situations.
- The running costs, which include replacement filters and power to the fan, should be taken into account.

Video detection is suitable for very large spaces such as churches or halls where the smoke would cool and stop rising before it reached conventional detectors sited at ceiling height. Fixed video cameras are linked to a computer, which is programmed to recognise the movement of smoke and raise the alarm. The expense can be offset by the fact that fewer cameras than point detectors in a conventional detection system are needed, and the system can incorporate some security features. If the premises are smoke-logged when the fire brigade arrives, they can rewind the tape to find the origin of the fire and thus make firefighting more effective.

Voice alarms cut the time from actuation to people responding (the response time) and thus cut the total evacuation time, which may allow some leeway in other fire safety provisions.

Review of fire separation and compartmentation

Compartmentation is the division of a building, by fire-resisting walls, partitions and ceilings, into separate fire compartments to limit the size of fire and to stop it spreading from one part of the building to another, or into staircases and other exit routes. In historic situations, improvements should only be necessary if a fire risk assessment has shown that the fire safety arrangements are not adequate and the means of escape or the building's fire performance are in need of improvement. Particular problem areas that can lead to undetected fire spread include undivided roof spaces; voids behind panelling, which sometimes interconnect with the roof space; and continuous floor voids which pass over compartment walls and partitions.

Perforation of fire-resisting ceilings by recessed downlighters and placing of electrical equipment in voids behind panelling should be avoided. Doors in compartment walls should be fire-resisting and self-closing and should not be propped or wedged open. They should self-close effectively to sit squarely within the frames. Any excessive gaps caused by warping or dropping of the hinges should be subject to remedial action. Where there are panelled reveals, the panelling is often a weak point in the fire resistance of the assembly, so an investigation, and if necessary fire-stopping between the door frame and the substrate, will be required. Holes in compartment walls or ceilings, formed for the passage of cables or pipes, should be fire stopped and the holes sealed with mineral wool or other fire-resisting material.

The Regulatory Reform (Fire Safety) Order 2005

The **Regulatory Reform (Fire Safety) Order 2005** (commonly known as the RRO), introduced in 2006 as Statutory Instrument 2005 No. 1541, was enacted to replace over one hundred pieces of fire legislation enforced by a variety of bodies. The RRO is enforced by the local fire authorities and applies to all premises with the exception of the following: single domestic dwellings; offshore installations; ships; outdoor undertakings; vehicles and other forms of transport; mines and quarries; and borehole sites.

The person responsible for ensuring compliance with the legislation in the workplace is the employer, except where the terms of a lease or contract place an obligation for repair or maintenance on someone else. '**The**

responsible person' (whether employer or otherwise) has a number of duties:

- to take general fire precautions to ensure the safety of employees and other persons in the premises
- to undertake a fire risk assessment and review it as necessary
- to record the significant findings of the risk assessment
- to apply the principles of prevention
- to arrange and record the planning, organisation, control, monitoring and review of the preventative and protective measures
- to eliminate or reduce the risk from dangerous substances
- to ensure that the premises are provided with appropriate firefighting equipment, fire alarm and detection
- to take measures for firefighting, including the training of competent persons, and arrange any contacts necessary in the emergency services
- to make sure that exits and exit routes are kept clear, that there are enough exits for the occupants of the building, that they are adequately signed and unlocked, and that they are lit by emergency lighting if necessary
- to establish and practise evacuation drills and nominate sufficient competent persons to implement the procedures
- to have procedures in place to prevent persons being exposed to serious or imminent dangers, including restricting access to areas of danger
- to take adequate precautions in respect of dangerous substances and make arrangements for informing the emergency services of their presence
- to ensure that there is a regime for adequately maintaining fire safety equipment and systems
- to appoint one or more persons to assist in the preventative and protective measures
- to provide information to employers of other persons and to self-employed working in the premises
- to provide initial and periodic training to employees, to take place during working hours
- to cooperate and coordinate with other responsible persons in premises that are multi-occupied

In addition, all employees have a personal duty of care to take precautions and inform others when risks arise.

The **principles of prevention,** which are the duty of the responsible person, involve

- avoiding risks
- evaluating the risks that cannot be avoided
- combating risks at source
- replacing the dangerous by the non-dangerous or less dangerous

- developing a coherent overall prevention policy which covers technology
- organising work and other influencing factors relating to fire and the working environment
- giving collective preventative measures priority over individual protective measures
- giving appropriate instructions to employees

Eleven guides accompany the RRO, and these fortunately recognise the significance of historic buildings and the need to ensure that a balance is struck between ensuring that sufficient measures are in place for the safety of people and maintaining the character of the building by avoiding extensive alterations. Should the design and nature of the historic building preclude the introduction of fire safety features, it will be necessary to manage the building in a way that limits the number of occupants, either staff or members of the public, inside the building; limits activities in the building; and provides adequate supervision within the building.

The RRO offers alternatives to conventional fire precautions: a fire-engineering solution; the upgrading of existing doors and partitions in a sympathetic manner to improve their fire resistance; and the consideration of installing specialist fire-detection or suppression systems.

Provision and maintenance of appropriate first response firefighting equipment

British Standard 5306 Part 3 gives appropriate guidance on the level of provision, siting and maintenance of fire extinguishers. The correct size and type of extinguisher should be used for the particular type of fire (Figure 12.1) and staff trained to use it safely and effectively. Hose reels and other automatic means for fighting fire should be considered for remote properties where the quick attendance of the fire brigade cannot be guaranteed.

Access for firefighting must always be available to all parts of the building and site, and consideration needs to be given to avoiding conflict between security measures and means of escape and the external and internal fire brigade access (Figure 12.2). The optimum degree of access is detailed in Approved Document B5, to allow rapid deployment of fire brigade ladders, hoses and other rescue equipment. However, this is not always possible for some sites – say, town centre sites, islands, walled palaces and castles – and a risk assessment might highlight the need for special compensatory measures, such as provision of

- a dry riser with inlet close to the available fire appliance access
- private hydrants and fire pumps
- ladders
- an automatic fire-suppression system

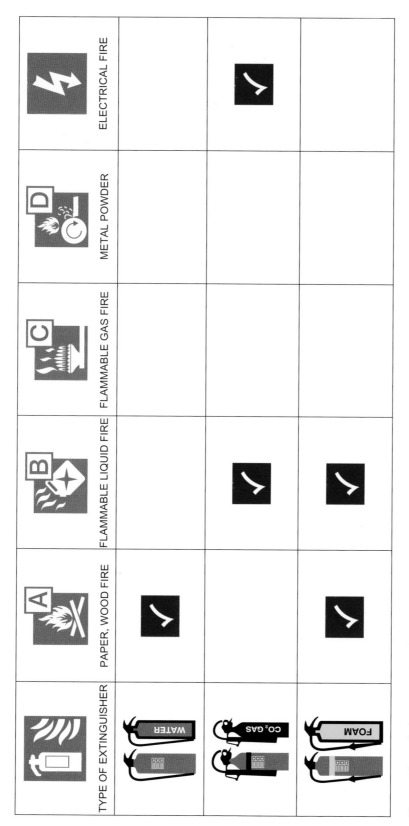

TYPE OF EXTINGUISHER	PAPER, WOOD FIRE	FLAMMABLE LIQUID FIRE	FLAMMABLE GAS FIRE	METAL POWDER	ELECTRICAL FIRE
WATER	✓				
CO₂ GAS		✓			✓
FOAM	✓	✓			

Figure 12.1 Which extinguisher for which fire?

Figure 12.2 Grade I-listed Stoke Rochford Hall, now a residential conference centre, near Grantham, Lincolnshire, was partially destroyed by fire in January 2005. Good access is vital to effective firefighting to limit damage.

Staff fire-training

Requirements for staff training will depend on the size and complexity of the building and its use. For small premises a brief tour and explanation of the fire procedures will be sufficient, but in larger premises the training should include

- basic fire legislation
- an understanding of fire science, including the triangle of fire, fire spread, fire growth and the dangers of smoke
- basic fire safety, including causes of fire and housekeeping
- the fire strategy for the premises including the provision of and reasons for compartmentation, means of escape, fire-warning systems, emergency lighting, firefighting equipment, and signs and notices
- the safe use of firefighting equipment, raising the alarm, evacuating the premises and calling the fire brigade

Regular inspection of residential apartments

Residential apartments pose one of the higher risks in mixed-use premises. The use of real fires, candles, deep-fat fryers, electric blankets and other sources of ignition are difficult to control in these situations, and sometimes the only solution is to educate occupiers on the dangers of fire; enforce good housekeeping; and ensure that the fire safety provisions are maintained to a high standard.

Fire safety requirements for building and maintenance contracts

A new risk assessment should be undertaken and clear procedures and enforcement carried out whenever there are contractors on site, such as for exhibition displays or building works, especially hot work, where there will be additional hazards. Where **caterers** are used for events, the contract should be clear about what operations can and cannot be carried out, what areas can be used, and who has the authority (preferably site staff) to make sure that the conditions of contract are adhered to. Menus should be agreed in advance, preferably to eliminate hazards such as deep-fat frying or the use of blowtorches; additional safeguards should be put in place if these are essential. Problems that might arise in the middle of an event can then be avoided.

The additional threats which **building works** pose can include

- loss of fire separation caused by the removal of doors or repair of partitions or ceilings
- temporary isolation of fire detectors to avoid false alarms caused by dust
- additional fire loading caused by the temporary storage of building materials and packaging
- additional sources of ignition caused by temporary lighting, plumbing works, sparks from cutting gear, burning paint and lead burning – these ignition sources should be controlled by a system of Hot Work Permits, or better still the banning of hot work altogether
- poor water supplies because hydrants have been covered or have not yet been fitted
- poor fire brigade access because of temporary hoardings or site huts

Damage control team

Damage control will need to be considered if the building contains artefacts, paintings or other valuable, historic or irreplaceable collections. A salvage plan, which is part of the counter-disaster manual, should be drawn up. This plan should identify

- personnel responsible for salvage operations, including the salvage officer and his or her deputy
- training of the salvage teams
- salvage priorities (Figure 12.3)
- salvage procedures
- emergency first aid conservation
- further treatment procedures

Figure 12.3 A devastating fire at the seventeenth century Wardington Manor, near Banbury, Oxfordshire, in 2004. The Manor contained Britain's greatest private collection of atlases, which was saved by villagers forming a human chain to pass the books to safety.

Salvage priorities (snatch lists) are best in the form of photographs of the items, their position in the room and building, any special measures needed to remove them, such as manual handling requirements, removal techniques and equipment required, and order of priority. The value of the exhibits should not be included, for security reasons. If a room is completely filled with items of similar value it is still worth sorting them into an order of removal, perhaps by order of rarity, importance, ownership or simply ease of removal.

It is particularly difficult to keep up-to-date **contact lists** for management teams, members of salvage teams and equipment suppliers. A worthwhile exercise is to occasionally try to contact people on the lists at different times of the day, in the evenings, at weekends and other unusual times to see if the existing method of making contact is still efficient.

Regular liaison with the local fire brigade

Fire brigades have a duty under section 1.1(d) of the Fire Services Act 1947 to familiarise themselves with the premises they are likely to attend. They will therefore usually be agreeable to an invitation to look around the property and perhaps take part in exercises.

Justifying work to historic fabric

There will probably be a whole range of possible actions to take to improve the fire performance of a historic building, not all of which may be desirable. The following questions may help in deciding which course of action to take:

- What factors have been identified as the biggest threats to the building and its contents?
- Can these threats be reduced to an acceptable level without involving upgrading, such as by reducing the fire load, or changing the use of the building or parts of the building?
- If improvements are necessary, are they reversible and sympathetic to the appearance of the building, and do they avoid damage to the historic fabric?
- Will the improvements be effective? For instance, the provision of a fire alarm and detection system that is not monitored will not provide any protection when the building is unoccupied.
- The provision of an automatic detection system may cut down the time before a fire is discovered, but is it reduced sufficiently that it is unlikely the fire will spread to adjoining spaces? If not, another layer of improvements, such as a sprinkler system or local water mist system, may be necessary.
- Will the improvements be affordable and, if not, is there a more cost-effective alternative?

Inventories, drawings and photographs

If records are in the form of original documents, archives and plans, perhaps of historical significance in their own right, it may be prudent to keep 8 copies on site and store the originals elsewhere.

Lightning protection

A comprehensive risk assessment should indicate whether the provision of lightning protection is justified. English Heritage, in conjunction with the Ecclesiastical Insurance Group, has produced a technical advice note on this subject.

Inspection and maintenance of heating systems and electrical equipment

The manufacturer's instructions should be followed when testing and servicing equipment including boilers, chimneys and flues, with correct inspection intervals and maintenance by competent persons. The electrical mains system and portable electrical equipment should be tested regularly by a competent person at the intervals recommended in the latest edition of the IEE Regulations. The use of multi-sockets and extension leads is to be discouraged.

Finally, it is important to give regard to the history of fires in the building and in buildings of a similar type and to consider whether the introduction of particular fire safety measures would cause irreversible damage to the historic fabric.

13 The effects of road traffic vibration on historic buildings

Ian Hume

Vibrations and buildings

The effect of vibration on buildings and their occupants is a very technical and complex subject. Vibrations can be caused by passing road traffic, by railways, both surface and underground, by users of the building and by numerous other sources including blasting and building works, particularly piling. When heavy goods vehicles pass, windows vibrate, ornaments rattle and the building's occupants may feel vibrations. As well as being technically complex, it is a very emotive subject.

The response to vibrations by the inhabitants of the building may range from mild annoyance through to grave alarm, probably via sleepless nights, but it must be remembered that the human body is a very sensitive instrument and it will 'register' the most minute sensations. Unlike sophisticated scientific equipment, the human body sometimes has difficulty in sorting out the effects of vibration from effects caused merely by noise. The human mind and body are affected by thoughts and opinions whereas scientific equipment takes measurements without any such psychological distractions.

Vibrations from road traffic

A passing lorry generating a lot of noise will draw attention to itself, and the observer may therefore be more susceptible to a level of vibration that, without the accompanying sound, might pass unnoticed.

The condition of the road surface near the building has a very significant effect on levels of vibration; vehicles on a smooth road surface create much lower levels of vibration than similar vehicles travelling at similar speeds on an uneven surface. Poor road surfaces with badly filled potholes or service trenches will generate vibrations, particularly if the traffic is fast-moving and/or heavy. However, Building Research Establishment (BRE) Digest 353 (1990) *Damage to Structures from Ground-borne Vibration* states that 'although vibrations induced in buildings by ground-borne excitation are often noticeable, there is little evidence that they produce even cosmetic damage (i.e. small cracks in plaster)'.

Between 1986 and 1988 members of the Conservation Engineering Branch of English Heritage (the author was a member of the team involved in this work) collaborated with the Transport and Road Research Laboratory (TRRL) to investigate the effects of vibration on historic buildings in varying conditions. The results were published as TRRL Research Reports Nos. 156 and 207. It was found that ground-borne road traffic vibration was the most significant source of building vibration; however, when the road surface is even, airborne vibrations dominate. Peak vibration levels were, as might be expected, greater on the upper floors, and on walls at the front of buildings, than at foundation level. Despite the relatively high vibration levels, crack movements measured on existing cracks were small, and much lower than those observed for normal variations in temperature and humidity.

Window pane vibrations were found to be relatively high, but at one site (a church with only a narrow footpath between the wall face and the kerb) where stained glass windows exposed to high levels of airborne road traffic vibration were compared to similar windows at much greater distances from the road, no differences in their condition that could be attributed to traffic vibration were found.

During the investigation it was the task of the English Heritage Conservation Engineering Branch to inspect the buildings, to report on the cracking and other signs of distress and to assess the possible causes. Some fractures in the buildings were clearly attributable to settlement, some to thermal and climatic movements and others to decay or overload. Most were patently nothing to do with the effects of passing road traffic. One village corner shop had suffered major damage when a large van suddenly appeared in the sales area, but this had little to do with the vibrations that it caused!

Some cosmetic damage – cracking of plaster, for example – might be attributable to traffic vibrations, but even this is a very difficult question to resolve. It was difficult to draw 'scientific' and quantitative conclusions from the work done in collaboration with TRRL, but it was concluded that vibrations from road traffic did not cause any problems to the structure of a fairly robust historic building, although they might possibly cause problems to fragile buildings, probably exacerbating existing cosmetic damage. However, it was also the view that these fragile buildings were in such a poor condition that they demanded repair even without the effects of road traffic vibrations being taken into account.

It is also very likely that the effects of traffic vibration on a building would become intolerable to the occupants long before structural damage was caused.

Conclusions

Clearly road traffic vibrations cause major problems to those people who have the misfortune to live in properties affected by large volumes of heavy traffic. It would be interesting to hear of any cases where road traffic vibrations are thought to be causing problems to the structure of buildings rather than just being tiresome for the occupants.

Other sources of vibration, such as nearby piling or blasting, may well create vibrations of a much more serious level, which will have a greater potential for damage and therefore must be treated accordingly.

14 Scaffolding and temporary works for historic structures

Ian Hume

Temporary shoring

Where alterations are being made, temporary shoring may fulfil an important role in the stability of the building. There are many instances in the conservation and repair of historic structures that demand that some primary load-carrying element is taken out for replacement. Temporary support will be called for. Sometimes this will mean the insertion of a single telescopic prop; in other cases, the temporary works may be a major engineering undertaking in their own right. All temporary works need careful thought if partial or even total collapse of the structure is to be avoided.

The engineer responsible for the structure, as well as the contractor, must consider the temporary works at an early stage, and both must be satisfied that they are properly designed and constructed to a competent standard. Temporary works, both shoring and scaffolding, must not be allowed to damage the historic fabric. It should also be borne in mind that major repairs to one structure may jeopardise the integrity of its neighbours.

While the temporary works, particularly where they form part of a contract for the restoration of a historic structure, must remain the responsibility of the contractor, it is vital for the engineer to be closely involved with their design and at the very least to see the details of all temporary works before their construction on site begins. The engineer will, in all probability, have a number of advantages that the contractor will not have. The engineer will have had a longer period of involvement with the structure than the contractor; he will have visited the site more frequently, have a greater understanding of the problems of the structure and a greater understanding of the construction, and therefore will have a greater understanding of what the temporary works will need to achieve. In many instances, particularly in the case of a smaller job, the engineer will also have engineering skills that will not be available to the contractor. With a historic structure, there will be no second chance. If collapse occurs or even if damage is caused, rebuilding or repair is a poor alternative to the original structure in its original condition.

No temporary work is too small for an engineer to be interested in. Clearly, the amount of information to be supplied by the contractor prior to the commencement on site will vary according to the complexity of the case. However, the simplest of temporary works can be undersized or unbraced, can provide support in the wrong place or may even be omitted altogether.

The contractor, and in particular the operatives, should be briefed about the value of the historic structure. If they are aware that it is of historic value and interest and not just another old building, there may be hope that they will take more care with their work. Temporary works must be designed with public safety in mind and also must be constructed so as to avoid providing easy access for children and vandals.

Scaffolding and temporary works for historic structures

Scaffolding and temporary works are a fundamental necessity of any building project, and when they are erected in or around historic structures it is vital that they do not cause damage. They must be capable of being constructed without the need for major intervention into historic fabric.

The basics of scaffolding and temporary works in historic environments are not greatly different from those for any existing structure. However, this section attempts to highlight some important points that need special attention if damage to historic fabric is to be avoided. In the non-historic situation damage caused by improperly erected scaffolding and temporary works, while being tiresome and causing unnecessary expenditure, can often be repaired without serious detriment to the structure. Where historic fabric is concerned, however, any damage is permanent; significant detail may be lost or an important facade permanently scarred. All badly erected scaffolding and temporary works, whether to a historically important structure or not, has the potential to allow the collapse of either the scaffolding itself or the structure, with disastrous and possibly fatal consequences. Experience indicates that when things go wrong it is usually owing to a lack of attention to seemingly minor details.

There are two types of scaffolding: access scaffolding, and shoring and support scaffolding. Neither should be expected to carry out the function of the other unless it has been specifically designed so to do. 'Independent tied' **access scaffolds** will normally be provided to gain access to historic building facades for painting, maintenance or other work. They consist of two rows of standards (the vertical supports) connected by ledgers and transoms (the horizontal elements). They are termed 'independent' because this type of scaffold derives no vertical support from the structure, and 'tied' because they must be tied to the structure for horizontal stability. Because of the need to avoid damage, tying to the facade of a historic building can present difficult problems. Longitudinal bracing must be used. **Shoring and support scaffolding** are temporary works erected either because there is a danger of collapse or because it is necessary to remove some vital supporting member for renewal or alteration. Obviously, the loads to be carried by shoring can be very great and failure can be disastrous, causing major damage to historic fabric.

Responsibility

The failure of a single telescopic prop supporting a major element of a structure under repair could have serious consequences. Therefore as the dangers do not necessarily relate to the size of the project, the architect or engineer should examine the contractor's proposals for all scaffolding and shoring. It must be ensured that schemes are erected so as to conform to those proposals. Care must be exercised to ensure that the contractor's responsibility for temporary works is eroded as little as possible.

While all elements of the permanent works are covered by specification clauses that are often extensive, the same situation is rarely true of scaffolding and temporary works, the correct construction of which is equally important. As damage to historic fabric is permanent and must be avoided at all costs, all contract documentation for works to historic buildings should include a section concerning scaffolding and temporary works. If the scaffolding or temporary works are of a major nature, the employment of an experienced scaffold designer should be considered.

Necessary features and common problems

The following are some of the features that can make scaffolding dangerous, unsuitable for its purpose or damaging to historic fabric. There are many more.

Scaffolding to building interfaces

Scaffolding, however well constructed, is always likely to move slightly, and a tube end rubbing on a wall face can easily cause permanent scarring. All tube ends that either touch a wall or are within 25 mm of one should have plastic end caps. All other points of contact or near contact between scaffolding and historic buildings should be protected in some way. All standards should sit on timber sole plates to spread the load, and floors beneath should be protected with polythene sheet, old carpet or similar materials to prevent damage.

Fixings to masonry

Where fixings are made to stone or brickwork, it must be ascertained that the masonry is adequate for this purpose. Such a fixing to a facade could dislodge a stone or an area of brick, endangering the safety of the scaffold. All fixings made to the wall of a historic structure must be of stainless steel for two reasons: first, because ordinary mild steel fixings will corrode and cause rust stains and also possibly split masonry; and secondly, because stainless steel fixings, which will not corrode, can be reused.

Foundations

Soil should be well rammed to ensure that there are no cavities, and timber sole plates at least 230 mm × 40 mm should be used. Where the ground is not firm or where the length of time that the scaffolding is to remain erected exceeds six months, railway sleepers or similar-sized timbers are more suitable. Foundations should always be level and should never be undermined. The foundation and the standard or prop set on it should be concentric to avoid inducing bending moments or eccentric forces.

Typical faults include rotten or missing sole plates, foundations dangerously out of level, and eccentric or undermined props and scaffold standards. Piles of bricks and other unsuitable foundations must not be used. Historic buildings often have basements outside the periphery of the ground floor that may well be incapable of supporting scaffolding. Sometimes there are below-ground water storage tanks that may not be capable of supporting a great weight.

If excavations are required to provide proper foundations for scaffolding or temporary works, there may be a need to provide archaeological supervision.

The foundations for access scaffolding or for a shoring scaffold may not always be at ground level. Sometimes it is necessary to erect such structures on roofs or floors, for example on the aisle roof of a church in order to gain access to the clerestory wall. In these instances it is important to ensure that the supporting structure can safely bear the weight and that floor or roof finishes are not damaged.

Vertical members

Out-of-plumb vertical members produce eccentricity of loading within individual members and horizontal forces in the structure as a whole. As historic buildings often have overhanging cornices and other projections, correct setting out of the bases of standards needs to be considered in the light of what is directly overhead.

Ties

Badly fixed and incorrectly positioned ties and an insufficient number of ties are frequent problems. Any tie taken out to enable work to proceed must be replaced as soon as possible. Through ties which 'hook' back to the inside face of the wall must have protective coverings, but such ties may not be suitable where there is panelling to the inside face. Through ties are simple to use with sash windows. The sash can be raised to allow the tube to pass through; the resulting gap can be sealed temporarily with plastic sheeting or hardboard and the sashes screwed to each other to prevent unauthorised entry. Casement windows are more difficult. If they carry leaded lights it may be possible to remove one small pane, but casements with a single glazed sheet may need to be taken off their hinges and stored safely.

Regrettably, some scaffolders just smash a window to get their fixings. This is particularly likely in a derelict building. Reveal ties (which use screw jacks to grip against the reveals of a window) must also be given good protection to ensure that they do not damage the building facade.

Decking

Very often conservation and repair work involves temporarily removing materials from the structure and storing them on the scaffolding. Slating and tiling a roof are typical examples. Excessive loading on platforms should be avoided unless the scaffolding has been specifically designed to carry heavy loads.

Shoring

Shoring must be competently designed and account must be taken of wind, dead and superimposed loads, slenderness ratio of members, slenderness ratio of structure, bracing, foundations, fixing to permanent structure, permissible stresses of materials, safety factors and any other relevant considerations. The main difficulty with shoring historic structures is to ensure that temporary works do not cause damage in the process of being installed.

Telescopic props

These may need bracing if they are over 2 metres high or if they carry heavy loads. They must be plumb and must be properly founded. It is common to find a missing support pin being replaced by a short piece of reinforcing bar or something even less satisfactory, such as a large nail. Only the manufacturer's high-tensile steel pin should be used.

Temporary roofs and temporary buildings

Such structures are often erected to protect historic structures after a fire or other disaster or during roof repairs. In relation to their area or volume they are, by nature, light structures. As a consequence, their need for lateral stability and resistance to wind uplift is a major – though often ignored – requirement. It is usually advisable to seek the help of a structural engineer in the erection of such structures. The contractor should always be required to provide a drawing of his proposals and, in any but the smallest of cases, supporting calculations.

Earthing

All scaffolding structures that are at risk from lightning strikes should be properly earthed.

Access to the building

Historic buildings often have important interiors, and these must be well protected. Carrying a seven metre length of steel scaffold tube into a building is not easy, and major damage can be caused by a scaffolder inadvertently hitting a door frame or a panelled wall with the end of a tube. It may be wise to provide stout protection to vulnerable surfaces.

Workforce

Efforts should be made to ensure that the workforce is aware of the value of the historic fabric. It must be ensured, particularly in the early stages of a contract, that proper attention is paid to the details discussed above. Scaffolders may not always bother to use plastic caps in the necessary locations, or when installing through ties they may simply smash the glass, not understanding that old glass can be important. It is vital to ensure that supervisors and the general workforce are aware of such details and that there is close supervision.

Conclusion

Scaffolding and temporary works are not always given the consideration they deserve. Consequently there is risk of damage to the historic fabric either in relatively minor ways, such as scarring of surface finishes, or in more serious ways, such as partial collapse. There is the additional risk of injury or death to members of the workforce or to passers-by.

Documentation produced by the architect or engineer and the contractor needs to be commensurate with the scale of the job, bearing in mind that failure of even a small element can cause serious problems. Even if only a single telescopic prop is proposed, it is important that some proper estimate of the weight to be carried is considered and reference made to appropriate literature to ensure that the proposed prop can carry the weight safely.

Architects and engineers involved in historic buildings work – or indeed any other building work – should have a clear understanding of the requirements of scaffolding and temporary works and be aware of the consequences if something goes wrong. The safety and success of scaffolding and temporary works in the historic building field rely heavily on two things: forethought and attention to detail.

With a historic structure, there will be no second chance.

Bibliography and further reading

British Standard BS 5973: 1993 *Code of Practice for Access and Working Scaffolds and Special Scaffold Structures in Steel.*
British Standard BS 5975:1982 *Code of Practice for Falsework.*
Health and Safety Executive, SS10 *Tower Scaffolds* (Health and Safety Executive construction summary sheet, 2002).
Health and Safety Executive, SS49 *General Access Scaffolds and Ladders* (Health and Safety Executive construction summary sheet, 2001).
Health and Safety Executive, GS42 *Tower Scaffolds* (Health and Safety Executive guidance notes, 1987).
National Association of Scaffolding Contractors, *Basic Scaffolding Check Guide* (n.d.).
Wilshire, C. J., *Access Scaffolding* (Thomas Telford, London, 1981).
Brand, Ronald E. *Falsework and Access Scaffolds in Tubular Steel* (McGraw Hill, 1975).

Index